John V. Caffaro
Allison Conn-Caffaro

Sibling Abuse Trauma
Assessment and Intervention Strategies for Children, Families, and Adults

Pre-publication
REVIEWS,
COMMENTARIES,
EVALUATIONS . . .

" **O**ver the last two decades, there has been a proliferation of research and writing on child maltreatment. Debates have ensued over children's memory, suggestibility, and truthfulness. Research has mushroomed on child sexual abuse and child abuse and neglect. There has even been focus on the perpetrator and the nonoffending parent. One area, however, has almost consistently been ignored: the area of sibling abuse. This book is a welcome and required addition to our developing literature on abuse."

Judith L. Alpert, PhD
Professor of Applied Psychology,
New York University

" **T**his book affords significant attention to the trauma of sibling abuse. Until this impressive work by Caffaro and Conn-Caffaro, we have not paid enough attention to sibling relationships in our research and practice on family violence and child abuse and neglect. The authors bring considerable insight and clinical experience to the issue of sibling abuse. This book will enhance practitioners' knowledge of sibling abuse dynamics and treatment strategies and make a contribution to the entire field by encouraging a broader discussion of the life-span developmental impact of sibling abuse."

Linda M. Williams, PhD
Director of Research,
Stone Center,
Wellesley College,
Wellesley, MA

Sibling Abuse Trauma

Assessment and Intervention Strategies for Children, Families, and Adults

THE HAWORTH MALTREATMENT & TRAUMA PRESS
Robert A. Geffner, PhD
Senior Editor

New, Recent, and Forthcoming Titles:

Sexual, Physical, and Emotional Abuse in Out-of-Home Care: Prevention Skills for At-Risk Children by Toni Cavanagh Johnson and Associates

Cedar House: A Model Child Abuse Treatment Program by Bobbi Kendig with Clara Lowry

Bridging Worlds: Understanding and Facilitating Adolescent Recovery from the Trauma of Abuse by Joycee Kennedy and Carol McCarthy

The Learning About Myself (LAMS) Program for At-Risk Parents: Learning from the Past—Changing the Future by Verna Rickard

The Learning About Myself (LAMS) Program for At-Risk Parents: Handbook for Group Participants by Verna Rickard

Treating Children with Sexually Abusive Behavior Problems: Guidelines for Child and Parent Intervention by Jan Ellen Burton, Lucinda A. Rasmussen, Julie Bradshaw, Barbara J. Christopherson, and Steven C. Huke

Bearing Witness: Violence and Collective Responsibility by Sandra L. Bloom and Michael Reichert

Sibling Abuse Trauma: Assessment and Intervention Strategies for Children, Families, and Adults by John V. Caffaro and Allison Conn-Caffaro

From Surviving to Thriving: A Therapist's Guide to Stage II Recovery for Survivors of Childhood Abuse by Mary Bratton

"I Never Told Anyone This Before": Managing the Initial Disclosure of Abuse Re-Collections by Janice A. Gasker

Breaking the Silence: Group Therapy for Childhood Sexual Abuse, A Practitioner's Manual by Judith A. Margolin

Sibling Abuse Trauma

Assessment and Intervention Strategies for Children, Families, and Adults

John V. Caffaro
Allison Conn-Caffaro

HMTP

The Haworth Maltreatment and Trauma Press
An Imprint of The Haworth Press, Inc.
New York • London

Published by

The Haworth Maltreatment and Trauma Press, an imprint of the The Haworth Press, Inc., 10 Alice Street, Binghamton, NY 13904-1580

Cover design by Jennifer M. Gaska.

Library of Congress Cataloging-in-Publication Data

Caffaro, John V.
    Sibling abuse trauma : assessment and intervention strategies for children, families, and adults / John V. Caffaro, Allison Conn-Caffaro.
        p.   cm.
    Includes bibliographical references and index.
    ISBN 0-7890-6007-8 (alk. paper).
    1. Sibling abuse. I. Conn-Caffaro, Allison. II. Title.
RJ506.S53C34   1998
616.85′822—dc21   98-8166
                                                                                                CIP

CONTENTS

ABOUT THE AUTHORS

John V. Caffaro, PhD, is Associate Clinical Professor of Psychology at the California School of Professional Psychology–Los Angeles. He is also in private practice, specializing in the treatment of post-traumatic stress and adult survivors of child abuse trauma in Del Mar, California. Dr. Caffaro speaks and writes on the topics of family trauma, sexual abuse, and sibling relationships. Prior to joining the faculty at CSPP, he served as clinical consultant to a number of child and family abuse treatment programs in San Diego, California.

Allison Conn-Caffaro, MFCC, is in private practice in Del Mar, California, where she specializes in working with families, children, and survivors of abuse trauma. She is a bilingual Mental Health Consultant with the University of California–San Diego's Child and Adolescent Psychiatry Service, as well as Clinical Instructor of Family, Play, and Group Therapy at the UCSD Department of Psychiatry. Allison and John have presented workshops and seminars at national conferences for child/family abuse professionals since 1991.

Electronic mail may be sent to: jvc@cts.com.

Foreword

In the outpouring of writing about child maltreatment—welcome as it may be after years of silence—the focus and emphasis has sometimes been driven more by fad and sentiment than by knowledge and reason. Topics such as child neglect, for example, which dominate caseloads, receive little attention, while sexual abuse, which comprises only one in eight substantiated cases (and a declining proportion, at that) has in some circles become synonymous with the idea of child abuse itself.

Maltreatment by siblings is another form of the problem whose widespread prevalence has been known for a considerable period of time, but which has generated disappointingly little specific scholarly and clinical attention. There is no question that cross-generational violations of trust and responsibility are morally reprehensible and have a potential to create developmental trauma that is compelling. But I am also inclined to blame the neglect of sibling abuse in part on the ethos of the present historical era, which has relished the themes of cross-generational conflict and intragenerational solidarity. It can hardly be a coincidence that in our era's slang "brother" and "sister," "bro," and the like are such terms of endearment while "mother" is an epithet.

This book is a welcome arrival at a time when I think the child maltreatment field is open to new horizons and a more mature and diversified outlook. It provides a detailed focus on this neglected issue, and nicely integrates research, theory, and the considerable clinical experience of its two authors. It is written with a healthy and complex appreciation of broader issues in the field of family violence and family therapy, and gives a great deal of thought-provoking case material for those interested in understanding more about sibling abuse dynamics and potential treatment strategies. I sincerely hope it will be a catalyst to even more sustained attention to the topic of sibling relationships, which, as the book persuasively argues, is such an important ingredient in child and life-course development.

David Finkelhor
Family Research Lab
University of New Hampshire

Preface

Several years ago, during lunch with a colleague, the conversation turned to our professional activities. We mentioned that we were beginning to write a book on abuse between siblings. She seemed genuinely curious and asked a few questions about the topic. Then our lunch order was ready and we went to the pickup counter, where our food was waiting.

When we returned to our table, our companion said she had a story to tell us. She described her childhood in a suburban community east of Los Angeles with an absent father, an alcoholic mother, and her older brother. Almost casually she told us how her adolescent brother began to sexually abuse her when she was six, and how he sold her to his friends for one dollar each until she was eleven. At first her voice had a reporting quality, as if she spoke about someone else's life. When she described how often he threatened and hurt her when she tried to refuse, her voice held a pain that we imagined was there at the time of the abuse. In only a few minutes, her normally calm and subdued demeanor had changed into something like awe about these traumatic events, as if she still could not quite believe that they had happened to her.

Sexually abused children learn about victimization before they learn about sex. As a result they are often unable to separate fear from desire and pain from pleasure in consensual sex as adults. Siblings who force sex on their brothers or sisters breed fear, anger, shame, humiliation, repulsion, and often guilt in their victims. Many sibling offenders are also victims of physical or sexual abuse.

Betrayals such as our colleague's do not encompass the wide range of abusive interactions that pervade some children's siblinghood. Sibling assault or physical abuse (particularly between boys) is such a normative event in our culture that parents or professionals cannot easily find reliable information about its prevalence, causes, and treatment. The problem is complicated by the commonly held view that it is often difficult to discern victim and offender roles in sibling assault cases. Indeed, in some instances of reciprocal physical violence between siblings, the children are victimized alternately. Yet significant numbers of children also grow up bullied and physically hurt by their closest genetic relatives. Their worst nightmare lives under the same roof with them—often in the same room. Child-on-child (including intersibling) violence may be our country's most closely kept secret; and as long as society communicates that violence is an acceptable solution to problems, we may have difficulty ending it.

Experts agree that incest or assault is usually accompanied by what is called psychological maltreatment or emotional abuse. Child abuse professionals agree that psychological maltreatment can be even more harmful than other, more highly publicized forms of abuse. It is difficult to imagine a family context more frequently associated with emotional abuse than the sibling world. Siblinghood provides a training ground for teasing, as well as manipulative, coercive, and sometimes threatening behavior, which children unleash, after field testing, on extended family and nonfamily peers. Furthermore, once solidly established, such cruel behavior seems quite resistant to extinction and often can be observed between adults, who appear to be suspended in an earlier sibling universe.

In this book we are concerned with the way to evaluate and treat victims of sibling abuse when there are identifiable victims and offenders. By now it also may be obvious that siblings are often subjected to a range of parent-child as well as child-child trauma and victimization. Many of the examples cited here reflect this tragic reality.

Our book is not only about child abuse; it is also about our fantasies of abuse. It is about the images we cannot summon up on our own or are afraid to acknowledge. It is about the stories we need to hear; the explanations we require to deal with abuse trauma. Without such an understanding we would be left with only the truth—and the truth of sibling abuse is often too harsh to tell.

John V. Caffaro
Allison Conn-Caffaro

Acknowledgments

Writing a book such as this involves the collaborative support of many individuals who contributed their time and expertise to a lengthy and rewarding process. Special recognition is due to the adult survivors of sibling incest and assault who volunteered to be a part of this project. Without them, our book could not have been written. Our clients, who humble us daily with their courage and commitment to healing and growth, deserve special thanks for teaching us so much about our humanity.

In addition, a number of people read this book in part or in its entirety at various stages of the writing and gave us wise editing advice, helpful criticism, and practical suggestions. We want to thank Bob Geffner, our editor at The Haworth Maltreatment and Trauma Press, for his unwavering support and incisive feedback on several versions of the manuscript. He guided our progress through completion, and we appreciate his collaborative spirit at all levels of the process. We would also like to thank David Finkelhor for his invaluable comments, feedback, and key suggestions.

We also thank Tama Sogoian, Gloria Isaacs-Giraldi, and Karen Feinberg for their assistance in reviewing the manuscript and offering many helpful criticisms and revisions. We appreciate the research support provided by the California Association of Marriage and Family Therapists (CAMFT) in 1995. John is grateful to the California School of Professional Psychology–Los Angeles for providing much-needed institutional support to complete this book, and to colleagues, particularly Susan Regas and Victor Cohen, for sustenance and unconditional friendship throughout this process. Allison is appreciative of the support she has received from colleagues at University of California–San Diego Child and Adolescent Psychiatry Service—especially Bob Knight, for his flexibility and understanding and David Kerr, for his artistic contribution to the Sibling Comic Strip. We are also grateful to our research assistant, Meredith Merchant, who provided attention to detail through-out the text.

We also thank our formal and informal teachers for being who they are and for their many gifts to us over the years. Some we have known only through their writings or at a distance. We are grateful to Eliana Gil for providing family therapists with a model of clarity and practical know-how for treating children and abusive families. Our gratitude also extends to John Briere, Christine Courtois, and Judith Herman for their unwavering commitment to excellence in training professionals who treat adult survivors of abuse trauma. And we are deeply grateful to many personal teachers as well: to Erving and Miriam Polster, who mirror the teaching of moment-to-moment awareness in all their endeavors and provide a source of deep inspiration to us as clinicians and as human beings; to Robert and Mary Goulding, for their integrative vision of brief psychother-apy long before it was fashionable; and to Betsy Gross, who served as an early inspiration for understanding the importance of sibling relationships and dynamics in our work with families at the Child Sexual Abuse Treatment Program.

We also want to express our appreciation for family and friends who offered their support, encouragement, and understanding throughout the process of writing this book. Finally, we wish to thank all of the many participants in our workshops and presentations across the coun-try who provided us with invaluable feedback and encouragement to continue this project to completion.

Introduction

Graduate and postgraduate education focused on sibling development and abuse is underemphasized or entirely overlooked in clinical training programs across the nation. This gap in the curriculum indirectly favors an overrestrictive focus on the parent-child relationship, with a conspicuous disregard for the assessment and treatment of sibling-related problems. Theoretical perspectives across disciplines also attend to the parent-child relationship without adequate inclusion of siblings. In this book we describe an eclectic, sibling-informed approach to individual and family psychotherapy, guided by the effects of abuse trauma on the development of sibling relationships. In addition, informal discussions with colleagues and workshop participants, as well as a review of the family therapy literature, reveal that clinicians largely would benefit from increasing the skills and knowledge essential for treating sibling-specific abuse problems. We believe that our book fills a void in the training and education of abuse trauma professionals, and validates sibling experiences as an important part of human development.

A primary purpose in writing this book is to enhance practitioners' knowledge of sibling abuse issues. We hope our work will stimulate a dialogue between clinicians and researchers, centered on these concerns. We would like to broaden the context for discussions of abuse trauma by proposing that standard medical and psychological examinations include routine screening for histories of victimization by siblings. We offer suggestions, based on clinical experience, for using individual and family modalities in treating cases of sibling abuse. Our intent is to encourage innovation throughout the treatment process by providing additional perspectives and techniques regarding therapy with sibling incest and assault victims and survivors. Research and clinical experience suggest that the child welfare system should expand its definition of "protective issues" to include sibling abuse cases. This step would educate society in general on the traumatic effects of intersibling abuse. We would also encourage efforts by schools to detect sibling violence and establish prevention programs.

We provide some essential information on sibling development to clarify the context in which sibling relationships unfold. We also incorporate research on sibling relationships into our clinical approach for treating victims and survivors when appropriate. This book focuses primarily on assessment and treatment; its success is linked to its utility for clinicians who treat children, families, and adults exposed to sibling abuse trauma. The clinical material and experiences portrayed here represent children, families, and adults who we believe have not been described adequately elsewhere. Similarities exist between characteristics of parental and sibling abuse victims, and are noted in numerous places throughout this book. But the potential for reciprocal physical and sexual interaction sets siblings apart from victims of parent-child abuse and encourages the stereotype of mutuality. Although we acknowledge that some level of conflict and sexual contact between siblings can be nonabusive, this book is centered on sibling activity that has traumatic effects on an identifiable victim. In addition, unlike parent-child abuse, many cases of sibling incest or assault must be treated without disuniting the family. Sibling offenders frequently remain in the home even after disclosure. This fact provides unique challenges to individual and family clinicians treating sibling abuse victims.

We limit our focus to the abuse of one sibling by another. Furthermore, the abuse is generally presented from the victim's point of view. Within these parameters, we adopt a life-span perspective that includes discussion of child, adolescent, and adult sibling issues. Rather than choosing to concentrate solely on sibling incest or assault, we apply a more inclusive, integrative approach to the study of sibling abuse trauma. This is predicated on the belief that an understanding of these types of sibling abuse is enhanced by exploring the dynamics and features common to both.

We assume that our readers have a basic knowledge of the principles of individual and family therapy with child abuse trauma victims and adult survivors. A growing body of literature explicates the principles of abuse-focused therapy with children, families, and adults (Briere, 1992; Gil, 1996; Herman, 1992). Many of the principles established for treating victims of parent-child abuse also apply to victims of sibling abuse. Our contributions in this book are:

1. An eclectic, sibling-informed approach to treating victims and survivors of sibling incest or assault.
2. A broadening of the context for addressing sibling-related concerns with child victims and adult survivors.
3. A heightening of readers' awareness of sibling incest and assault concerns with regard to assessment and treatment of individuals and families.

A book on sibling relationships is inherently family-based. Yet the unique circumstances of child abuse treatment frequently require a modification of traditional systemic approaches. In treating victims or perpetrators of family violence, safety and accountability are front-and-center issues for the clinician. It is very likely that certain kinds of therapies work for children from some kinds of families but not others. For example, therapy with other family members present is not always in the abuse victim's best interest. Sibling offenders frequently require individual and group abuse-focused treatment before they can benefit from family therapy. Alternatively, family-based therapy may be one aspect of a multi-modal approach to treatment that includes individual, group, and family intervention. Often therapy proceeds sequentially—family members are added only after significant individual gains are made. In recognition of these and other important variants in the course of therapy, we have included a number of diverse clinical examples, including some in which family-based treatment is contraindicated. In either case, psychotherapy focuses on relationship and interaction, whether between members of a family system, between an individual client and therapist, or in a group of unrelated persons.

This book is divided into three sections. Part I begins with an overview chapter that underscores the need for clinical and research data on sibling abuse, states the purpose and scope of the book, and orients the reader to abuse as viewed from a sibling perspective. In Chapter 2, we review sibling relations from a life-span perspective and present a developmental context for healthy sibling functioning in a nonabusive setting. Chapter 3 examines the effects of abuse on the sibling dyad and sibling relationships in an abusive family system. We describe individual dynamics common to sibling incest and assault, particularly the offender's misuse of power, control, and authority. Family environment factors such as gender roles and inadequate parental supervision are explored in some detail as they relate to the development of sibling incest and assault.

Part II begins with a comprehensive discussion of sibling incest: Chapter 4 examines individual and family contextual factors that are essential to an understanding of sibling incest. In this chapter, we also discuss gender issues germane to the development of sibling incest, with subsections on issues that may be gender-specific for both male and female victims of same-sex incest. This chapter ends with a summary of concerns unique to sibling incest offenders, and explains the harmful effects of sibling incest for victims and families. Chapter 5 covers similar ground with respect to sibling assault victims and survivors. Chapters 4 and 5 are organized according to risk factors identified in our research as well as in the child abuse literature. Instances of psychological maltreatment are cited throughout this section because such abuse often co-occurs with sibling incest and physical assault.

Part III contains some of our central ideas regarding assessment and clinical intervention with children, families, and adult survivors. In Chapter 6, we propose cogent factors in reaching accurate decisions on assessing sibling abuse: relationships among family members, and a summary of offender risk characteristics. A Sibling Abuse Interview is presented and discussed. Chapter 7 describes guidelines specifying how and when to address sibling issues when working with sibling abuse victims, cultural influences, and other clinical considerations with children and families. In Chapter 8 we provide an eclectic, multidimensional approach to treating child and adolescent victims of sibling incest or assault and their families. Principles of abuse-focused therapy are linked with an ecologically based approach to guiding various clinical decisions and interventions. Chapter 9 covers similar ground with respect to therapy with adult survivors. Chapters 8 and 9 contain numerous clinical examples and are meant to illustrate viable solutions to complex treatment situations. The inclusion of individual, sibling, and family methods is designed to encourage a multilevel approach to clinical intervention. Appendixes contain research information and tables, as well as a depiction of an additional sibling-oriented intervention.

To illustrate important aspects of evaluation and treatment, we supply case examples at various points in this book. Client confidentiality has been protected rigorously in the reconstruction of these cases. When presenting case examples, we have altered some details of the client's age, gender, occupation, or other identifying information. When we provide dialogue, either we reconstructed it from notes or memory, combined the stories of several cases into one presentation, or we obtained explicit permission to reproduce segments from actual research transcripts or audiotaped interviews.

PART I:
THE CONTEXT OF SIBLING DEVELOPMENT AND ABUSE

Chapter 1

The Sibling Domain

Irreconcilables fought for supremacy in us; peace could never be made: at best a smoldering sort of armistice might be reached after many battles.

Tennessee Williams, on his
relationship with his sister, Rose

Siblings often constitute our ongoing sense of family. Brothers and sisters provide one another with life's longest intimate relationships, generally outlasting ties with parents by twenty to thirty years. Friendships may come and go, and marriages begin and end, but sibling connections remain. Thus our siblings potentially share more of our lives, genetically and contextually, than anyone else. Nonetheless, in assessment and clinical intervention with abusive families, sibling relationships are often overshadowed by parent-child interactions.

Although the study of siblings has a long history, previous researchers concentrated on outcomes associated with birth order, family size, and sibling spacing in nonclinical families. The results of these early studies were inconsistent. More recently, researchers have focused on development (Buhrmester, 1992) and on the personalities of individual siblings in the same family (Hetherington and Clingempeel, 1992) as well as on links between sibling and other social relationships (Bryant, 1992; Dunn, 1988). The prevalent theme in many of these studies is that sibling relationships and their contribution to developmental outcomes can be understood only in the context of processes involved in other family relationships (Hetherington, 1994). This observation becomes evident when applied to the study of intersibling abuse. For example, clinical experience supports the routine assessment for histories of sibling abuse in adults who are being treated for abusing their own children. Such assessments are often overlooked, however.

The negative effects of child maltreatment have been the subject of numerous clinical studies. Theories of child development and abuse trauma most often focus on a child's relationship to his or her parents. The effects of abuse trauma on the sibling relationship are rarely documented so systematically. There is evidence, however, which suggests that in times of crisis the underpinnings of a sibling relationship are likely to surface and be clarified. Anna Freud's (Freud and Dann, 1951) experience in the Hampstead nurseries with children raised in concentration camps offered early indication that a supportive relationship between siblings in situations of intense deprivation can prevent some of the more devastating consequences of trauma.

The increased interest in sibling relations in recent years may be explained by the changing characteristics of our country's population:

- Demographic trends show the emergence of a generation of adults with more siblings than children.
- Of women born in the early 1950s, 17 percent are remaining childless in contrast to 9 percent of women born in the 1930s.
- Census Bureau figures project that as much as 20 percent of the adult population may not marry.
- Eighty-three percent of the population was raised with at least one sibling in the family.

Family size also has declined steadily in recent years. Because Americans are living longer, the importance of siblings as potential caretakers is increasing. Researchers suggest, and siblings agree, that a deep-seated sense of obligation generally exists between brothers and sisters. A shared family history exists as well. What if that shared history includes intersibling abuse? How are sibling relationships shaped by these traumatic experiences? In this book, based on our clinical experience, interviews, and empirical findings, we explore some possible answers to these questions.

Sibling relationships include all of the interactions, verbal and nonverbal, of two or more individuals who are members of the same sibling subsystem and who have parents in common. Victims of stepsibling and half sibling assault and incest are included in our description of siblings because violence has similar mechanisms and effects when it occurs in these relationships. Siblings share some knowledge, perceptions, attitudes, beliefs, and feelings regarding each other, beginning when one sibling first becomes psychologically aware of the other.

SYSTEMS THEORY AND ABUSE TRAUMA

According to family systems theory, family members are part of an interactive, interdependent network in which the behavior of each individual or subsystem modifies that of other individuals or subsystems (Minuchin, 1985). Although individuals are regarded as important components, an ecologically based model also emphasizes contextual influences at the level of the family, the community, and the culture. This school of thought has not consistently incorporated basic tenets of abuse trauma theory and practice. Most family system investigations of child abuse trauma continue to focus on father-daughter incest, despite recognition that sibling incest and assault occur more frequently. Studies acknowledging the harmful effects of sibling incest have begun to appear in the literature (Abrahams and Hoey, 1994; Canavan, Meyer, and Higgs, 1992). By contrast, research examining the effects of childhood sibling assault on adult relationships is conspicuously lacking, although it is pandemic in families (Finkelhor and Dziuba-Leatherman, 1994).

Only 11 percent of child abuse research over the past three decades specifically addresses sibling concerns. Relatively few studies of child abuse trauma incorporate a systemic approach to assessment or treatment; notable exceptions include Belsky (1993), Friedrich (1990), Gil (1996), and Trepper and Barrett (1989). These authors collectively maintain that child maltreatment is not the result of a single factor or system but rather the consequence of interactions among multiple factors and systems. In addition, developmental levels of the individual child, sibling, and family system all affect the potential for abuse. We assert that no single approach is sufficient to explain the complexities common in working with sibling abuse victims and survivors. Rather, one perspective (abuse trauma) informs the other (systemic); each is critical for an adequate understanding of the dynamics.

DEFINITIONS AND TERMINOLOGY

The inability to accurately and consistently define sibling incest or assault has created serious problems for clinicians, researchers, and child and family protection agencies. Below we define the terms used frequently in this book:

Sibling assault occurs when one member of a sibling dyad nonaccidentally causes physical harm, injury, or death to a brother or sister. It consists of a range of behaviors including pushing, hitting, kicking, beating, and using weapons to inflict physical harm. Several other conditions are often present in families in which sibling assault occurs. Siblings may be more likely to develop an assaultive relationship as a result of problems among family members, overall system dysfunction, external environmental influences, and role rigidity among siblings that results in the solidification of victim/offender status. For the purposes of our study, the survivor's subjective perception was an important criterion in establishing the presence of sibling assault. We adopted criteria established by Graham-Bermann, Cutler, Litzenberger, and Schwartz (1994, p. 88) for inclusion under our definition of adult survivors of sibling assault. All three of the following were required to establish the presence of sibling assault in our study's participants (see Appendix D):

- Individuals who perceived themselves as being "picked on a lot" by one sibling in particular
- Individuals who would characterize their childhood sibling interactions as violent and abusive
- Siblings who perceived a higher level of conflict with childhood brothers and sisters in the home than with others

Although we acknowledge that some sexual contact between siblings can be nonabusive, we concentrate here on *sibling incest* that is experienced by the victim as traumatic. This includes sexual behavior between siblings for which the victim is not developmentally prepared, which is not transitory, and which is not motivated by age-appropriate curiosity. It may or may not involve physical touching, coercion, or force. Noncontact sibling incest may encompass behavior that is intended to sexually stimulate a sibling or the offender. It can include unwanted sexual references in conversation, indecent exposure, forcing a sibling to observe others' sexual behavior, taking pornographic pictures, or forcing a sibling to view pornography (Wiehe, 1996).

Pure types of child maltreatment probably do not exist in reality. Most of our clients and many of the participants in our study suffered multiple forms of abuse. *Psychological maltreatment,* one of the most prevalent forms of intersibling abuse, is also difficult to define, and has only recently received significant public or professional attention. Sibling psychological maltreatment often persists under the guise of "teasing." Child abuse researchers (Garbarino, 1986; Hart and Brassard, 1987) regard such maltreatment as more prevalent and potentially more destructive than other forms of abuse and neglect. Our definition of psychological maltreatment includes the following:

- Emotional abuse that includes neglect of a sibling, as well as exposing a sibling to violence by peers or other siblings
- Comments aimed at ridiculing, insulting, threatening, terrorizing, and belittling a sibling
- Rejecting, degrading, and exploiting a sibling
- Destroying a sibling's personal property

Navarre (1987) observes that emotional abuse is probably an inherent or core element of all forms of child maltreatment. Detection of sibling psychological maltreatment is complicated by the fact that professionals and parents have tended to accept emotionally abusive behavior as a normative aspect of sibling and peer interactions. Thus many sibling victims of emotional abuse tend to overlook or deny this form of abuse. Unfortunately, however, many of these victims accept and internalize the abusive messages received from their brothers or sisters. Psychological maltreatment has the potential to distort perceptions and assumptions regarding oneself, others, the environment, and the future. Its presence in other types of maltreatment suggests that it has broad effects on later psychosocial functioning (Briere, 1992).

Finally, *sibling victim* in our book refers to a child or adult who is the target of sibling incest or assault while it is still occurring. *Sibling survivor* is the adult who was abused in childhood by a sibling. We offer these definitional guidelines with the understanding that many factors need to be considered when faced with questions about the abusive nature of "consensual" sex play or "reciprocal" violence between siblings.

A FOCUS ON SIBLING VICTIMS

Early sibling relationships may influence our current lives more strongly than we realize. For example, an abuse victim's psychological adjustment is frequently associated with the degree of acknowledgment and support forthcoming from nonabusive family members, including siblings. Treatment that includes siblings, where indicated, actually may accelerate therapy and consolidate treatment gains for abuse survivors. Psychotherapists often are underprepared to help clients cope with the complexities of their bonds to brothers and sisters. Many research participants reported that although they had spent months and sometimes years in therapy, the subject of their sibling relationships had never been raised.

As we examine the data, the need for greater attention to the victims of sibling abuse becomes clear. Sibling incest may be among the most underreported forms of sexual abuse: very few of the adult survivors of sibling incest who participated in our study indicated that it was a one-time event. Increased awareness and understanding of the dynamics of sibling incest and assault might result in more accurate and more reliable reporting procedures.

KEY POINTS

- Siblings have received increased attention in recent years, though little is known about the effects of intersibling abuse on sibling relationships.

- A systems perspective that is informed by the literature on abuse trauma is crucial for understanding the dynamics of sibling abuse.
- *Sibling relationship*, for the purposes of this book, is defined as all of the interactions of two or more individuals who have parents in common, and includes stepsiblings and half siblings.
- *Sibling assault* occurs when one member of a sibling pair deliberately causes physical harm to a brother or sister. It may consist of pushing, hitting, kicking, or using weapons to inflict physical harm.
- *Sibling incest* is defined as sexual behavior between siblings which is not age-appropriate, is not transitory, and is not motivated by developmentally appropriate curiosity. It may or may not involve coercion or force.
- *Psychological maltreatment* may include verbal comments aimed at ridiculing, insulting, humiliating, threatening, or terrorizing a sibling, as well as exploiting a brother or sister and destroying his or her property. Psychological maltreatment is probably an inherent element of all sibling abuse; it tends to be minimized by victims, offenders, and society in general.

Chapter 2

Sibling Development Across the Life Span

When my siblings and I had measles, my sister Sophie was very ill, high fever and delirious. In the delirium she was heard to say over and over, "I want my mummy, no not your mummy, I want my mummy."

Anna Freud

Social scientists ignored sibling relationships for a surprisingly long time, given the developmental significance accorded to child-child interactions by major theorists (e.g., Piaget, 1965; Sullivan, 1953) and to sibling rivalry by both clinicians and personality theorists (e.g., Adler, 1959). Systematic studies of siblings began to appear in the literature approximately ten years ago. Much of this research, however, explored infancy and early childhood, and examined specific interactions between siblings rather than broad dimensions of relationships. Recent investigators are more likely to describe relationships so as to include a focus on siblings' and parents' perceptions (Buhrmester, 1992; Raffaelli, 1991).

SIBLING DEVELOPMENT IN INFANCY AND EARLY CHILDHOOD

Sibling relationships begin much earlier than the moment when brothers and sisters first meet face to face. Early on, with their parents' help, siblings begin to formulate what it will mean to them to have a younger brother or sister. They engage in developmentally appropriate fantasies about sharing interests, teaching a younger sibling their acquired mastery of the world, having someone to play with, or feeling powerful because they are no longer the baby of the family. Conversely, most siblings have some trepidation at the thought of sharing their parents' attention. They may feel rejected because Mommy and Daddy want another baby, or may wonder what their new role will be in the family. They may have trouble sharing their possessions, or may refuse to help prepare for the care of their younger sister or brother.

How a parent addresses a child's concern about an impending birth sets the foundation of the sibling relationship. In better-functioning families, parents initiate the development of sibling ties by involving their children throughout the pregnancy. Mothers may encourage the development of positive sibling relationships by allowing children to feel fetal movements, attend checkups, and hear their younger brother's or sister's heartbeat. Parents also can help their older children understand their baby brother's or sister's development and early needs by discussing the baby as a little person with feelings and needs. They can take time to discuss their older children's feelings and thoughts, and can answer questions in developmentally appropriate ways throughout the birthing process. In this way they acknowledge an older child's continued importance in the family. Parents who promote positive sibling relationships begin to shape a new and important role for their children—that of an older sibling.

After the birth of a new child, parents still strongly influence the sibling relationship. When this influence is handled effectively, they can instill a positive sense of identity in the older child. For earlier-born children, this supports their adjustment to a new role that they value because of the benefits received, primarily in relation to their parents. Older siblings, for example, may not be skilled at handling infants. If parents interpret this clumsiness as malicious, they may chastise the child. This might lead to the development of shame, along with increased anger and resentment toward the new sibling. Conversely, if parents understand that their older children simply may be unskilled, they have an opportunity to instruct and support bonding between the siblings.

Older siblings may not be interested in interacting with their baby sister or brother because the time together will not necessarily always be enjoyable. Parents can enhance the relationship by highlighting moments when older siblings make the baby smile and laugh, or by pointing out something about the older sibling's behavior that the baby likes. Throughout this process, older children come to experience the beginning of a positive relationship with their younger sibling. Consequently the threat of jealous, angry feelings and subsequent abusive behavior is reduced.

As children develop, they generally become more interesting playmates for their older brothers or sisters. Simultaneously, parental influence over the sibling relationship lessens. By age four, second-born children spend more time talking and playing with their older siblings than with their parents (Dunn, 1993). Still, parents provide guidance as they facilitate conflict resolution skills and aid in developing values around sharing, empathy, communication, and boundaries. At this developmental stage, a family's subsystem organization becomes more prominent. Healthy sibling development requires the maintenance of appropriate subsystem boundaries. In better-functioning families, the integrity of the sibling bond is preserved by a lack of parental intrusion. Siblings are able to develop separate relationships that do not include their parents, and the parents refrain from involving children in the spousal subsystem. They are able to respect the sibling subsystem boundary while remaining engaged in their children's lives.

Siblings who develop better relationships are generally supported in developing both their unique and their shared characteristics and interests. Some families tend to accentuate differences between siblings, and some support similarities; greater tolerance for both emanates from a family system that can incorporate and validate an array of qualities. The labeling of children is common to most, if not all, families: One child is the "smart one," another is the "musically gifted one," and so on. Problems emerge when these roles are defined rigidly within the family, thus limiting the range of skills and identities embraced by each child.

Even in caring families, labeling can lead to resentment and can restrict siblings' behavior. Families that produce stronger sibling ties are those which give permission to discuss these resentments. This often leads to the realization that there is room in the family for everyone. Helping each child to explore a variety of interests assists in the process of differentiation, which is vital to strong sibling ties. Ideally siblings can maintain an emotional connection while each is discovering his or her likes, dislikes, values, and beliefs. Stronger ties result when siblings share interests and maintain respect for differences.

Increased interest in childhood relationships has recently spawned a burst of empirical research on children's relationships, not only with their parents but also with their siblings, friends, and peer groups, and on the links between and among these relationships. Furthermore, social interactions that develop as children mature are widely acknowledged as important components of their cognitive development. One area of particular interest is the exploration of factors that account for differences between siblings who grow up in the same family. Not all sibling differences can be explained by genetics (see Dunn and Plomin, 1990 for additional information).

Families in which siblings develop supportive, close relationships ares notable unlike those from which they emerge with mutual animosity or distance. Children are highly responsive to emotional interactions and to the quality of other relationships within the family, such as marital and parent-sibling dyads. This sensitivity has been demonstrated in studies by Dunn and Munn (1985), and Cummings (1987). In particular, low levels of paternal acceptance and involvement have all-pervasive negative effects on children; this suggests the importance of a father's influence on his child's development. In one study (Stocker and McHale, 1992), levels of conflict were lower among siblings who described their relationships with their fathers as warm and as characterized by equal treatment of each child. This is not meant to suggest that a father's (or mother's) presence always benefits the sibling relationship; children from multiproblem intact families may suffer more extensive maladjustment than children from some fractured homes.

Summary: Sibling Development in Infancy and Early Childhood

- In better-functioning families, parents initiate sibling ties by involving children throughout the pregnancy.
- By age four, second-born children spend more time talking and playing with older siblings than with parents.
- As the sibling relationship develops, parents must be able to respect the sibling subsystem while remaining engaged in their children's lives.
- Stronger sibling ties result when children learn to share interests and to maintain respect for each other's differences.
- Siblings are highly responsive to emotional interactions and to the quality of other relationships in the family, such as marital and parent-child dyads.

ADOLESCENT SIBLING DEVELOPMENT

During adolescence, sibling relationships begin to change in a manner that mimics the development of parent-child relationships. As younger siblings mature, their interactions with older siblings become more egalitarian. Throughout adolescence, siblings continue to be important sources of attachment for one another; older siblings are preferred to younger ones as confidants (see Ross and Milgram, 1982, for information regarding sibling coinfluence in adolescence and adulthood). During adolescence, siblings frequently become companions who link each other to larger social environments. Customarily this is accomplished when older siblings bring friends to the house, and when younger siblings accompany their brothers and sisters on social occasions with friends. These and similar events expose younger siblings to nonfamilial social situations.

Later childhood and adolescent sibling patterns apparently set the stage for subsequent peer and adult relationships. One critical skill that ordinarily solidifies within the sibling subsystem during adolescence is conflict resolution. Sibling conflict is valuable in that it helps to define interpersonal boundaries and rules for family relationships. Regulated aggressive contact between siblings can be important in developing social skills that enable children to learn how to surrender without debasing themselves, and to win without humiliating others.

Parents, because of their early influence on sibling relationships, play a major role in the way sisters and brothers learn to deal with disagreements. Bank and Kahn (1982) outline three specific parenting styles, and how these styles influence the development of conflict resolution skills between siblings. The two styles that are associated with sibling assault (conflict-avoiding and conflict-amplifying) will be presented in greater detail in Chapter 5. The third style, described as powerful parents, can enhance the children's ability to work through their anger with one another. Powerful parents model appropriate and effective conflict resolution skills in their own relationships. They encourage their children to express their respective positions and feelings, and facilitate the development of their abilities to compromise. Whenever possible, they allow their children to resolve differences with one another with minimal parental interfer-

ence. They intervene, however, when facilitation is requested or
necessary, or when siblings are in genuine danger of hurting one
another.

Sibling conflict is present to some degree even in better-functioning households. Each child struggles to develop his or her own
identity and to establish family and community status against the
standards set by his or her brothers and sisters.

SIBLING RELATIONS AND FAMILY DEVELOPMENT

Sibling relationships also are influenced by the changes accompanying the family's transition through developmental stages. Even
a close, harmonious siblinghood in the early years does not ensure
that a happy relationship will continue. Siblings must endure
changes in family constellation, residence, finances, and relationships with extended-family members; these changes then converge
with individual developmental changes such as attending and
changing schools, peer groups, puberty, and romantic interests.
Some observers believe that because sibling relationships are so
firmly rooted in ambivalence, they are likely to be more stressful
and more volatile than most other human relationships; love and
hate are viewed as the two sides of the sibling coin. On one side is
sibling rivalry. On the other, balance is provided by psychological
closeness, supportive caretaking, direct instruction, and facilitative
modeling of developmental milestones.

Parental influence, which contributes heavily in the beginning to
shape sibling roles, continues to affect older siblings' manner of
resolving these critical issues. Equal treatment of children is probably an idealized goal for many parents; it is rarely obtained consistently. Dunn and Plomin (1990) reported that in families with more
than one child, the parents feel and behave rather differently toward
each child in regard to both warmth and discipline or control. We
found that these differences in parental treatment greatly influence
sibling relationships, especially in families that share additional risk
factors and lack protective mechanisms for sibling abuse.

Better-functioning parents are generally available to their children on both physical and emotional levels. They take an active
interest in their children's lives, and regularly respond with support

and nurturance when one of their children is hurt. Better-functioning parents consistently spend quality time with their children.

This is not to imply that functional families are without stress. A functional family fulfills its main psychosocial purpose of supporting and protecting its members most, but not all, of the time. Adequate parents recognize that difficulties in their relationship often translate into difficulties in the overall family system; they seek assistance, when it is indicated, in resolving couple problems. If other systemic difficulties arise, these parents are aware enough to notice the changes and respond to them. It is tempting for clinicians to emphasize dysfunctional aspects of these accommodations to new situations and to mislabel transitions as pathological. Pathological labels, however, should be reserved for those families who become more rigid under stress, and avoid exploration of more functional alternatives.

According to Minuchin (1985), functional families are open to internal and external feedback. Furthermore, they are flexible enough to change and adapt to family members' needs but stable enough to provide continuity throughout the family life cycle. For example, parents can observe their children's developmental changes and modify their parenting styles as indicated. With regard to discipline, developmental adaptation might be accomplished by transitions in parental intervention: "time out" for younger children; an earlier bedtime, no television, or no outside playtime for latency-age children; and limited phone time, decreased allowance, or house, room, or car restrictions for adolescents.

Responding to a child's developmental needs requires continuing attention. During infancy and early childhood, children benefit from secure attachments to caregivers and want to spend much time with them. As they begin to explore their environment, they need parents to allow them more space, even while maintaining proximity. At this stage, parents can aid in children's development of personal boundaries by honoring their newly discovered ability to say "no" and by allowing for safe, limited periods of privacy when desired. Later, children require greater freedom to develop sibling and peer relationships. Parents who are sensitive to these changes will respect their children's relationship boundaries. Adolescents generally benefit from a good deal of freedom; yet they often continue to require a great amount of parental availability for guidance and support as they develop their abilities to make important decisions.

Clearer generational boundaries allow parents to acknowledge each child's uniqueness without losing sight of his or her equality to the others. Although siblings in these families may develop different characteristics, skills, and roles, their differences are not treated as deficits but are supported and encouraged. Healthier sibling relationships provide brothers and sisters with opportunities to develop roles that prepare them for adulthood (e.g., by role-playing mother/father, doctor, teacher, cook, or entrepreneur). In better-functioning sibling relationships, childhood enactments generally are less rigidly defined; they enable sisters and brothers to explore roles beyond traditional gender stereotypes.

If better-functioning parents develop "favorites" among their children, their partiality tends to shift with changes in developmental stages or activities so that all siblings generally receive equal amounts of attention overall. In one of our clinical families, for example, the mother acknowledged a special fondness for her three children from their infancy through toddler stages. She enjoyed the closeness and the feeling of being needed by them. Conversely, the father became more interested in his children as they learned to communicate in more mature ways. Although both parents were loving to their children overall, each preferred specific developmental stages, during which time each child received more attention.

Another characteristic of better-functioning families is that the older siblings serve as stable and nonabusive secondary attachment figures for their younger sisters and brothers. Lamb (1978) reported that both infants and older siblings interacted more with their mother than with each other in triadic situations; thus he concluded that the siblings were not attached in these families. Stewart (1983), however, observed younger children without their mothers and noted that they used their older siblings as a secure base of exploration in the presence of strangers; the older siblings comforted and reassured the younger by serving as substitute attachment figures. This level of safety within the sibling bond appears to be critical to sisters and brothers in forming enduring, nonabusive relationships.

ADULT SIBLING TIES

Cicirelli (1980b) studied the influence of siblings from nonclinical families on one another into adulthood, and found that they rarely broke off their relationship or completely lost touch. He also discovered that most of these siblings had close feelings of affection for each other: "There is an attachment bond between siblings that accounts for the persistence of sibling relationships over separations of time and distance" (p. 14). Pulakos (1987) and Ross and Milgram (1982), who studied late adolescent and adulthood sibling relationships, confirmed Cicirelli's findings. They demonstrated that most adult siblings were increasingly close to each other into adulthood, and that these feelings originated in childhood.

The quality of a child's relationship with siblings influences subsequent attachments with friends, colleagues, and spouse. Close, intense sibling relationships may be associated with lesser involvement with peers in childhood as well as adulthood. For example, close sibling bonds in adulthood can leave little room for spouses, and therefore can cause greater distance in couple relationships. Conversely, an intensely close bond with a spouse may leave little room for a relationship with one's siblings. Chronic power differences evident in an abusive sibling dyad also can influence other peerlike relationships. In one study (Sutton-Smith and Rosenberg, 1970), children who took low-powered roles with their siblings had high-powered roles with friends, and vice versa. Victims of sibling incest or assault may establish patterns in peer relationships, based on frozen childhood sibling roles, which persist into adulthood.

One individual who exemplifies this dynamic entered treatment for help in dealing with the harmful effects of having sexual relations with his older sister. She initiated the incest when he was only eight years old, and it represented much of the physical contact he remembered from his childhood. Although he suffered conflict about it as he matured, they maintained a sexualized relationship well into adulthood. When the incest began, she taunted her brother repeatedly by promising sexual contact only if he begged for it or performed some favor. Thus he developed a humiliating, low-powered role with his sister. As an adult, however, he achieved an extraordinarily high-powered role in relation to his peers: He be-

came a top executive in a large corporation, such that he command-
ed respect and authority wherever he went. This did not mean,
however, that he maintained equal or satisfying relationships. He
complained of lifelong difficulties in developing peer relationships;
those that existed were primarily hierarchical, and he was always in
charge. His marriage was more complex. It contained remnants of
the earlier sibling-related powerlessness; he felt that he was controlled and dominated by his wife, and he needed to be in charge.
He achieved this by having numerous clandestine affairs throughout
their thirty-year union.

KEY POINTS

- Relational skills developed between siblings in childhood and
  adolescence are the same skills that we bring to other intimate
  relationships throughout our lives.
- Initially, parents are the primary influence on children's definition of their sibling relationship and interaction. In better-functioning families, parents help to model appropriate conflict
  resolution, appreciate similarities and differences, and respect
  the integrity of the sibling subsystem.
- Parents who chronically select favorites, violate generational
  boundaries to develop parent-child coalitions, and/or compare
  their children with one another in unfavorable ways contribute
  to the development of conflictual and potentially abusive sibling interactions.
- By early adolescence, relationships with brothers and sisters
  take on their own identity. Each child's self-definition appears
  to be related more closely to sibling connections than to parent-child ties.
- In changes inherent in the family's transition through developmental stages, parents must respond and adapt to a child's
  changing needs and must modify parenting styles accordingly.
  Yet they also must provide stability and continuity throughout
  the family life cycle.

Chapter 3

Abusive Sibling Relationships

The family I grew up in was not the same family my brothers grew up in. They grew up in a family where they had to unite in secret misadventures just to find common pleasures. In the family I grew up in, my brothers were as much a part of its construction as my parents. They were part of what I had to experience, to learn from. They were part of what I had to overcome and shun . . .

Mikal Gilmore

Sibling ties only recently have been recognized as significant contributors to the development of childhood personality. Although child and family therapists traditionally have not treated the sibling subsystem, research supports some reasons why such a practice should be developed—especially in cases of sibling abuse.

Investigations of childhood sibling relationships (Dunn and Plomin, 1990) suggest two dimensions with important implications for abuse trauma professionals. First, siblings have separate relationships with one another that change when others intrude. Most, if not all, parents have stumbled upon their children engaging in suspicious or secretive behavior and have asked, "What's going on in here?"—only to be met by innocent looks and a vague "Nothing." Most sibling abuse studies rely exclusively on parents' reports. Many researchers believe that the incidence of sibling assault and incest are significantly underreported, in part because of this characteristic response by siblings to outside intrusion. Second, sibling victims may be reluctant to report an older brother or sister out of a sense of family loyalty and obligation, a fear of retaliation, or a concern that family members and/or child welfare workers will discriminate against the victim or the victimizer.

Clinical observation of siblings from abusive families should include interviews conducted with, as well as separate from, parents. Children often behave in one way in the presence of parental caregivers but have another set of roles, rules, and behavior specific to the sibling domain. A second empirical justification for interviewing siblings separately whenever possible is that siblings perceive the same family events differently. These nonshared experiences are thought to be important in determining personality differences in siblings reared in the same family of origin. They also may explain the complexity of attachments in the changing family system. At birth, every sibling enters a new developmental family. Each member of the family system accommodates to one another throughout life cycle changes. Therefore the sibling influence on childhood personality is generally covert, yet prominent throughout the life span.

OVERLAPPING RISK FACTORS FOR SIBLING ASSAULT AND INCEST TRAUMA

Even family therapists often make oversimplistic generalizations about abusive families (e.g., all incestuous families are "enmeshed"; abusive behavior always serves another nonabusive systemic function in the family). In fact, however, the dynamics of sibling incest and assault are varied and complex. Clinical experience and subjective reports by sibling abuse survivors suggest that some family characteristics may be common to both assault and incest (Conn-Caffaro and Caffaro, 1993). Yet it is not clear exactly which family dynamics, if any, contribute most substantially. Risk factors do not cause sibling incest or assault, but the presence of such factors makes sibling violence more likely under certain circumstances. Also, although one risk factor alone rarely determines overall risk, we believe it is valuable to study in combination the dynamic processes of the family as a whole, its individual members, and the broader sociocultural context.

Systemic Factors

Certain systemic risk factors characterize both sibling assault and sibling incest. For example, parental unavailability and lack of supervision are frequently implicated in both types of abuse. Parental caregivers themselves may be emotionally overwhelmed and thus unable to attend to their children's needs. They may work long hours, misuse drugs, suffer from a mental illness, or lack the parenting skills needed to be adequate caregivers. Parents may develop a special relationship with a favored child and may disregard the needs of the other children in the home. For these and many other reasons, lack of parental supervision and/or availability is consistently cited as an important characteristic in families where sibling abuse develops.

When parents fail to meet supervisory responsibilities, the resulting gap in authority may be filled by an older sibling. Children without appropriate adult supervision or guidance may turn to one another for support, nurturing, or validation. They may target anger intended for parents at their brothers or sisters. Researchers consistently report that increased access and opportunity between siblings are important risk factors for the development of incestuous relationships.

It is not unusual or necessarily harmful for older siblings to assume some caretaking responsibilities for younger sisters or brothers. Lack of supervision, however, in conjunction with other risk factors, may leave one or more children vulnerable to intersibling abuse. Sibling relationships characterized by gross power imbalances, role rigidity, and unclear individual and generational boundaries lay the foundation for abusive behavior. The development of good sibling relationships requires boundary maintenance; in abusive sibling interactions, one sibling repeatedly violates another's physical and psychological space.

Another systemic risk factor often implicated in sibling abuse is the differential treatment of children in the same family. As mentioned earlier, parents inadvertently place children in comparative categories such as the "smart one" or the "lazy one." This unidimensional labeling often inhibits sibling relationship development. In more extreme forms of differential treatment, parents develop favorites with whom they compare their other children negatively. This dynamic, common in families where sibling abuse occurs, becomes even more significant when parents are also generally unavailable to their children. In addition, parents may extend praise or lavish attention on the preferred child and spare him or her from abuse within the family. As a result, this child is often targeted for maltreatment by other "less favored" siblings when parents are not present. Also, a favored child may become abusive toward siblings because of his or her power, level of protection, and status in the family.

One of our clinical families sought treatment because their seven-year-old son, Danny, was biting their eleven-year-old-son, Eric, about once a week, often to the point of drawing blood. Eric recently had been in a great deal of trouble at school and at home. The parents were distressed by his behavior, but Danny's inception of violence led them to seek treatment. Both parents revealed an obvious preference for Danny in their descriptions of and behavior toward the boys.

A different story emerged from assessment interviews with the whole family, the parents, the siblings, and then each sibling individually. It became apparent that Eric was deeply wounded by his parents' preference for his younger brother. He expressed his hurt as anger and aggression toward Danny and his peers. Danny, on the other hand, was generally afraid of Eric because of the constant, largely covert assaultive behavior he endured at the hands of his older brother. During his individual interview, Danny denied any wrongdoing. His parents became suspicious and took bite impressions from each boy when the next biting episode occurred. They discovered that Eric, who desperately wanted equal treatment in his family, had resorted to biting himself and blaming it on his brother.

A child's perception that he or she is loved less is particularly significant to the development of sibling abuse, and can easily emerge after a new child is introduced into the home. When children perceive their parents as consistent and as behaving justly, less sibling conflict occurs. Feelings of rivalry and hostility arise when a child's sense of justice is violated. Some researchers (e.g., Bryant, 1978) hypothesize that children with a secure mother-child relationship are most likely to form friendly, nonantagonistic relationships with their siblings. In contrast, insecure children will tend to reenact aspects of the nonnurturant caregiver role in their relationship with each other (Teti and Ablard, 1989). This observation is especially significant for families experiencing sibling incest and assault.

The father-child attachment process also may have important implications for the sibling relationship, particularly with boys. Kromelow, Harding, and Touris (1990) suggest that father-child and mother-child attachments are distinct relationships predicated on different types of interactions in different contexts:

> While many fathers do not participate in caregiving behaviors often associated with "soothing and comforting," most fathers do play with their children and often in an affect-laden, boisterous manner. For securely attached children, father's very presence may be a salient cue for playfulness and increased affiliation with others. (pp. 527-528)

In families where the father is either unavailable or unable to provide for such well-modulated, interpersonally sensitive, safe play activity, children may suffer from the lack of an appropriate template for this behavior. A child's working model (Bowlby, 1973) of the attachment figure and the self thus may be impaired.

This differential attention strongly influences childhood sibling development. Children compare the amount of attention they receive from a parent with the amount their brothers or sisters receive. Researchers (e.g., Felson and Russo, 1988) suggest that rivalry is not simply an effect of interaction with parents; rather, the sibling relationship is impaired as a result of differential treatment. In fact, an accumulation of research with siblings of different ages suggests that differential treatment by parents is linked to the quality of the sibling relationship (see Dunn, Stocker, and Plomin, 1990 for additional information). This family dynamic affects the entire sibling subsystem, not only the child who receives less of the parents' resources. Preferential treatment by caregivers is an often insurmountable obstacle to the development of satisfying sibling relationships. If other abuse-related conditions exist in the family, and if protective mechanisms are lacking, problematic sibling relations frequently follow. A child may abuse a younger brother or sister in an effort to obtain scarce parental emotional supplies, or as a way to vicariously meet needs related to empowerment.

A child's perception that he or she is the least favored sibling may damage not only the sibling relationship but also the individual's self-worth (see longitudinal studies by Dunn, 1991 for additional information). Unresolved sibling difficulties in childhood and adolescence may affect one's self-image as well as relationships with others throughout life. According to Cicirelli (1985), adults with hostile feelings toward siblings tend to be cautious, rigid, anxious, stereotyped, and conventional. By contrast, those who perceived their siblings as jealous of them tended to be more self-assured, outgoing, sincere, and stable.

Finally, the larger ecological system surrounding the family may play a role. Researchers (Butler, 1980; Herman, 1990) have speculated that a relationship exists between sexism in the society and sexual abuse. Others (Finkelhor, 1984) suggest that child pornography may disinhibit the sexual abuse of children.

Summary: Systemic Risk Factors

- Parental unavailability and lack of adequate supervision of children in the home.
- Sibling relationships characterized by power imbalances, role rigidity, and unclear boundaries.
- One sibling repeatedly violating another's physical and psychological space.
- Differential treatment of siblings, which places children in comparative categories and causes parents to develop a "favorite" child, with whom they compare others negatively.
- The relationship between family functioning and larger ecosystem factors such as sexism in society or pornography.

Individual Risk Factors

An awareness of individual risk factors common to sibling incest and assault is also critical for effective evaluation and intervention. In focusing exclusively on the characteristics of abusive families, one risks shifting responsibility for the abuse away from the sibling offender by suggesting that the abuse is entirely the result of dysfunctional family operations. Taken to extremes, this notion supports collusion with the offender's denial of responsibility for the abuse. Although the importance of familial characteristics must not be underestimated, such dynamics cannot account totally for sibling incest or assault. Sibling abuse does not occur in every family with unavailable or absent parents. A thorough evaluation for abuse entails an analysis of the combination of individual and systemic factors unique to each family.

Sibling offenders, for example, often maintain thinking errors that minimize or distort abusive behavior. An offender's exploitative, coercive abuse may be motivated by an internal need for power and control over a younger, more naive sibling. A comprehensive evaluation would assess for cruel and sadistic behavior toward siblings, peers, and small animals. Many sibling offenders themselves are victimized by parents, older siblings, or others outside the family. Therefore it may be that the offender recreates learned behavior associated with his or her own trauma through the abuse of a vulnerable sibling. A history of victimization may play an important role in the development of deviant sexual behavior patterns. In many cases of sibling incest, an offender's deviant sexual arousal patterns also must be considered a risk factor. Adolescent sibling incest offenders, in particular, are often motivated by sensations associated with orgasm.

Motivation to commit sibling incest or assault may stem as well from other intrapsychic and interpersonal sources. Sibling offenders often lack adequate impulse control and may suffer from developmental deficits. As a result, they may be unable to feel empathy for victims or assume their perspective. In addition, offenders may lack adequate social skills and the emotional maturity needed to resolve conflict and develop meaningful, nonabusive relationships with a brother or sister. A pattern of drug or alcohol use and dissociative reactions to previous trauma also must be considered in evaluating the potential for sibling incest or assault.

Individual risk factors associated with the victim should also be identified. When offending siblings serve as emotional stand-ins for parents, victims may become dependent on their abusers and vulnerable to being manipulated, confused, or coerced. Under these circumstances, the lack of additional supportive relationships (in or outside the family) increases victims' risk for sibling abuse.

Developmental, physical, or intellectual differences also can render younger, smaller, and less sophisticated children vulnerable to abuse by siblings. Unusually frequent and ready access to a victim (e.g., sharing a room, spending large amounts of unsupervised time with an older brother or sister) may place a child at risk for incest or assault by a motivated sibling offender. Finally, a history of victimization may increase a victim's risk of being abused (see Table 3.1).

Table 3.1. Individual Risk Factors

Sibling Offenders

- Offender's thinking errors that distort or minimize abusive behavior
- History of victimization by parent, older sibling, or persons outside the immediate family
- Inadequate impulse control, empathic deficits, and emotional immaturity
- Willingness to use coercion or force to control victim (sadistic, cruel behavior)
- Drug or alcohol use
- Dissociative reactions to trauma

Sibling Victims

- Large developmental, physical, or intellectual differences between siblings
- Victim's dependence on an older, more powerful sibling
- Lack of other, supportive relationships
- Prior history of victimization
- Lack of sex education

For example, a study participant with a history of being physically abused by an older brother quickly began to feel intimidated, and decided, in the hope of avoiding further physical injury, not to resist his sexual advances.

KEY POINTS

- Sibling abuse trauma is the product of complex factors and interactions involving the victim, the offender, and the family environment. The sibling relationship in abusive families is determined by multiple individual and systemic characteristics.
- Parental absence and differential treatment of siblings are thought to play a significant role in intensifying mutual depen-

dency, sexual curiosity, and hostility between brothers and sisters. Under these conditions, opportunity and access to sibling victims increase.

- Poorly defined boundaries and imbalances in power also may promote abusive relationships.
- Individual risk factors for sibling abuse include offenders' thinking errors, which distort or minimize abusive behavior; a history of victimization; empathy deficits; inadequate impulse control and/or emotional immaturity; substance abuse; and a victim's dependence on an older, more powerful sibling.

PART II:
SIBLING INCEST AND ASSAULT

Chapter 4

Sibling Incest

When it first started, I was so unaware that it was wrong. I just remember that it pleased him so much, and I . . . looked up to my brother. And since what was going on was pleasing to him, I thought . . . "Oh, this is good."

Phyllis, age sixteen

Prior to the emergence of a multidisciplinary literature on child abuse and neglect, the rarely published studies of sibling incest were usually located in medical or forensic journals. As a result, information on this subject was not readily accessible to mental health professionals treating cases of sibling incest. Study of the topic was further complicated by disagreement over the type of sexual contact involved, age and sex differences between children, the question of consent or coercion, and the presence of harmful effects. Reported cases are still far less common than father-daughter incest because most parents who discover sibling incest are unlikely to deliver a son or daughter to the authorities. Consequently, advances in evaluation and treatment of sibling incest have been delayed. Although accumulating research substantiates the high incidence of sibling incest (Bank and Kahn, 1982; Finkelhor, 1980) and its harmful effects (Alpert, 1991; Laviola, 1992), society still tends to ignore it or, at best, to minimize the consequences for children and families.

In recent years, research with sexual abuse victims and survivors has greatly increased our knowledge of incest trauma. Studies reveal that sexual abuse trauma is associated with serious psychosocial symptoms in childhood and in adult life. Indeed, evidence suggests that violent victimization is a major traumatogenic influence in child development (Boney-McCoy and Finkelhor, 1995).

The effects of sexual abuse trauma also differ at various developmental stages. A victim's age and level of development are particularly relevant with regard to his or her capacity for understanding and dealing with incest. Children of varied ages think and act differently, and differ in their emotional functioning. Experiences that may be traumatic to an adult may not be perceived in the same way by a child. On the other hand, experiences that are extremely traumatic to a young child may not trouble an adult.

In addition, family and community reaction, support, and comfort help a child make sense of the incest and are directly related to his or her ability to cope with its traumatic effects. Sibling incest, once disclosed, frequently disrupts a family's organization, dividing the family into teams (victim or offender) that compete with one another for power, resources, and support. Without intervention, the result is often a loss of social and familial mechanisms for stabilization and compassion.

The duration, nature, and pattern of the incest also determine the extent of the trauma to the victim and his or her family. The more frequently children are traumatized, the more likely they are to suffer symptoms. For example, siblings chronically abused by their brothers or sisters are more likely to have pervasive and malignant symptoms than children who were traumatized once and who can remain in an emotionally supportive family. Duration of the abuse may be important in predicting later problems, but less important than other characteristics such as the relationship to the offender, the severity of the abuse, and the use of force (Urquiza and Capra, 1990). In addition, children sexually victimized by brothers or sisters may be the target of emotional, sexual, and/or physical abuse by parents or other relatives. Several investigators are studying the effects of a range of victimizations on a child's response to trauma (Boney-McCoy and Finkelhor, 1995; Briere and Runtz, 1990; Claussen and Crittendon, 1991). Most of these studies, however, focus on the effects of parent-child incest trauma on victims.

Although many of the findings associated with parent-child incest apply as well to sibling victims and offenders, unique differences also exist. For example, age differences between the victim and the offender may be relatively small, and the family often remains intact postdisclosure. Family characteristics, the extent and duration of the incest, the relationship between the victim and the offender, and family and community reaction to the abuse may differ substantially in sibling incest cases.

The harmful effects of sibling incest are easy to underestimate for several reasons. First, no generational boundary is violated when one child sexually abuses another in the same family. (With parent-child incest it is self-evident that a parent violates such a boundary by engaging in sexual behavior with his or her child.) Further, it is not always obvious, particularly to those without specialized training in sibling abuse trauma, that sibling incest exceeds the limits of developmentally appropriate sexual exploration, that coercion or force has been used, or that a victim and an offender can be identified. Finally, for many victims the role and the significance of sibling incest in their lives are overshadowed by a simultaneous history of parent-child abuse. This minimization persists despite evidence that female victims of sibling incest are often violated severely (O'Brien, 1991), are frequently forced or coerced into sexual acts by older brothers (Laviola, 1992), and are often significantly younger than their offenders.

In most cases of sibling incest, older brothers molest younger sisters. Thus many of the clinical observations and examples, as well as much of the research material in this chapter, apply to older brother-younger sister incest when not otherwise specified. The information on sibling incest presented here is meant also to pertain to stepsiblings and half siblings; the distinctive dynamics of stepsibling relationships are discussed more fully in Chapter 8. According to Courtois (1988), older brother-younger sister incest has three main variations: (1) when a pubertal brother uses his younger and less experienced sister for sexual experimentation; (2) when a socially inept or parentally neglected brother substitutes a sister for unavailable female peers or for the lack of affection or nurturance; and (3) when a brother who may be much older and who himself may have been physically and/or sexually abused forces a sister into sexual activity through violence and coercion (p. 76). These categories may overlap in any particular case.

A thoughtful discussion of sibling incest must begin by delineating how to distinguish between abuse and mutually consensual sexual exploration and curiosity. Forward and Buck (1978) state:

> If the children are young age-mates, if there is no betrayal of trust between them, if the sexual play is the result of their natural curiosity and exploration, and if the children are not traumatized by disapproving adults, sibling sexual contact can be just another part of growing up. In most cases, both partners are sexually naive. (p. 85)

The possibility of nonabusive sexual contact between siblings contributes to a myth of mutuality regarding sibling incest, even among professionals who tend to view parent-child incest as abusive. Sexual contact between siblings is generally considered to be abusive when there is a large age difference between the children (regardless of the form of sexual activity) and/or when the activities go beyond normal exploration to include oral-genital contact or intercourse. Sibling incest frequently, but not always, includes force or coercion by older or more powerful brothers or sisters. The average age of sibling incest victims at onset of the abuse is nine years old (DeJong, 1989; Laviola, 1992; O'Brien, 1991). Sibling incest offenders are generally much older, averaging about fifteen years old. Yet at least one investigator (O'Brien, 1991) observed that 25 percent of participants in a sibling offender study were peers within three years of their victims' age. Physical size and strength, intelligence, and developmental differences also can create situations of power and dominance between age-mate siblings.

Abusive sibling incest also includes sexual behavior that may not appear to be forced but nonetheless is based on coercion or manipulation. Both siblings may engage willingly in the behavior as an attempt to cope with unmet needs for affection and affiliation (see the discussion of pseudoconsensual incest in Chapter 8). The sexual contact usually is not limited to developmentally appropriate, transitory activity (i.e., the result of normal curiosity). Sibling incest may include attempts at intercourse, oral/genital contact, or other compulsive sexual behavior that continues over an extended period. It may or may not involve physical touching. Noncontact sexual abuse, also known as "hands-off abuse," can include unwanted sexual references in conversation, indecent exposure, forcing a sibling to observe others' sexual behavior, taking pornographic pictures of the sibling, or forcing a sibling to view pornography (Wiehe, 1996). Even noncontact sexual abuse may produce harmful effects in children (Boney-McCoy and Finkelhor, 1995).

Summary: Characteristics of Sibling Incest

- Sexual contact is forced on a child by an older brother or sister.
- Attempts at intercourse, oral/genital contact, or other compulsive sexual activity may extend over long periods.
- May include unwanted sexual references in conversation, indecent exposure, forcing a sibling to observe sex, forcing a sibling to view pornography, or taking pornographic pictures of a sibling.
- Behavior is not limited to age-appropriate developmental curiosity. May not appear to be forced, but nonetheless is based on manipulation, fear, threats, and/or coercion, or may occur while the victim is unconscious.
- Sexual contact occurs when both participants are engaging in the behavior as an attempt to cope with unmet needs for affection.

Motivation to commit sibling incest is determined by multiple individual and family factors:

- The development of a compulsive, deviant sexual arousal pattern
- The exertion of power and control over a younger and less experienced sibling
- The need to fulfill critical emotional and/or physical needs unmet within the family
- Individual and/or family beliefs that minimize or distort incestuous behavior

Because many sibling incest offenders are themselves victims of abuse, it also appears that the offender may be recreating his or her own trauma through the abuse of a vulnerable sibling. Being a victim of sexual abuse plays a role in the development of deviant sexual behavior patterns, but it is only one of many variables. Finkelhor (1984) suggests that incest offenders must overcome not only external impediments to committing incest, but also internal inhibitions against acting on the motivation. Often these inhibitions are reduced by drug or alcohol use, inadequate impulse control, or a lack of empathy for the victim. Sibling offenders also must overcome resistance by the victim. Systemic factors such as absent and neglectful parents, unclear boundaries, modeling of sexual and violent behavior at home, and differential treatment of siblings also place vulnerable children at risk.

Although guidelines provide a useful framework for differentiating sibling incest from mutual sexual exploration between children from the same family, the victim's subjective experience is also important. An experience that feels exploitative, frightening, or confusing should not be ignored, regardless of the participants' age or the activity involved. If not addressed early and redirected, questionable, transitory sexual behavior between siblings can easily become a pattern of relating to family and nonfamily children. The ambiguity or absence of judicial protocols regarding sibling incest challenges our usual understanding about reporting and securing protective services for children and families. To some degree this explains why we do not know how often sibling incest occurs.

Some researchers estimate that sibling incest is five times as prevalent as incest between a parent and a child (Bank and Kahn, 1982; Smith and Israel, 1987). No reliable figures are available, however, because it is rarely reported to police or clinics and is documented and recorded unevenly by child protective officials. In a study that first drew national attention to sibling incest, Finkelhor (1978) conducted a survey of sibling sexual experiences among college students in New England. Of the nearly 800 students surveyed, 15 percent of the women and 10 percent of the men reported some type of sexual encounter with a sibling. Although the study established that sexual experiences between siblings are fairly common, sibling behavior could not easily be categorized as either incest or sex play because many types of sexual activities were studied together.

Incest that appears consensual may sometimes be based on fear, particularly in pseudoconsensual incest dyads, where siblings appear to be age-mates engaged in a mutually consensual activity. Furthermore, age differences between siblings may be largely irrelevant in determining consent. Laviola (1992), who studied seventeen cases of older brother/younger sister incest, observed that more than half of the women reported the age difference between themselves and their offenders as five years or less. Even so, the victims perceived themselves as having been coerced into the activity. The magnitude of a child's experience with sibling incest appears to be directly proportional to the complexity and the subjective emotional significance of the experience. Bank and Kahn (1982) suggest that siblings seldom initiate incest simultaneously: "One sibling is always a little ahead, pushing to break through the incest barrier; yet erotization can develop and continue by mutual consent" (p. 171). In addition, although all incest is family-based, sibling incest is more likely to be successfully concealed. Unlike some cases of parent-child incest, it does not require the nonparticipating parent's collusion. Whether the parents are naive, suspicious, or even vigilant, children determined to sexually exploit their siblings usually succeed.

CHARACTERISTICS OF SIBLING INCEST FAMILIES

Parental Absence and Unavailability

Any description of sibling incest must examine the family environment. As preconditions for incestuous sibling relationships, previous investigators (Bank and Kahn, 1982; Smith and Israel, 1987) emphasized siblings' high accessibility to each other and the parents' inability to meet their children's needs. When important caretaking relationships are unreliable, extreme sibling reactions may be activated. In instances of severe child maltreatment, victims may form strong attachments to their sibling offenders, who serve as emotional stand-ins for unavailable parents. Outright parental abandonment or loss also can be a precursor to sibling incest. For example, a thirteen-year-old adolescent client who had always felt very close to her mother but was unhappy with her new stepfather became extremely depressed when her mother suddenly died of can-

cer. Her fifteen-year-old brother was even more despondent because his relationship with the stepfather was competitive and
openly antagonistic. At night the girl could hear her brother crying
himself to sleep. After several nights of this, she began to visit his
room to comfort him and to meet some of her own needs for support
and connection. Her brother rapidly sexualized their mutual need
for nurturance, and she became pregnant. She was admitted to an
adolescent acute psychiatric facility after a suicide attempt.

When parents are unavailable, the amount of unsupervised time
spent with a sibling usually increases, and this relationship assumes
greater developmental significance. Siblings who feel ignored or
abandoned may turn to one another for the warmth and comfort
they originally sought from parents. Boundaries may become
blurred and sexual tension may increase, resulting in an increased
risk of incest. Siblings' high accessibility to one another, unusual
sleeping arrangements, and eroticized interactions should always be
evaluated. Alternatively, an aggressive older sibling may coerce or
groom a younger child into sexual activity, confident that the younger one will be too ashamed or too much afraid of being blamed to
disclose the secret to underinvolved parents. In DeJong's (1989)
study, 83 percent of the sibling incest victims lived in single-parent
homes and were often left to be supervised by their offenders. Most
sibling incest seems to occur in families that lack parental leadership or appropriate role modeling. One adult survivor described the
unusual circumstances in which her mother discovered the incest,
and her mother's subsequent reaction:

> My brother, at fourteen, had a dream in which this man came
> to him and said, "What you are doing is wrong, and you've got
> to stop and tell your parents." So he woke up my mom in the
> middle of the night, saying something like "Dad's going to kill
> me, Dad's going to kill me." At first my mom thought he was
> having a bad dream and told him to go back to sleep, but then
> he told about what happened. He only told her about one
> particular incident that had occurred probably a few days prior.
> My mom said to him, "Don't ever do that again." Then she
> came into my room, and it was totally dark, and she said,
> "Well, Ben told me what happened." And I remember feeling

really ashamed, like I was caught. She said, "What were you thinking? You could have gotten pregnant." I didn't even have my period yet. I was still just a little kid. My mom didn't even know. Then she said to me, "It takes two to tango, you know," and left the room. And then it was never talked about again until I was about fourteen. My brother, by this time, was having some real problems—doing drugs, hanging out with the wrong crowd—and my mom was worried.

Once when she got really angry with him, she said, "Well, you raped your sister!" I was shocked . . . I had never thought of it like that. I just remember clinging to my mom and feeling very confused. First, she hardly mentioned it except to blame me. Then, four years later, she's calling it rape.

The Family Sexual Environment

Parents influence their children even when they are largely absent or unable to supervise adequately. Adult modeling of inappropriate sexual attitudes and behavior is important in creating the context for sibling incest. An exaggerated climate of sexuality is often present in the family. More than forty years ago Weinberg (1955) reported a "loose sex culture" as one of the background factors in such families. He described families that spoke openly about sex in obscene language, and where parents did little to supervise their children's sexual activity. More recent studies of sibling incest (De Young, 1982; Smith and Israel, 1987) cite families in which the daughter has been abused by her father before becoming her brother's victim.

One client, Shirley, is the third of five siblings. She has two older brothers and two younger sisters, one of whom is her younger twin. Shirley reported that when she was a child, it was her job to "run the house." She prepared dinner and did the dishes from the time she was six. (She had to stand on a chair to reach the kitchen sink.) Her father began to sexually abuse her, by his own admission, "the day she arrived home from the hospital." The incest continued into her adulthood. He began forcing intercourse with her when she was only seven, and burned her stomach with a cigarette lighter or a lit pipe if she tried to resist. Shirley shared a room with her two sisters; eventually they witnessed each other's abuse.

Shirley felt especially close to her twin sister as a child, stating that there was no real difference between the two of them. She worked hardest to prevent their father from molesting her. Often at night, as soon as she heard her father leave his room, she got up and pretended to use the bathroom, which required her to walk by her sister's bed. This sometimes had the effect of delaying or preventing her father from entering her twin's bed. Shirley, however, had no control over her older brothers, who were exempted from household duties and for whom she was expected to care when their father was away. Her brothers knew that she was being molested, and constantly tormented and teased her about it. During her high school years, her brothers coaxed her into their room and persuaded her to engage in petting and fondling, which eventually led to intercourse.

Shirley believed at the time that this was normal adolescent acting out:

> When you have five kids in four years, that's an awful lot of kids in one age group. I just thought it was . . . any good Catholic family that has that many kids that close together . . . like my classmates are not talking about it, but their brothers and sisters are probably doing it too. But it always felt wrong, and if we got caught we knew we'd be busted.

This type of hypersexualized environment distorts and prematurely heightens a child's sexual arousal patterns. In the absence of appropriate adult supervision, this family climate can lead to imitative behavior by sibling offenders; such behavior is stimulated by, and in reaction to, parent-child sexual abuse.

Family sexual abuse may be repeated transgenerationally in this way. A research participant who frequently witnessed sex between her parents said that they made little effort to prevent her and her siblings from observing their sexual activity:

> I remember my dad fondling my mom all the time when she was cooking. I can see her standing there at the stove stirring something. My father would just walk in, stick his hand down her pants, sit there, and touch her. Another time, I think he had just come back from a long trip. I remember he walked in,

threw his suitcase down, and the next thing you know, they were having sex on the couch . . . the front door was still open.

A sexually repressive family environment has also been associated with sibling incest. Smith and Israel (1987) reported that the mothers in about one-third of the families not only did not stimulate sexuality but were devoutly religious, rigid, and puritanical about sexual matters. Such parents have been termed *erotophobic* (Friedrich, 1990); they are thought to contribute to a sexually repressed climate in the family by responding to incest with tremendous anxiety and excessively punitive measures designed to reestablish control over their children. A mixture of messages in the environment, such as repressive norms and permissive sexual attitudes and behavior, confuses family sex roles and intensifies a child's sexual curiosity and rebelliousness.

Another survivor, Nora, described how her parents' rigid religious instruction pervaded the household. While her mother was having extramarital affairs, she was being molested by a half brother. An inconsistent climate, in which strict prohibitions against any kind of sexual communication were coupled with tacit denial of sexual behavior occurring in the family, left Nora confused, unprepared, and unprotected from abuse. In high school, for example, she dated a young man who tried to rape her. When she returned home, disheveled and bearing a huge mark on her neck, her mother behaved as if she did not know what the mark was. When Nora explained that it was a hickey and that her companion had tried to rape her, her mom refused to comment, except to demand that her daughter pray for forgiveness. The next day, Sunday, Nora was so embarrassed that she wore bandages on her neck and made up a story about what had happened to tell her church friends.

By contrast, Nora's relationship with her older brother was tense and highly sexualized. Beginning in childhood, her half brother constantly made lewd remarks, grooming her for incest. Nora's parents were often gone, and her brother was a constant threat. He frequently tried to peer into her room while she was dressing. Once, while they were home alone, he walked in on her in the shower after picking the bathroom lock, pressured her into playing strip poker, and showed her pornographic material he had hidden in the backyard. Her brother could also be violent. Once he physically assaulted her when she tried to tell her mother about his behavior. On another occasion, he tortured her cat and two rabbits to send her the message that he meant business. Ultimately he forced Nora to have intercourse several times during her adolescence, and threatened her with violence if she told anyone.

The abuse did not end when they became adults. Years later, armed with only a partial recollection of her childhood, Nora tried to confront her brother about some of the details of her abuse. He acknowledged the incest and helped her to fill in some of the missing details. Then he sent Nora a photograph of herself at the age of fifteen. Below the picture he had scrawled, "What a beautiful girl you were." He began to phone her regularly to recount lurid details of his earlier sexual activity with her. Nora stated, "I finally realized . . . he was getting off on it all over again. It made me sick." She began to worry about the safety of her own children and had to change her phone number to end the obscene calls.

Parental Favoritism

As stated earlier, differential treatment by parents can increase a family's susceptibility to sibling incest. Chronic favoritism toward one child at the expense of another creates conditions ripe for family disequilibrium. Children are continually comparing the amount of attention they receive from parents with the amount their brothers or sisters receive. Siblings who perceive themselves as less favored, or who actually *are* less favored, may retaliate against a weaker sister or brother. Inadequate supervision by parents allows for increased access, through which an older sibling can express his or her anger at parents by aggressive behavior against a younger sibling.

Also, a favored child already predisposed toward sexualized aggression, as a result of being raised in an abusive home, may direct his or her rage toward a scapegoated sibling. Armed with the power and status inherent in the favored child role, the sibling offender feels sheltered from the risks usually associated with incest. In the following example, Jana's victimization was related to several factors, including her brother's powerful position and her own status as the only biracial member of her immediate family.

Jana's mother, Holly, was married to Leon for several years; Jana's older brother, Leon Jr., was their biological son. Leon and Holly divorced after the disclosure that Holly was having an affair with a man named Darryl, who later fathered Jana. Three years later, Holly and Darryl separated; Jana's mother eventually remarried Leon.

Jana felt like the outsider for a number of reasons, including the fact that her father, Darryl, was black. To her stepfather, Jana was a constant reminder of a previous rejection by Holly. Leon's constant fighting with Jana had escalated to physical abuse by the time Jana reached adolescence. She and her mother were somewhat close, but Holly could not shelter Jana from the family's verbal and physical assaults. Holly still felt guilty about her infidelity and was unable to protect herself from the beatings she received from Leon, which she attributed to his "temper."

Jana's half brother was the preferred child, and was left to "keep her in line" when their parents were working. Leon Jr. exerted his power over his sister by picking fights with her and then wrestling her to the ground or up against a wall. He then grabbed at her breasts and rubbed his penis against her, over their clothing. Confident that his father would believe whatever he said, Leon Jr. threatened to tell lies about her, which would ensure a beating if she revealed anything about the abuse.

One day at school, Jana began her menses. Unaware of what was happening to her body, she panicked. She assumed that she was pregnant and feared that her stepfather would kill her. Desperate for support, she spontaneously disclosed the sexual abuse to the school nurse. When her parents learned from the child welfare authorities that Jana had disclosed the sibling abuse, Leon Sr. ordered that Jana be immediately sent to live with relatives. He said he would not tolerate lying designed to retaliate against him by hurting his son. Jana's mother was inclined to believe her because she had witnessed suspicious exchanges between Leon Jr. and Jana, but she was afraid to stand up for her daughter. Her husband made it more difficult by framing the crisis as a test of her loyalty to him or to Jana's father, Darryl.

Victimized siblings may be targeted because of gender, ethnicity, physical appearance, or for possessing a personal quality deemed unacceptable or inferior in the family. Under such circumstances, sibling incest places the victim in a double bind. Disclosure, which is difficult in any case for most victims, is complicated by the offender's favored status in the family. The victim usually recognizes the resulting dilemma for herself and her family: She must ask her parents to believe her version of events in the face of the offender's denial. Further, the offender's favored status greatly reduces the chances that the victim will receive parental support. This point is critical because supportive, confiding relationships with parents can mitigate the effects of stressful life events. A family member's acknowledgment of the abuse can be an important ingredient in the victim's stability and healing process, beginning with disclosure. The absence of an advocate can increase the harmful consequences of abuse-related stress (Brown and Harris, 1978). Isolation from external resources and support only increases traumatic stress, perpetuates role rigidity, and contributes to family dysfunction.

Rigid Gender Roles

Male and female roles in sibling incest families are often shaped by rigid gender stereotypes. These roles and the family rules that maintain them are usually enforced by a powerful male figure, in sibling incest as well as parent-child incest families.

Gender differences also are crucial in understanding the dynamics of sibling incest. Researchers such as Furman and Buhrmester (1990) report that girls generally perceive themselves as less powerful than boys in sibling relationships. This inherent power difference should be a critical component of evaluation and intervention with sibling incest dyads. Brothers and sisters who assume rigidly gendered male or female family roles often enter into powerful alliances that can exacerbate sexual tension between them. Families that are organized and segregated by gender are overrepresented in cross-cultural studies of sibling incest (Taggart, 1992). Gender segregation is apparently a necessary, though not a sufficient, condition for the existence of sexual hierarchies (Sanday, 1981; Schlegel, 1977). Furthermore, sibling incest is feared especially in societies where brothers have authority over their sisters, parallel to a fear of father-daughter incest in societies where husbands have authority over their wives.

Separate and unequal rules based on power imbalances lead to uneven application of consequences for behavior. As a result of gender-based power differences in offender and victim roles, an older brother and a younger sister dyad is most at risk for sibling incest. As one research participant explained,

> My brother was the hero of the family. He was the firstborn, and there was a great deal of importance placed on him being a male. My father tended to talk to him about the family business and ignore us girls. My mother would hang on every word he said. She still lives for any kind of connection with him. If he ever messed up or did something wrong, my parents would soon forgive and forget. When I finally confronted them about Shawn molesting me as a teenager, at first they didn't believe me. Later, they suggested that I just get over it.

Secrecy

A characteristic common to incest families in general is the preponderance of secrets. In the last two decades, public awareness and understanding of parent-child incest have increased tremendously, largely because of a proliferation of research, education, and media attention. Yet despite this information explosion, society still does not adequately recognize or understand sibling incest. The literature contains relatively few references to sibling incest, and few resources in the community are geared for victims whose offenders are identified as their brother or sister. We know of more than one client who attended a community incest survivor group only to return and say that she or he did not feel understood or included. Shame and guilt often keep sibling incest survivors from disclosing their abuse even in treatment.

Gale, a twenty-seven-year-old woman, entered individual therapy for assistance with chronic anxiety attacks. These had occurred regularly since her mother's death about two years earlier. Gale thought the anxiety might be related to her work; she was a flight attendant and often felt an attack coming on as she prepared to board a plane. She had previously sought treatment, but was disappointed by the results. Gale attended ten sessions of cognitively oriented therapy that focused on her anxiety attacks. This had significantly reduced the frequency and duration of her symptoms, but they had not disappeared. She remained weary of flying and was generally lethargic.

We reviewed Gale's history once again. When asked a casual question about her mother's death, Gale mentioned that the last time she saw her stepbrother was at the funeral, where he had made a pass at her. In reply to further inquiry, Gale described an incestuous relationship with her stepbrother, which began when she was seven and continued until she left home for college. The first incident occurred when her stepbrother, then an adolescent, had accompanied her on a flight to Texas to visit their grandparents, and molested her aboard the plane. She had not previously told anyone about the incest.

The tendency to conceal is not limited to sibling incest. Intergenerational patterns of abuse are common in families in which sibling incest occurs. Extramarital affairs appear to be prevalent (Smith and Israel, 1987); in contrast, offenders in parent-child incest families often lack the confidence to venture outside the home to meet their sexual or emotional needs. Smith and Israel report the presence of extramarital affairs in 76 percent of the sibling incest cases they studied. They conclude that by modeling secretive sexual behavior, the affairs implicitly give permission to siblings already vulnerable to incestuous activity. Confused by their parents' behavior, children can be pushed into a sexualized pseudoadult version of parental conduct, designed to ensure against being left behind. The incest then must be concealed as another element of secrecy in the family drama.

Coercion and Force

Apparently one of the most reliable predictors of poor adjustment to any type of victimization is the use or threat of violence (Helfer, 1987; Koss and Harvey, 1987). Estimates of coercion in sibling incest range from 25 to 100 percent of the cases studied (DeJong, 1989; Laviola, 1992; Russell, 1986). Because the relationship between coercion and sibling incest can be subtle and complex, it is often difficult to determine the degree to which force or coercion is present. What appears to be consent is frequently based either on fear or on the child's inability to give consent. Differences in victim and offender sex roles also may play a part in the child's inability to identify coercive aspects of the incest.

One client, introduced to sex by his adolescent sister when he was nine, remembered the incest as pleasurable and as begun at his initiative. Yet when he began to explore events surrounding the activity in greater depth, he recalled that she actually initiated the incest. Once it was established, his sister held out the promise of sex contingent on certain behavior, vaguely defined as "being a good boy." The client, intensely stimulated by the sexual contact, begged for sex while his sister devised ways to humiliate him because of his arousal. Even though the potential consequences of disclosing the incest were never discussed, he carried a tendency toward secrecy into adulthood. Because he recalled desiring the sexual contact with his sister, he felt implicated as a coconspirator, sharing the responsibility, blame, and self-punishment. In this case, the power difference between siblings was such that the offender, in effect, defined her brother's reality. Apparently her engaging in the incest behavior implied that she viewed it as appropriate. He accepted this interpretation of events and never questioned either her judgment or his role as a collaborator in the abuse.

Coercion and related aggression account for some of the most harmful aftereffects of incest trauma. In Finkelhor's (1980) study, while one-quarter of the participants reported coercion in sexual activity with siblings, the same respondents held the most negative perceptions of the experience and were the most silent about them. Laviola (1992), in studying harmful effects of sibling incest on younger sisters, discovered that force was used to maintain the behavior when it involved attempted or full intercourse. While it was occurring, victims felt negatively toward both their brothers and the activity. When less invasive sexual activity, such as fondling, was maintained through coercion, sisters experienced some positive feelings toward their offenders but blamed themselves for the incest and developed distorted self-perceptions based on supplying sex to men. In these instances, victims apparently internalized an offender's belief system, which demonstrated that they were worthless, wanted the abuse, and were responsible for it.

At other times we have observed that some sisters submitted to sexual contact with a sibling because the association with their brothers brought them special status. Jeanne, an overweight client with a long history of entering casual, unsafe sexual encounters, described how, when she was six, her nine-year-old brother coaxed her into participating in incest:

> I didn't want to participate and he would say, "Come on, please." He always had hamsters throughout our childhood, and he would say, "Well, I'll let you hold my hamster." And even though I knew I could have held it anyway, it was like, "Well, OK." I got so I wanted to please him because he was my older brother. And I felt kind of special that he'd chosen me. He was manipulative, almost making me feel sorry for him. He would whine, "Oh, please, please," . . . kind of like begging. That's what I remember.

MALE VICTIMS

As we stated earlier, the great majority of sibling incest involves older brothers molesting younger sisters. Studies (Hunter et al., 1993) also suggest that a preponderance of females who do become sibling incest offenders have been physically and sexually abused, most often by males. In multiproblem families with a pattern of intergenerational abuse, sisters sometimes sexually abuse younger brothers. Female sexual offenders' behavior is relatively understudied; yet women commit 3 to 13 percent of all sexual abuse (Kendall-Tackett and Simon, 1987; McCarty, 1986) and 1 to 24 percent of sexual abuse involving male victims (Finkelhor et al., 1990; Finkelhor and Russell, 1984).

Significant numbers of boys are sexually abused, but the majority are victimized by male offenders. Boys sexually victimized by their sisters are a minority of male victims. They are also much less likely to disclose their abuse, however, possibly because of gender role socialization regarding self-reliance and because of varying societal definitions of abuse based on the gender differences between the victim and the offender. Boys have a gender-based tendency not to talk freely about feelings or to share problems and concerns. In addition, boys are implicitly taught not to demonstrate or display vulnerability. Expressions of guilt or shame, having been victimized, and feelings of powerlessness all may be perceived as weakness. There is also some indication that boys are less willing than girls to disclose information about sexual abuse. Because most sibling incest offenders are boys, concerns about homosexuality loom large for male victims. Disclosing same-sex abuse to peers or parents might threaten a boy's developing masculinity or create the risk of being stigmatized. For all of these reasons, current estimates of the prevalence of male sibling incest victims are probably low.

Few clinical or empirical studies have examined boys sexually abused by their sisters. Research, however, has established that victimized boys present sequelae of abuse-related reactions, some of which appear to be gender-specific. Gender-based differences exist in stress, coping, adaptation, family relationships, and societal values. For example, boys externalize behavior in response to stressful situations, while girls typically internalize (Achenbach and Edelbrock, 1983). According to Urquiza and Capra (1990), two main clusters of problems persist for male victims: disturbances of conduct and inappropriate sexual behaviors. Finkelhor (1986) suggests that premature exposure to sexual contact may leave male children confused and disoriented about their sexuality. Male victims also may experience tremendous conflict about pleasurable sensations resulting from abuse or from expectations of sexual activity in relationships. Sexual abuse by a male, particularly severe abuse, disinhibits a boy's sexuality; sexually compulsive or offending behavior may result. Furthermore, boys sexually abused by older sisters may not perceive the relationship as abusive. Although scant research exists to illuminate this type of male victimization, it may contain elements of coercion and also involve the victim's inability to give consent.

Even when a brother and a sister perceive the sexual relationship as mutually satisfying, the male victim can suffer adverse consequences. Jim, for example, reported that once his older sister had initiated the incest, he repeatedly asked her—indeed, begged her—for sex throughout his childhood and adolescence. On the rare occasions when she agreed, he felt tremendous pleasure and gratitude. More frequently, however, she taunted him and then denied him access, leaving him feeling helpless and inept. A similar problem developed in Jim's long-standing marriage: he and his wife rarely agreed on sexual matters. He spent much of the time either "being good" and hoping for sexual access or engaging in extramarital affairs, where he was totally in charge of the sexual activity.

In another instance, an adult survivor recalled that he was often left in his older sister's care as a child. They developed a close, special relationship based on covering for each other and defying the rules, which led to beatings from their mother. The siblings' unhappy relationship with their mother seemed to cement their bond, which met some of their needs for nurturing and affection. He described the family interactions associated with his sister's abuse:

> My older sister and I were strong, and our mom was always trying to break us. She could hit; there were times when she could hit the hell out of us and we wouldn't cry. And it would piss her off. You get hit, you don't cry, she hits you harder. When my sister would baby-sit the rest of us and one of us kids did something wrong, she would say, "Okay, I'm going to have to spank you. Come with me." She'd take you into the bathroom and we would not get spanked. She'd hit the belt to her hand . . . like we were getting spanked. And of course, we'd make screaming noises. But to get out of the spanking, you had to touch her. You had to fondle her, and she'd touch you . . . She'd sit on the toilet, spread her legs. I was a little kid, maybe five or six.

BROTHER-BROTHER INCEST

Studies cite varying percentages of male sex offenders who victimize boys to whom they are related. These percentages range from as low as 30 percent (Urquiza, 1988) to as high as 97 percent (Friedrich, Beilke, and Urquiza, 1988). Fathers and father figures, however, do not account for all of these offenders. Studies tend to include both fathers and other male relatives in the larger category of older male relative; thus it is difficult to calculate the proportion of sibling offenders in this aggregate. Consequently we know little about the family dynamics, the harmful effects, or the prevalence of brother-brother incest.

Brother-brother incest can occur in large families where older brothers have ample unsupervised contact with younger siblings.

Children who are reared in families exposed to numerous stressors, and who lack adequate protective resources, are especially vulnerable to multiple forms of abuse and neglect. Such a family environment set the stage for Tom to experience a series of traumatic events, including molestation by an older brother.

Tom and his wife initially requested treatment for marital problems. Early in therapy, Tom disclosed that while home alone one evening with his fifteen-year-old daughter, he began drinking and fondled her breasts and buttocks. His daughter resisted his advances, and disclosed the incident to her mother a few days later. An abuse report was filed with Child Protective Services, and an investigation was conducted. Tom moved out of the home.

During his individual treatment, Tom revealed that as a child he had been sexually abused by an older brother. Indeed, his childhood was filled with physical and sexual abuse trauma. Tom was the youngest of seven children, raised in a rural section of the deep South. He described his father as cruel, violent, and rejecting. His mother, he said, meant well but was largely unavailable. There was little parental supervision at home. Tom's father had multiple affairs, and his mother had been depressed and bedridden since his early childhood. As a result, his oldest sister provided the little parenting Tom received in his early years.

One session, which centered on Tom's fear of a security check related to a new job, triggered a litany of terrors from childhood. His fear was related to continued self-blame for the sibling abuse and the fear that it would be discovered. He told of being continuously assaulted and shamed by two older brothers, as well as by neighborhood boys, throughout high school. Jack, the brother with whom he shared a room while growing up, began abusing him sexually when Tom was seven. Jack also bartered sexual contact with his younger brother to the neighborhood boys in exchange for cigarettes and pocket change. Tom had been raped at age twelve by a much older student in the school bathroom, while others looked on. His brother Jack warned him that he would die if the rapist ejaculated inside him. For months afterward, Tom was depressed, anxious, and suicidal. He lay awake nights, staring at the ceiling and waiting for death to arrive.

SISTER-SISTER INCEST

One of the least studied areas of sexual abuse is the occurrence of incestuous female sibling relationships. The few cases of sister-sister incest reported in the literature (Fortenberry and Hill, 1986; Russell, 1986) suggest that most, if not all, offenders had been molested by fathers and/or older brothers before sexually abusing their sisters. In addition, when sisters participate in group sexual victimization with one male or more, they often play an adjunctive rather than a primary, initiating role (Russell, 1986). This point is consistent with our findings. Andee, the youngest of four siblings, spoke to us about the group victimization experience she endured when she was eight years old:

> There would be this guy baby-sitting for all four of us, and all I remember is that there was this game that we played. My two older brothers would turn off all the lights, and everybody would start running around, trying to find each other. I don't know what the game was called, but we'd be in the living room and everyone would touch and feel each other. Once or twice during this game, my sister held me and would put her hand down my pants. And then, later, I watched my brother have intercourse with her.

Girls are much less likely to be sexually abused by a sister than by a brother. Previous research also suggests that sister-sister incest may be less upsetting and may result in fewer traumatic effects for victims. Russell (1986), for example, found that sister-sister incest was associated with less force or coercion, was shorter in duration, and was less violating than incest perpetrated by male offenders. All four of the sister-sister incest victims in our investigation, however, reported they had no contact with their female sibling offenders in adulthood. (Two of the four were abused both sexually and physically.) Any hypotheses generated from this finding must remain speculative. Nonetheless it is clinically interesting.

Empirical studies of sibling relationships reveal fairly consistent findings regarding intimacy: sister dyads tend to have the closest ties (Adams, 1968; Cicirelli, 1989; Cummings and Schneider, 1961). To our knowledge, however, nobody has investigated how this intense bond might both influence and be influenced by sister-sister incest. Predisposition toward stronger sibling attachment may make female survivors of sibling abuse trauma more vulnerable to the effects of a disturbed, emotionally cutoff sister bond. Also, sister-sister relationships are marked by a special intricacy and intimacy, almost as if women see aspects of themselves reflected in their sisters (McGoldrick, 1995). The differences in siblings' subjective experiences make these contacts invaluable sources of information and reality testing. Sisters often provide corroboration for what it was like to grow up in the family. Additional research is needed to determine whether adult survivors of sister-sister incest suffer from gender-specific harmful effects related to their inability to develop and maintain satisfying relationships with their sisters in adulthood.

SIBLING INCEST OFFENDERS

A thorough examination of etiology and family and individual characteristics pertinent to sibling incest offenders is beyond the scope of our book. Clinicians, however, who treat child victims of sibling incest often provide at least collateral services to child offenders as well. Recognizing the characteristics of sibling incest offenders and their deleterious impact on aspects of the victim's experience helps clinicians to understand abuse-related injuries. And some of the harsh, self-punitive thinking patterns of incest victims and survivors can be traced to an internalization of the thinking errors of their offenders (Salter, 1995). Therefore we offer a brief review of the literature on sibling incest offenders.

Numerous studies suggest that early childhood sexual experiences play an important role in the development of later sexual offenses (Becker, 1988; Cantwell, 1988). Thus it is axiomatic to conclude that many adult incest offenders themselves were victimized at an earlier age and are reenacting traumatic childhood experiences with someone else. The sibling sexual abuser's background also appears to be important in understanding the development of their offending behavior; a history of physical abuse in childhood has been reported consistently in several studies of male sibling incest offenders (Adler and Schutz, 1995; O'Brien, 1991; Worling,

1995). Studies of female adolescent offenders, however, although not limited exclusively to siblings, indicate that the great majority report a history of sexual and physical abuse. It is quite possible that boy victims are more likely to reenact their trauma through violence toward others, whereas girls may tend to turn their trauma inward through revictimization or self-injurious behavior. In addition, Worling (1995) and O'Brien (1991) rated the families of male sibling incest offenders as severely disturbed in comparison with families of nonsibling adolescent sex offenders.

The multiple pathways resulting in sibling incest offenses have yet to be determined. At present, the literature contains no studies comparing a sibling incest sample with a nonclinical control group with respect to histories of physical abuse. It seems clear, however, that an understanding of sibling incest is enhanced by focusing on the interplay between physical and sexual abuse histories in victims who become offenders. Victims do not necessarily repeat their own form of victimization, but childhood victims are more likely to grow up to victimize others (Finkelhor and Dzuiba-Leatherman, 1994).

Until recently, abuse-focused clinicians generally divided themselves into two mutually exclusive camps: victim therapists and offender therapists. Viewing a child as both a victim and an offender requires great flexibility on the part of the therapist. Furthermore, child and adolescent sibling incest offenders are quite a heterogeneous group. Some require intervention weighted toward the offender side; others require a victim-focused approach. As with adult offenders, no single profile applies to all. One sibling incest offender expressed her guilt and confusion as follows:

> I wish there was a way for those of us who did abuse our siblings . . . that there was a way we knew how to deal with that. Yeah, you can work on it in therapy, but that's a very hard thing to bring up—to talk to another human being about. I'm forty-three years old and I've finally said it. Yet it has always been there. I have always carried that guilt. And I know I can't be the only female . . .

Some clinicians might suggest that there are significant differences between intrafamilial and extrafamilial offenders, but such a dichotomy is easily overdrawn. For example, parent-child incest has traditionally been thought to be the result of family dysfunction. This assertion that families rather than offenders are responsible for parent-child incest, however, has been challenged by Becker and Coleman (1988), Herman (1981), and Salter (1988). Several investigators report that incestuous and nonincestuous adult child molesters have much in common (Becker and Coleman, 1988; Panton, 1979). Apparently a substantial number of incestuous fathers engage in extrafamilial sex offenses as well (Abel and Rouleau, 1990).

To our knowledge, similar information about sibling incest offenders is unavailable. In a study of 170 adolescents, however, O'Brien (1989) reported that the sibling incest offenders had committed the greatest number of sex crimes and were more likely to have two or more victims. Both O'Brien (1989) and Worling (1995) report that the sibling offenders in their studies were more likely than other types of adolescent offenders to have been sexually victimized, most often by their fathers. Therefore it seems clear that children who are sexually abused and then become offenders are making a powerful statement that their earlier trauma has not been resolved. The success rate in treating sexual offenders in general is quite low (Finkelhor, 1987; Pence, 1993). Thus therapy must be undertaken cautiously, with an eye toward maintaining the safety of victims and other children.

Shame and fear of being judged keep many adult sibling incest offenders from speaking about their behavior. For numerous reasons, they are often reluctant informants regarding prior sexual offending. More reliable information is probably provided during treatment than in an initial evaluation. During our research interview with Leslie, for example, we were struck by the open and straightforward manner in which she described her own sexual victimization in her family of origin. Her tone suddenly changed, however, when she spoke of her role as an offender with her younger sister Rhonda:

> I have great difficulty with the fact that I used my younger sister for a long period of time. I have never talked about this. It's just something I try to work through on my own. But to be

fair, if I'm going to say that my brothers did it to me, I have to own up to what I did to my younger sister. She and I shared a bed, and I would mess around with her when she was asleep. I don't know that she ever woke up.

Leslie found it difficult to acknowledge her role as an offender. Sometimes she assumed tremendous shame and guilt, secretly wondering if her offense explained why she and her sister had limited contact. At other times she struggled with accepting responsibility for her contribution to the strained relationship with her sister. On the surface, she described a sibling relationship characterized by manipulation and indifference: "She lives in Los Angeles, but we never see each other unless I go up there. When we were kids, if she wanted me to do one of her chores she could be real sweet. If I had something she wanted, I could be acknowledged. The rest of the time I was dead to her. That is basically how she still is now." It may be easier for Leslie to project angry feelings onto her sister than to experience the anger and self-loathing that initially might accompany acceptance of her role as an offender. Tragically, her inability to accept responsibility for sexually abusing Rhonda interferes with her capacity to understand and empathize with her sister.

TRAUMATIC EFFECTS

In determining the psychosocial consequences of sibling incest, one must take into account characteristics of the victim, the offender, and the family as well as interactions between them. Growing evidence suggests that incest trauma arrests development and affects the quality of the sibling relationship throughout life. Finkelhor and Browne (1985) used the term *traumatic sexualization* to refer to the sexual abuse survivor's inability to go outside the family to develop age-appropriate sexual attachments. The development of sexual feelings, attitudes, and behavior between siblings complicates the peer attachment process in childhood and adolescence.

Clinical experience suggests that sibling incest trauma also may affect the adult survivor's ability to form adequate, sustaining intimate relationships. Claire, a sibling incest survivor who agreed to participate in our research project, described her experience as an adolescent with her male peers:

> I was very shy. I was afraid of intimate relations. I was definitely afraid of boys because I thought they were going to hurt me the way my brother did. I never really had a boyfriend growing up . . . I was interested in boys, but not *really* interested in them. I knew exactly what they wanted, and I didn't want that. It totally distorted my idea of what a relationship was . . . the ones I always picked were the wrong ones.

For some, this difficulty with establishing intimate relationships may persist into adulthood. Russell (1986) reported that almost half (47 percent) of the victims of brother-sister incest in her investigation had never married. At that time, this nonmarriage rate was the highest among any of the incest survivor groups. Alpert (1991) later reported that 48 percent of participants in a study of adult survivors of sibling incest had never married. Results compiled from these studies warrant further investigation. Some authors (Colonna and Newman, 1983; Doherty, 1988) have suggested that because brothers and sisters are the first peer group for most of us, parallels may exist between the quality of the sibling relationship and mate selection in adulthood.

Many female adult survivors are victimized again as adults by being raped or battered (Briere and Runtz, 1988; Russell, 1986). Studies also link childhood sexual abuse to later prostitution (Bagley and Young, 1987; Harlan, Rogers, and Slattery, 1981). Russell (1986) reported that female victims of sibling incest who married were more likely to be subjected to physical violence in their marriages than women who were never incestuously abused (50 percent versus 18 percent). She also reported that victims were more likely to experience unwanted sexual advances by an authority figure than were women with no history of incest (58 percent versus 27 percent).

Our interviews also suggest that sibling incest can leave lasting effects on the relationship between survivors and their brothers and sisters. Efforts to differentiate from one's sibling are impaired, resulting in extremely fused or disengaged relationships in adulthood. Cicirelli (1982) estimated that only 6 percent of siblings reared in nonclinical families permanently sever emotional ties with one another. There are gradations, however, of what Bowen (1978) called "emotional cutoff," and many of the adult survivors in our study had little or no contact with their offenders. Sisters generally are more emotionally bonded to their siblings than are brothers. In one study (Cicirelli, 1980a) college-age women reported feeling as close to their "closest sibling" as they did to their mothers, and significantly closer than they felt to their fathers. Because most sibling incest victims are sisters, this predisposition for sibling attachment raises important questions about a female survivor's increased vulnerability to the traumatic effects of severing ties with a brother or sister.

Furthermore, relationships between sibling victims may be fractured by sibling incest. One adult survivor recalled that a sadistic older brother had tortured her while sexually abusing her. During the interview, she reluctantly acknowledged sending her younger sisters to him as her only defense. After that, he was less harsh with her. She still wakes up during the night plagued by guilt and feeling like an evil person for putting her sisters in harm's way in order to lessen her own trauma. She describes her adult relationships with each of her sisters with significant dissatisfaction. One has moved to another country and maintains no contact with her; she depicts the other as lost and dependent, with significant mental health problems, so that their visits always end badly.

Laredo (1982) applied the term *denial of impact* to describe the adult incest survivor's tendency to minimize the effect of the incest on his or her functioning. This denial causes many survivors to remain silent about their abuse long after it occurred. Our clinical experience suggests another explanation for this silence as well: society's ambiguous taboo against sibling sexual behavior, coupled with the strong possibility that the victim and the offender are age-mates, can make survivors feel guilty and cause them to assume that they were willing participants. This misperception only exacerbates a survivor's confusion and shame. Many of our research participants had undergone therapy and remarked that their therapists had not focused on their sibling relationships; thus it was easier for survivors to remain silent about their abuse. Some expressed the fear that their therapist would judge them harshly upon hearing their secret.

Another consistent theme raised by sibling incest survivors is a family member's failure to acknowledge the incest. Family members' reluctance to validate and support survivors increases the likelihood of impaired connections between siblings in adulthood. In addition, we hardly know how a family's decision not to prosecute a sibling offender affects the victim's perception of the event. Families and society are reluctant to acknowledge the harmful effects of sibling incest on victims; thus sibling offenders remain in the home after disclosure more often than incestuous mothers or fathers. Other harmful effects include a finding that adult female survivors may have difficulty in relating to their sons. Meiselman (1978) suggested that a young son may reactivate early conflicts associated with the sibling incest. In one of the few studies comparing sibling incest victims with victims of parent-child incest, Meiselman noted that sibling victims engage more often in oral-genital contact, had more often experienced periods of sexual promiscuity, and more often reported a history of rape.

More recent investigators (Patton, 1991) suggest that sibling incest also results in more pregnancies than father-daughter incest because offenders have greater access to victims and penetrate them more frequently. Questions about the scope of the incest are complex, and depend somewhat on developmental factors. Younger offenders may be more likely to respect a victim's unwillingness to continue the incest, and an older victim may be more able to resist a brother's or sister's manipulation or sexual aggression. Evidence suggests, however, that older brothers may behave more like parents in maintaining the incest without regard for their sisters' protests.

Younger siblings who lack basic sex education also can suffer harmful effects long after the incest has ended. Sarah, for example, recalled that at age seven she was pressured into letting her older brother look at her chest (to see if her breasts were growing). He persuaded her to allow him to suck on her breasts, saying that it would help them grow. She felt that she had to let him do this. He then came to her regularly to "check" on whether they had grown. Once she said to him, "It's only been a week. Why are you asking me again?" Sarah recounted these events during her interview when she made a connection, for the first time, between her sibling incest experience and breastfeeding her own children: "With both of my children, I had horrible times, and I think it's related . . . horrible mastitis . . . hospitalized with it. The ducts were just plugged up . . . there wasn't anything physiologically wrong."

KEY POINTS

- Sibling incest historically has been viewed as a harmless, mutually consensual, educational, and (under certain conditions, such as between consenting age-mates) positive sexual experience for both participants. Research over the last decade, however, suggests that factors such as duration, the presence of force or threat, and age and sex differences between participants increase the likelihood that victims will perceive the incest negatively.
- Age differences should not overshadow other important concerns such as the victim's and offender's gender, physical size and strength, intelligence, and developmental sophistication. Each of these characteristics may create situations of power and dominance between children of similar ages. Even while evidence accumulates regarding prevalence and traumatic effects of sibling incest, society's response remains tentative.
- A crucial aspect of effective evaluation and treatment with child victims and adult survivors of sibling incest is the ability to recognize the wide range of family dynamics and aftereffects that manifest in each case.
- Characteristics of sibling incest (duration, nature, and pattern) also influence the traumatic impact on the victim and his or her family. Many children victimized by a sibling are exposed to multiple traumas including sexual, physical, and emotional maltreatment by parents.
- Many findings associated with sibling incest are derived from studies of parent-child incest. Nonetheless, differences exist. The harmful effects of sibling incest are easy to underestimate because no generational boundary is violated and the presence

of coercion may be difficult to determine. In addition, it may not be easy to establish victim and offender roles.

- Certain family characteristics are consistently associated with sibling incest. One of the most commonly reported is parental absence coupled with emotional neglect. When parents become chronically unavailable, siblings may have greater unsupervised access to each other. If boundaries are already blurred, sexual tension can easily increase, and incestuous behavior may result.

- Aggressive or violent older siblings can coerce younger children into incest activity. The levels of coercion and force can be subtle and complex in sibling incest dyads. A victim's consent, for example, may be based on fear. Gender often reflects an inherent difference in power, and victims are easily implicated as coconspirators in the process. Gender and birth order interact with systemic characteristics to conspire against younger female siblings. Researchers (Finkelhor, 1980; Laviola, 1992) suggest that coercion and related aggression account for some of the most harmful effects of sibling incest.

- The family's sexual climate is important; either an exaggeratedly sexual environment or a rigidly repressive atmosphere can provide the context for sibling incest. It also may set the stage for multiple victims and offenders in the same family.

- A combination of individual and systemic factors accounts for sibling incest. Clinicians must be careful not to assume a therapeutic stance that holds families and nonoffenders responsible for the incest behavior. A view of sibling incest as the exclusive product of systemic dysfunction not only dangerously minimizes the offender's responsibility, but also neglects the offender's specific intrapsychic issues that contribute to the incest behavior.

- Sister-sister dyads may be the least studied group of victims and offenders. Because of closer ties and stronger identification between sisters, the betrayal usually associated with incest may be particularly traumatic for female survivors.

- Many sibling offenders are victims of abuse. Although a history of victimization does not necessarily cause current behavior, some offenders appear to be reenacting previous abuse experiences with a brother or sister. It is crucial to understand the interplay between physical and sexual abuse histories in victims and offenders.

- Clinical and judicial systems are unsure how to intervene most effectively with sibling incest families. Sibling incest offenders, despite documented higher rates of sex crimes and more extensive, more intrusive sexual contact with victims, are the least likely of juvenile sex offenders to be adjudicated. Professionals in criminal justice and in the child protective and mental health systems have often reinforced the family's resistance to treatment by inadequate investigation, deciding not to prosecute, failing to specify appropriate requirements for treatment, and failing to deliver appropriate treatment.

Chapter 5

Sibling Assault

I was a very fearful little girl . . . very imaginative, and much brighter. My older brother and sister were stronger and bigger than me. They tormented me regularly and I would scream and cry and my parents did nothing. Now, I think that I have chosen friends with whom I can't succeed, and I have often chosen friends who want me to fail.

Diana Trilling

Many of us remember being afraid of a neighborhood bully as children. At times, feeling threatened, we may have stayed a little later at school in the hope of avoiding insult or attack. Or perhaps a late-afternoon errand to the local convenience store to buy milk or a newspaper became a mad dash through enemy territory. We knew that if we could make it back home, we would be safe. But what if our bully lived at home?

It seems reasonable to suggest that the intermittent bullying many of us experienced as children is qualitatively unlike the chronic victimization children endure when a brother or sister is the source of the violence. Violence between children growing up in the same family often has substantial, long-lasting effects. Sibling assault, or physical abuse between siblings, is by most accounts the most frequently occurring form of family violence as well as one of the most underreported and least understood.

To complicate matters, distinctions between normal power tactics and sibling assault remain vague and undefined by courts, child protective services, clinicians, and families. Thus it is especially difficult to identify and respond to sibling relationships characterized by excessive aggression. Factors associated with sibling assault include inner rage, impulsivity, the desire for power and control, needs for parental attention or approval, a history of childhood victimization, drug use, external stressors, and deficient interpersonal skills. Family stressors often interact with some combination of these factors to create conditions conducive to sibling assault. Studies (Steinmetz, 1977; Straus, 1979) suggest that most victims of sibling assault are eight years old or younger; many children, however, are victimized well into adolescence.

For siblings, aggression and rivalry have neither simple forms nor simple causes. It can be difficult to distinguish between normative and abusive sibling interaction, in part because the point at which sibling aggression escalates into assault has yet to be established. An exploration of sibling assault might begin by drawing logical distinctions between assault and normative rivalry. Historically, rivalry is the dimension of sibling relationships that has received the greatest attention. Much of this attention has focused on the negative, hostile aspects, despite evidence that rivalry and conflict do not adequately reflect the differences between sibling pairs.

Contemporary research suggests that rivalry should not be regarded simply as one pole on a unitary dimension, with friendly cooperation at the other end. Rather, investigators report that two relatively independent positive and negative dimensions portray sibling interactions more accurately (Dunn, 1993). The independence of these dimensions is evident in the varied combinations of hostility and friendliness found in different sibling pairs. For example, some siblings are both quarrelsome and frequent playmates; others are low on both negative and friendly dimensions. Still other sibling pairs are high on one dimension or the other. It appears that rivalry alone is not sufficient to explain the presence or absence of sibling assault. Indeed, in more functional families, sibling rivalry has substantial benefits. It may aid siblings in the process of differentiation, help them learn how to negotiate to meet their needs, and facilitate the development of conflict resolution skills. Table 5.1 lists criteria for distinguishing between normative rivalry (adopted from Bank and Kahn, 1982) and sibling assault.

In addition to physical injury, increasing evidence suggests that victimization resulting from sibling assault has serious short- and long-term effects on mental health. Graham-Bermann and Cutler

Table 5.1. Characteristics of Sibling Rivalry and Sibling Assault

Sibling Rivalry
• Conflict between siblings in which the reward is possession of something that the other also wants.
• Conflict between siblings that strengthens their relationship.
• Fierce but balanced comparisons between siblings with regard to achievement, attractiveness, and social relations with peers.
Sibling Assault
• A repeated pattern of physical aggression directed toward a sibling with the intent to inflict harm, and motivated by an internal emotional need for power and control.
• Physical aggression directed toward a sibling that aims to leave the other feeling humiliated, defeated, and/or unsafe.
• An escalating pattern of sibling aggression and retaliation that parents seem unwilling or unable to stop.
• Role rigidity resulting in the solidification of victim and offender sibling roles.

(1992) observed that adults from high-conflict sibling dyads experienced lower self-esteem and greater anxiety and depression than did those from sibling dyads involving less conflict. They concluded that childhood sibling violence has the power to shape the adult survivor's emotional life and worldview.

Our clinical experience is consistent with this finding. A thirty-nine-year-old sibling assault survivor, in treatment for symptoms of depression, described her life as a series of hills and valleys. While speaking about her wish to change jobs, she said:

> I'd like to leave the hospital where I work for something more challenging, maybe private practice, but then I think I can't compete with the other professionals out there. And how could I deal with the insecurity of working for myself? I'm always worrying about money now, with a regular paycheck! It seems that I've needed something to worry about most of my life. Even when things are going okay, I imagine that any minute something horrible could happen. As a kid, I used to worry

about whether or not my brother liked me, and this is the same
brother that used to regularly beat and torture me.

  Sibling narratives are among the most universal family dramas.
Early abuse often leaves a lasting emotional impression as we try to
make sense of lifelong conflicts with our brothers or sisters. Far more
often than is acknowledged, clinicians listen to tales of lengthy emotional cutoffs and unilateral separations between adult siblings. In a
therapy culture where parent-child relationships are most significant, it
is easy to minimize or diminish a client's report of a sibling cutoff,
even though such disconnects can be powerful determinants of adult
behavior.
  A group member named Ethel, with an acknowledged problem of
dealing with anger in peer relationships, began such a narrative one
day by describing how she grew up in the "perfect" family. Everything
was highly structured, no one ever lied, and each person had a place—
except her. Previously at this juncture in her story, Ethel had described
strong disapproval by her mother. On this occasion, however, with
support from the group leader, she spoke of her struggle to deal with
an older sister who was everything her family wanted Ethel to be. Not
only did Ethel perceive her sister as smarter, more attractive, and more
popular; she also knew how to fit into their family. Ethel, on the other
hand, could not measure up. She always felt one-down in relation to
her sister. In her words, she was "not quite making it." Thus Ethel
became what she called "inappropriate". She developed a hair-trigger
temper and became physically violent toward her sister.
  The violence typically began when Ethel felt ignored. She then did
or said something to anger her sister, such as calling her a derogatory
name. This upset her sister, who sometimes reacted by throwing
something at Ethel. Then they were "off and running," with Ethel on
the offensive. She always had long fingernails and, being athletic,
was much stronger than her sister. "I would love to beat her up. I
would just tear at her on the floor, running around, scratching, biting,
beating, slugging, screaming. Even now, recounting this, it feels
really good. I still feel like I want to do all that to her."
  Ethel acknowledged how angry she still felt toward her sister and
family. She next disclosed that although she had been in treatment
for years, she had never recounted her violent sibling behavior. Nor

had she realized its significance to her ongoing struggle with anger. When asked how she thought her sister would respond to her now, Ethel shrugged. She honestly did not know; she and her sister had not spoken to each other for years.

Persistent sibling conflict is one of the most common family complaints that parents bring to mental health professionals. Parents actually can contribute in various ways—both knowingly and unknowingly—to the escalation of sibling rivalry into assault. Unavailable parents with serious skill deficits have difficulty in modeling or teaching effective problem-solving behavior. Siblings in such families are more likely to resort to assaultive behavior as a means of resolving conflict.

In addition, social learning theory suggests that harsh physical punishment by parents models assaultive behavior, which siblings may imitate in turn. In a home climate where physical abuse is tolerated, a child learns that behaviors such as hitting, slapping, and pushing are appropriate ways to solve problems. Victims also receive the message, "You deserved to be treated like this." Such messages can have profound effects on a child's self-esteem into adulthood. In research based on a national violence survey (Straus and Gelles, 1990), parent-child physical abuse was associated with higher rates of sibling violence and child-to-parent violence by both girls and boys (Hotaling, Straus, and Lincoln, 1990). In fact, in the study by Hotaling and colleagues (1990), sibling violence was related more closely to parent-child physical abuse than to spousal assault.

Children also have opportunities to observe that the parents who teach them not to hurt one another nevertheless sometimes administer emotionally or physically hurtful discipline. These events teach children to regard sibling aggression, which may escalate into assault, less seriously.

Family stress factors (e.g., financial instability, alcohol or drug abuse, marital discord, single-parent families) also may contribute to the development of sibling assault. Peripheral fathers, for example, are overrepresented in families experiencing sibling assault, and lower levels of paternal acceptance and involvement have pervasive negative effects on children. In the past decade, significant numbers of fathers have vanished from their children's lives. Furstenberg, Morgan-Philip, and Allison (1987) suggest that many men cannot separate their relationship with their children from their relationship with their former spouse. When the marriage ends, the paternal bond often withers in a few years.

Important developmental distinctions also exist. According to Finkelhor:

> Childhood is a period of enormous change in size, strength, cognitive capacities, gender differentiation, relationships, and social environments—all of which may affect the potential for victimization. Moreover, the impact of these changes, which interact with one another, is not simple. (1995, p. 178)

Power and control issues are often reciprocal between siblings who are close in age. Patterson (1986) suggests that siblings show considerable similarity in aggressive behavior, and that siblings and their parents "shape" each other's aggressive behavior through spiraling patterns of coercive interaction. The gradual equalization of size and strength between siblings of different ages may account for the decline in sibling violence from 90 percent among three- and four-year-olds to 64 percent among fifteen- to seventeen-year-olds (Straus, Gelles, and Steinmetz, 1980).

Age differences appear to be more important between children reared with siblings as caretakers, though this depends somewhat on the role and function assumed by older siblings in the family. One of the most consistent research findings in this area is that each child's contribution to a sibling interaction is strongly influenced by whether the child is older or younger. Overall, older siblings are a salient feature in the lives of their younger brothers and sisters. Baskett (1984) observed that younger siblings were more likely to attend to an older sibling's behavior than to that of a parent. In addition, younger siblings often passively accept aggressive acts initiated by older siblings.

Firstborns, especially boys who use physical force, are viewed as more powerful and bossier than younger siblings (Bryant, 1982). Several explanations are hypothesized. For example, firstborns generally are considered more likely to engage in hierarchical power relationships with their parents. In relationships with younger siblings, they tend to model their parents' power tactics. In response, younger siblings often react in ways aimed at upsetting the older siblings' power.

In Debbie's family, this pattern became violent and had serious consequences:

> My dad would come home drunk, and my mom would be angry and slap him in the face. She'd slap him, but never more than twice. Because if you went more than twice . . . the trophies started flying, the shelves started falling, and we were hiding. When my dad came home in this kind of mood, we knew right where to go. And if you did something that day that Mom was going to tell Dad, you knew that you were really going to get it, and he'd be hitting you . . . he don't know how many times he's been hitting you, he don't know how long he's been hitting you, he just knows that he's been hitting you. And then Gary, my oldest brother, would treat my younger brother Mark the same way. I remember one time he got angry with my brother and they went out to the car, and Mark put his hands in to get something and Gary slammed the trunk down. I just remember all the blood.

Finally, the developmental effects of age and sex must be considered during an evaluation for sibling assault. Boys and girls mature at different rates; some researchers have suggested that particular combinations of siblings' age and sex can raise or lower the level of sibling violence. Straus, Gelles, and Steinmetz (1980) found that the sex of the sibling group, in contrast to differences between individual children of each sex, is a major determinant in the level of sibling violence. In their study, rates of sibling violence were consistently higher in families with only male children than in families composed only of girls. Furthermore, differences between all-girl and all-boy families increased markedly as the children grew older. For example, the rates of sibling violence for ten- to fourteen-year-old boys in all-boy families was more than double the rate for girls in all-girl families. For the oldest age group (fifteen through seventeen), rates for all-boy families were roughly twice as great as for all-girl families.

PANDEMIC FAMILY VIOLENCE

Sibling assault is by far the most common form of family violence (Gelles and Cornell, 1985). According to national surveys (Gelles and Straus, 1988; Straus, Gelles, and Steinmetz, 1980), physical aggression between siblings is far more prevalent than spousal and parent-child abuse combined. Yet despite such evidence, sibling assault receives relatively little research attention. The incidence of sibling assault has been documented, however, in a number of important investigations. Steinmetz (1981) states that violence between siblings may also be the most potent form of family violence in that it represents the child's first opportunity to engage in violence witnessed and experienced with peers. In an earlier work, Steinmetz (1978) reported that 70 percent of the young siblings studied, with an average age below eight, used physical violence to resolve conflict.

In a study of college students, Straus (1979) found that 62 percent of his sample had used physical force on brothers or sisters during the past twelve months. Straus, Gelles, and Steinmetz (1980) conducted a national survey of 2,143 families and discovered that eight out of ten children with siblings committed acts of violence against a brother or sister every year. Abusive behavior directed toward a sibling in these studies included pushing, shoving, slapping, throwing objects, kicking, biting, hitting with a fist, beating up, hitting with an object, and threatening to use or using a knife and/or gun. According to parents, the more severe acts of violence were committed by a large number of siblings.

When researchers Graham-Bermann and Cutler (1992) examined adults' recollections of sibling abuse, only 8 percent of their college-age sample reported that they had been abused by a brother or sister during childhood. The researchers made no effort, however, to distinguish between sibling victims and offenders. Victims may be less reluctant than parents or sibling offenders to identify cases involving severe violence. In a recent study (Kolko, Kazdin, and Day, 1996) comparing children's and parents' reports of family violence, the highest levels of violence (over 90 percent) were reported by children in reference to sibling assault. The authors concluded that children's reports contribute to the identification of violent families beyond those identified by parents' reports alone.

It seems likely, then, that empirical studies which rely exclusively on parents' reports risk underreporting the incidence of sibling assault. Parents probably do not know about every instance of sibling assault that occurs in the family; therefore they may underestimate rates of sibling violence at home. Because parents learn to expect sibling conflict, they may not be alarmed when it occurs. They may abandon efforts to reduce sibling violence, or may intervene only in intense disputes.

During one family assessment interview, for example, the presenting problem was a recent suicide attempt by the second oldest sibling. The therapist observed that the two youngest boys were calling names and making threatening statements to each other ("Just wait till we get home"; "Wait till the next time you're acting all cool with your friends"; "You're such a chump"). The boys' parents ignored their behavior, which escalated rapidly to punches, kicks, and throwing elbows on the sly. Within ten minutes, the boys were openly hitting each other in a contest to see who could get in the last punch, while the parents continued to ignore them.

The therapist intervened and asked the parents, "What do you do when they do this at home?"

> **Mother:** Do what?
> **Therapist:** Hit, kick, . . . and behave in hurtful ways toward each other.
> **Mother:** Oh, that. Well, we tried to get them to stop, but it's been going on for years. [The boys were seven and nine years old.] Finally, we just gave up. I figure I grew up with only one brother and we fought, but we didn't fight like that. So I just thought after a while, when we couldn't get them to stop, that that's how brothers are. They horseplay a lot, and you can't do anything about it. But I yell at them sometimes to stop if the noise gets to me, especially at Tim [the older one] because he should act his age more.
> **Father:** That's how it was with me and my younger brother, we fought all the time. Boys are just rougher than girls.

Both parents denied that their sons' behavior ever got out of hand. Direct questioning, however, revealed that they had made two trips to the emergency room and several to the doctor's office for stitches, concussions, and a loose tooth, all as a result of the sibling violence. The more abusive episodes generally occurred after the mother had intervened to protect the youngest child. Also, a few years earlier the father had punished the eldest boy excessively, thereby initiating an investigation by CPS. This same child was assaultive toward his three younger brothers.

A number of researchers contend that although aggression is a regular feature of the sibling relationship, the overwhelming majority of their subjects were both victims and perpetrators of sibling violence (Brody, Stoneman, and Burke, 1987; Roscoe, Goodwin, and Kennedy, 1987). Moreover, family interaction studies of parent-child physical abuse implicate various child characteristics (e.g., oppositional behavior, special physical status) in accord with interactional perspectives that emphasize the role of multiple determinants (Ammerman, 1991). Factors such as physical size and strength, intelligence, and developmental stage, however, can override the existence of reciprocity, and can create situations of power and dominance even between age mates.

In addition, a younger sibling may be trained or coerced to "fight back" and inadvertently may provoke further abuse. In such cases parents, failing to perceive sibling aggression as a problem, may not intervene. The resulting physical and psychological injury to victims can be as damaging as in less evenly matched sibling pairs.

What of sibling assault cases in which the violence is clearly not mutual? A pattern of predictable victim and offender sibling roles based on inherent inequality strongly suggests abuse. A few studies identify the characteristics of sibling assault when one sibling is primarily the perpetrator, and the other the victim. Graham-Bermann, Cutler, Litzenberger, and Schwartz (1994) conducted an investigation of young adults' recollections of high-conflict or violent sibling relationships during childhood and adolescence, in which 28 percent of the subjects experienced some type of high conflict in their sibling dyad. Further, this study revealed that when levels of conflict characterized as violent, abusive, or both are assessed, birth order and gender differences become salient characteristics of the sibling dyad. The authors suggest that the sibling dyad most at risk for serious conflict involves an older brother and a younger sister.

Parents sometimes may be unable to observe intersibling assault because of the unique, somewhat exclusionary aspects of siblinghood described earlier. Pressure to remain loyal to an older brother or sister, combined with the fear of adult consequences, motivates children to maintain secrecy about assaultive sibling episodes. Jeff, for example, was an adult survivor in our study who told how much he had idolized his older brother, Dave, as a child. Dave was popular at school and a good athlete. Jeff was small for his age, and developed a rich inner life based on books, music, and art. He grew up in a large family without his father's stable presence, and his mother constantly compared him unfavorably with his older brother. As a result, he vacillated between resenting Dave and seeking his approval. Dave often humiliated Jeff publicly. Once, for example, he stole Jeff's towel and clothing from his gym locker so that Jeff was forced to walk naked around the locker room, asking if anyone had seen his clothes. Jeff knew better than to report on his brother when they returned home because he knew his mother would call him a baby and a tattletale. Also, Dave might retaliate. Besides, he secretly hoped that by demonstrating to his brother that he could "take it like a man," he would gain Dave's approval.

Finkelhor and Dziuba-Leatherman (1994) believe that sibling assault should be grouped into a category of child victimization that they term "pandemic" because of its frequency in our society. The rates of peer and sibling assault against younger children have virtually no equivalent among adults (Pagelow, 1989). Society tends to treat inter-sibling violence as relatively inconsequential. Yet it is not clear to the child why being beaten up by a peer (or sibling) is less traumatic or less violent than being physically abused by an adult (Greenbaum, 1989). Furthermore, Straus and colleagues (1980) estimate that nearly 2 million children at some point have faced an angry brother or sister wielding a gun or a knife. Pandemic victimizations such as sibling assault deserve greater attention, if only because of their alarming frequency and the possibility that they may powerfully influence a child's everyday life and development. Viewed in these terms, sibling assault is unique among types of childhood victimization.

A PRECURSOR OF FUTURE VIOLENCE

Sibling rivalry is widely accepted as a normal characteristic of family life. Unfortunately, the same may be true for physical violence between siblings. Intersibling violence, however, sets the stage for violent interactions with peers, and later with spouses and children. Gully, Dengerink, Pepping, and Bergstrom (1981) suggest, on the basis of empirical evidence, that violent sibling interactions, particularly for children in the perpetrator role, may be more important than other family interactions in socializing individuals to behave violently in the future.

Gully and colleagues (1981) report that being the recipient of sibling violence actually may inhibit later violent behavior. The results of their study suggest that a tendency to engage in aggressive behavior is acquired through interactions in the family. Loeber, Weissman, and Reid (1983) reached a similar conclusion regarding the potential for future violence in a study of chronic adolescent offenders. It appears that certain familial experiences, such as assaulting a brother or a sister, may be important in promoting violent behavior. This suggests the need, among adult perpetrators referred to treatment, for more explicit clinical assessment of a sibling offender role in childhood.

To illustrate, a client was referred to us for therapy in relation to anger management. During a particularly heated argument with his girlfriend, he had shoved her hard enough to knock her down. A psychosocial history provided by the domestic violence program, where he was attending group counseling, made no mention of any abuse trauma in his background. In response to a direct query, the client also denied the existence of abuse in his family history.

During our first few meetings, we proceeded to construct a genogram together. It was revealed that as a child, the client was often assigned the primary caretaker role for his brother, who was just eleven months younger than himself. His parents, both drug dealers, were rarely at home. He reported an extended history of violent interactions with his sibling, well into their adolescence. Their fighting became more severe as time went on. Often one or both of them were injured, sometimes to the point of requiring medical treatment. The client did not characterize the conflict with his brother as abusive.

The sibling assault literature remains inadequate in addressing the complexity and the scope of this national child welfare concern. Finkelhor and Dziuba-Leatherman (1994) state the problem succinctly: "Sibling violence, the most frequent form of child victimization, is conspicuous for how little it has been studied in proportion to how often it occurs" (p. 174).

PSYCHOLOGICAL MALTREATMENT

Sibling assault is often accompanied by psychological maltreatment. Wiehe (1990) found that 91 percent of the adult sibling abuse survivors in his study reported emotional abuse in conjunction with either physical or sexual maltreatment. Family environments conducive to sibling assault are frequently characterized by chronic displays of emotional abuse and neglect. These clearly contribute to sibling assault victims' overall psychopathology. Yet the more highly visible violent behavior between siblings often overshadows and threatens to minimize the impact of psychological maltreatment. In fact, evidence suggests that emotional abuse, which is more common than violence, leaves long-lasting scars on sibling victims and survivors. According to Wolfe (1987), "the psychological nature of maltreatment is more difficult to record and is suspected to be more damaging to the child than physical injuries" (p. 18).

A younger, more dependent sibling may have no choice but to submit to intimidation and ridicule. Accepting such conditions entails learning to survive with constant fear as a "normal" way of life. In many cases, sibling emotional abuse carries the threat of physical retaliation should the victim protest or disclose the maltreatment.

Aggressive interactions between siblings often stem from some form of emotional abuse that can escalate into assault if left unaddressed by parents. An exchange of words, name calling, teasing, intimidation, destruction of personal property, or other methods of provocation commonly precede physical abuse. A look on a brother or sister's face, a sudden movement, or no reply at all can trigger a chain of complex events leading to assault.

In one case, a family came to counseling appropriately concerned about their eleven-year-old son, Donnie, who had recently burned down the garage and one room of their home after an argument with his mother, Sheila. The meeting was attended by Sheila, her second husband, Greg (stepfather to the boys), Donnie, and his eight-year-old brother Jason. The family revealed specific details about the argument that had precipitated the fire. The fight was about whether

Donnie should be allowed to "hang out" after school at his friend Seth's house, without adult supervision, until dinnertime when he usually returned home. Donnie's mother had allowed him to do this before her recent marriage to Greg. Greg thought that Donnie was too young to be without adult supervision for such an extended period; Sheila, reversing her former position, now agreed. She complained that he had run to his room and shut the door, preventing further discussion. "Yeah, after you called me a loser, and called my dad a loser," replied Donnie. Sheila admitted to saying that Donnie was "good for nothing" and was "wasting himself" when all he did was hang out at Seth's, and that he was "taking after his father."

Jason agreed, saying that Donnie never did his chores at home. Donnie kicked the leg of Jason's chair, and glared directly at him. Jason stopped in the middle of his sentence and said, "I just wish we all got along better." The therapists' efforts to explore this process were met with silence from both boys. The stepfather, however, said that Jason was afraid of Donnie and that Donnie had just given him a signal to keep his mouth shut or else risk getting clobbered when they got home. Greg had observed this sort of interaction between the siblings many times.

In a subsequent session with Jason and his mother, Jason revealed that Donnie sometimes terrorized him at night. They shared a room, and Donnie accused his brother of being "a bad brother" and an "evil person" for tattling on him to their parents. In fact, Jason rarely tattled on his brother. He explained, "My mom or Greg just find out things sometimes, and he thinks I told, but I didn't."

Jason also disclosed that his brother sometimes suggested that perhaps he should just suffocate or stab Jason in his sleep, or throw him out the window and put him out of his misery. Then Jason would not have to look at his "ugly, big-nosed, chipmunk face in the mirror anymore." Jason took these threats quite seriously. He frequently stayed awake as long as he could, afraid to fall asleep and be stabbed, dropped out the window, or smothered by his brother's pillow. Donnie sometimes put action figures with bags tied around their necks and knives in their chests in Jason's bed, or hung them on his bedpost or out the window to further terrorize Jason when he was angry. Donnie rarely hit Jason, but his emotional abuse already showed signs of having serious consequences.

Many parents and professionals tend to discount intersibling psychological maltreatment and to minimize its importance because it leaves no physical signs. In addition, detecting emotional abuse is difficult because parents and professionals alike tend to accept it as a normal occurrence in most sibling interactions. Television and the popular media frequently portray sibling interactions as if emotional abuse were acceptable. Often it is minimized ("all kids talk that way to their brothers or sisters") or excused as a variation on sibling rivalry. Parents who grew up in families where sibling emotional abuse occurred, and who are overwhelmed by multiple acute stressors, may not even consider these interactions problematic when they observe them between their own children. In addition, sibling psychological maltreatment can be subtle and may be masked by a veneer of functionality. Psychologically maltreated children, however, have been depicted as having difficult temperaments (e.g., excessively active or withdrawn) and as exhibiting more aversive behaviors than other children (Garbarino and Vondra, 1987).

Robyn, for example, lived in the shadow of her talented older brother, Richard, whom their mother clearly favored. She followed Richard everywhere when they were children, and became a tagalong business partner in adulthood. In his company, Robyn lacked opinions and even the inclination to have them. Despite her initial disinterest in the family business, Robyn's keen interpersonal skills and her perfectionism pushed the company to greater success. Still, Richard received all the praise and took all the credit. He never praised his sister's contributions, and made certain to intercept any positive feedback directed toward her. He demanded total allegiance and obedience and maintained complete authority over her life in almost militaristic fashion. He criticized her personal appearance, questioned her professional judgment (though it was often sound), and exploited her dependence on him by stating that he "only wanted the best for her." The two things that mattered most to Robyn—her mother's love and her own sense of self—lay exclusively under Richard's control.

Robyn made her first attempt to liberate herself by marrying a man who resembled her brother as little as possible. He was an undisciplined, free-spirited drifter who represented a window to an exciting life she could only imagine. Richard opposed the marriage, offering the man a substantial sum of money to call the whole thing off and disappear. This only strengthened their resolve. Married life, however, became another confirmation of Robyn's perceived inferiority. After only fourteen months, she filed for a restraining order and then a divorce, revealing a troubled relationship marked by spousal assault.

Although there are obvious distinctions between the types of sibling abuse (incest, assault, and psychological maltreatment), often they are all part of the same incident and the same family culture. Therefore it is important to acknowledge that sibling abuse victims are frequently subjected to multiple forms of abuse by the same offender. We have already discussed the use of force and coercion by sibling incest offenders, and its potentially damaging effects. Older siblings, when left in charge of younger children in the family, often abuse them emotionally by demanding that they do household chores or personal favors for them. The penalty for noncompliance may be ridicule, name calling, or even physical assault. This exploitation or manipulation frequently occurs along gender lines, when an older brother sets himself up as lord and master over a younger sister.

Detonia, sixteen, found herself in such a situation with her older brother Troy. They both were well-behaved young people who had managed to avoid the kinds of activities that often lead to trouble in adolescence. Detonia earned better grades than her brother; sometimes this was a source of contention between them. One day, Troy learned from a mutual friend that his sister had lied to their mother and attended a party against their mother's wishes. At the party, according to acquaintances, Detonia consumed alcohol and tried smoking pot for the first time. Troy began to blackmail his sister. He made her buy gas for his car, do his chores at home when their mother was away, give him money, and even write a five-page book report for his English class. He also began whispering "druggie" and "alkie" to her at the dinner table, just out of their mother's hearing. When they were alone, he called her a "loser" and a "drunkard," and told her to stay away from him.

CHARACTERISTICS OF SIBLING ASSAULT FAMILIES

Ineffective Parenting

Parents are highly influential role models for siblings, particularly in earlier childhood. Children are quite sensitive to emotional interactions and to the quality of other relationships such as couples and parent-sibling dyads. Therefore they are exquisitely attuned to the family environment. Accorded this early influence, parents play a major role in the way brothers and sisters learn to deal with conflict. In many families, sibling aggression can serve a positive, constructive function in that it forces brothers and sisters into a social "laboratory," where they learn how to manage and resolve disagreement. Developmentally varied sibling subgroups offer children a powerful opportunity to learn flexibility, play, and competence. The resulting aggressive give-and-take is one component of a constructive dialectic that characterizes ideal sibling connections.

To facilitate this social milieu, parents must offer a stable value system and must consistently apply its principles in order to help siblings settle disputes. Parental apathy and nonacceptance have pervasive negative effects on sibling conflict. Worse yet, when a parent's principles are capricious, bizarre, or arbitrary, sibling relationships can become chaotic, violent, or even murderous.

According to Bank and Kahn (1982), ineffective parents appear to fall into two groups: those who avoid conflicts and those who amplify them. Conflict-avoiding parents negotiate *for* children, as opposed to facilitating the development of skills that eventually would render them capable of reaching their own solutions. This situation contributes to conflict because parents act as referees and determine who is right and who is wrong, thus interfering with the natural cycle of conflict resolution between their children. As a result, children are forced to continue their conflict underground, outside the parents' sphere of influence. Conflict-avoidant parents typically have trouble respecting the boundaries of sibling conflicts, and remain ignorant or in denial about any sibling assault occurring at home.

Conversely, conflict-amplifying parents encourage conflict by indirectly supporting it as a means of resolving disputes between siblings. Sibling assault, engendered by parents who amplify conflicts, is widely underreported. Such parents often rationalize or dismiss their children's aggression as normal horseplay, and thus minimize actual injury when it occurs. In some cases, sibling assault may be related to the conflict amplifying the parents' dislike of, or unresolved conflict with, one of the children.

Boys in particular are often subject to conflict-escalating parental behavior because of differences in gender role socialization for male children. Brandon, a research participant, described how this dynamic was displayed in his family:

> After my mom got divorced she married Steve, who had two kids—George, who was two years older than me, and Tara, who was a year younger. My mom used to get mad at me sometimes and tell me I was just like my dad . . . I don't know if this was why Steve never liked me . . . he just didn't. He used to suggest all the time that George and I wrestle [George was on the high school wrestling team] . . . and he didn't have to say much; I knew he was rootin' for George. He'd say, "George, show me your new wrestling moves. You help him out, Brandon." Or he'd start a game of "keep away" that would always end up with me and George wrestling and fighting. I'd always be the one to end up with the busted lip or black eye or something, and Steve would always laugh it off. I was scared to really fight back, because if I ever hurt George, he came at me twice as hard. I hated when football season was going on, because that's when Steve really did this a lot, during half-time. I dreaded half-time . . . I still don't like football much.

Another common characteristic of families with ineffective parents is harsher, more frequent punishment of an older, dominant sibling. Felson and Russo (1988) reported that such parents are more likely to punish the more powerful sibling; this, in turn, stimulates more aggression on the part of the "weaker" sibling. Such a response begins a repetitive, nonproductive sequence of events that can escalate into sibling assault. Consistent, even-handed parental intervention in such cases is crucial. Most clinicians agree that in well-functioning families, a structure of accepted and constructive rules guides interactions within and between family subsystems. Families with serious problems of sibling aggression lack such a rule structure.

Parental Favoritism

Parental favoritism occurs in all families, but in better-functioning families the favored status rotates among the children with some regularity. Researchers (Elder, Caspi, and Burton, 1988; Ross et al., 1994) support the view that parents' differential treatment of children is associated with conflictual sibling relations. When parents make one child their consistent favorite, this behavior contributes to the development of sibling abuse in two primary ways.

First, the preferred child may develop an identity based on a sense of power, privilege, and entitlement. Such an identity can set the stage for aggression and violence between siblings. Marta depicted her relationship with her brother, who abused her physically and sexually, as "competitive." She also described him as the family hero: "He was the firstborn, and there was a great importance placed on him being the firstborn male. Whenever he messed up or did something wrong, my parents were always quick to forgive and forget."

Second, parent-child relationships characterized by favoritism or cross-generational coalitions may encourage a child who is left out to become increasingly resentful and aggressive toward the preferred child. The aggressive child may experience acute feelings of isolation and abandonment in witnessing positive interactions between a parent and a preferred younger brother or sister. The following example illustrates the negative effects of such a parent-child coalition on the sibling relationship.

Karin, who was large for a nine-year-old, lived in a foster home with her fifteen-year-old sister, Timara. Both had been removed from their biological family approximately two years earlier because of physical abuse and extreme neglect. Timara essentially raised Karin and was precociously mature and eager to please. As a result, her foster parents regarded Timara highly. They did not hesitate to show how proud they were of her good grades, her extra effort at home, and her overall pleasant manner.

Karin viewed her foster parents' regard for her older sister somewhat differently. "They show her off as if she's a movie star," she said. "And when they talk about me, they say, 'Oh . . . she's doing better' or 'Her grades are getting better, but she still has some problems with her temper.' They say it's hard to believe she's my sister because she's so good and I'm not."

Karin's ability to tolerate her foster parents' favoritism for Timara eventually wore thin. Her problems with her "temper" increased. Whereas previously she had expressed her anger and resentment covertly (e.g., by "accidentally" ruining Timara's belongings, or borrowing her things without asking), now her voice grew louder, and her outbursts became more frequent and more intense. Her anger finally escalated to the point where she began assaulting Timara physically. Once she pushed a wicker armoire over on top of her sister. On another occasion, she threw a chair and dishes at her sister, narrowly missing her head.

Consistent and fair-minded parenting has been established as an important component of healthy sibling development (Dunn and Plomin, 1990; Schacter, 1985; Stocker and McHale, 1992). Siblings often fight over ostensibly trivial concerns (e.g., "Who took my X-Men comic book?"). However, when sibling conflict is transformed into a competition for parental approval ("Choose me, reject him"), the stakes become high and the conflict can escalate quickly into assault.

Low levels of paternal acceptance and involvement can be especially harmful to siblings. In a longitudinal study by Brody, Stoneman, and McCoy (1994), a father's differentially negative treatment of his children was associated with negative dimensions of the quality of the sibling relationship. Research by others (Brody et al., 1992; Stocker and McHale, 1992) suggests that siblings' levels of conflict are much lower when they characterize their relationship with their father as warm, and believe that their father treats them with relative equality. These findings reveal the particular significance of father-child relationships in siblings' development, and highlight the primacy of a father's differential behavior in forecasting the quality of sibling relationships from middle childhood to early adolescence. In fact, a father's relative unavailability, compared with the mother's, may bestow a particular psychological salience on the paternal role and its relationship to the quality of sibling interaction. The father, as one basis of role identification (especially for boys), is an important model for empathy development and limit setting with regard to playful and aggressive behavior between siblings.

Sibling Deidentification

Differentiation in families requires that siblings be able to identify with some characteristics of their brothers and sisters, and to deidentify with others. Schacter's (1985) study of sibling deidentification makes some helpful distinctions between this phenomenon in normal families, where it seems to mitigate sibling rivalry and allow for conflict resolution, and in clinical families, where sibling deidentification appears to exacerbate conflict between the designated "good" and "bad" siblings, and sometimes leads to extreme violence. Schacter proposes that in pathological deidentification, the process of conflict resolution between siblings is somehow flawed. In dysfunctional families, a sibling role or identity becomes rigidified and predisposes a child to direct aggressive behavior toward a brother or sister perceived as different. Over the course of childhood, perceived differences may result in the solidification of inequitable victim and offender sibling roles. Naturally occurring dynamic cycles of conflict and resolution disappear. Instead the process becomes fixed: The "bad" sibling constantly harasses the "good" one, who is defined as the innocent victim. Such power inequities become permanent components of sibling interactions, often into adulthood.

According to Schacter (1985), the solution to this problem becomes the problem. To protect "innocent" victims, parents consistently intervene in sibling conflicts and sometimes prohibit fighting altogether. Much like the approach taken by Bank and Kahn's (1982) conflict-avoidant parents, this intervention style impedes the dynamic flow of sibling conflict so that vital education in conflict resolution and assertiveness skills is interrupted. The result is the development of internalizing symptoms for the "good" sibling and externalizing symptoms for the "bad" one. Hence family therapists recognize the familiar clinical observation that troubled children often come in "good-bad" pairs. Yet in sibling dyads where one child is already abusive to another, further physical or emotional abuse must be prevented. In these cases, protecting the victim and decreasing the frequency and intensity of sibling violence must take precedence over other goals. Sibling deidentification occurs most commonly between the first two children in the family, more often between same-sex siblings.

Spousal Abuse

Sibling relationships also may be harmed by chronic spousal abuse. When a child acts out violently against a brother or sister, he may be signaling his upset about incidents in which his father physically or emotionally abuses his mother. Each year at least three million American children ages three to seventeen witness violence between their parents.

Apparently there is an important connection between sibling violence and spousal abuse. Children exposed to parental violence learn to model assaultive behavior in both subtle and overt ways. Research (Margolin, 1995) suggests that they learn less about *how* to act aggressively than about the "conditions under which aggression may be applied in intimate relationships" (p. 31). Correspondent symptoms of growing up with interparental violence include accepting violence as a way to resolve conflicts, rationalizing the use of violence under stressful conditions, and devaluing females.

Graham-Bermann et al. (1994) also report a significant relationship between sibling violence and use of severe violence in the parental dyad. Serious physical violence between parents creates powerful templates for children. Children whose parents resolve conflicts through attempts to control, intimidate, and dominate may use similar strategies with peers and siblings. The multigenerational transmission of violence in families flows from adults to children, who then exhibit the same behavior when they reach adulthood. More precise assessment and identification of sibling assault in families characterized by spousal abuse would aid in early intervention designed to disrupt faulty intergenerational patterns in these multi-problem families.

Finally, chronic conflict between spouses regarding their children's disputes may give siblings the message that they should take matters into their own hands. Reid and Donovan (1990) discuss how frequent parental conflict about sibling disputes can cause children to reject parental authority and "fight it out themselves" (p. 50). The following example illustrates the relationship between sibling and parental behavior in one family:

> It doesn't matter what we do . . . they keep on fighting. It's like Douglas tries to be the parent and punish his sister and brother, and they don't like him to boss them around . . . so they gang up on him, and pretty soon they're all yelling back and forth, breaking each other's things, hitting each other . . . we just can't take it anymore.

Mrs. Walker, the exasperated parent in this example, is describing the presenting problem in an initial family therapy meeting. Soon she and her husband produced more details about how they responded to the sibling conflict:

> **Father:** Well, I work long, hard days and on my time off, I need to rest. I think I deserve that. I support my family the best I can by working all week and don't need to hear them fighting the entire time I'm home. I think she [Mrs. Walker] should have a better handle on the situation.
>
> **Mother:** Yeah, so I *never* get a break from working . . . because he just doesn't seem to realize that parenting is a full-time job for me—I don't get any time off . . . *ever*! I can't just work for the day and relax on the weekend or in the evening like him. [At this point the children begin arguing and calling each other names.]
>
> **Father** (raising his voice): Who can relax with all the yelling that goes on?
>
> **Mother:** Well, in case you haven't noticed, you're a significant part of the yelling. As soon as the kids disagree, you start yelling at me to do something, or punish them so they'll stop. They're just being kids at that point, and they haven't done anything wrong. [By now the children are tossing insults and punches back and forth, flipping rubber bands at each other, and threatening one another with "Wait till we get home."]
>
> **Father:** I know how it goes by now. That's just the beginning. They escalate from there, and you know it too. At least you should've noticed by now.

Mother: Well, if I'm the boss of the kids, I'll handle it my way. If you don't like it, you do something to make them stop as soon as they start fighting instead of when they're just playing. And maybe if you were more involved when it first starts, you wouldn't come in later and have to yell and scream at them to get them to stop fighting. If I'm so bad at it, why don't you do some of the work where the kids are concerned!

In subsequent family meetings, the therapist observed that the Walker children fought more aggressively in their father's presence. Conjoint sessions with the parents focused on Mrs. Walker's resentment toward her husband for his lack of involvement in coparenting the children. Mr. Walker disclosed that he felt neglected and undervalued in the family, and acknowledged his increasing withdrawal from parenting duties as a result. The couple became aware of how each was subtly contributing to the sibling violence as a means of indirectly expressing anger and dissatisfaction in their marriage. They were invited to explore effective alternatives to disciplining their children, and in particular were taught the importance of maintaining a united coparenting stance whenever possible. Remaining family meetings focused on providing the parents with opportunities to practice their new skills in a safe, supportive environment. A decrease in fighting between the parents, coupled with effective modeling of conflict resolution, led to a noticeable decline in sibling violence.

Boundary Problems

Another important family characteristic conducive to sibling assault is the lack of flexible and adaptive boundaries between family members. Clearer boundaries enable parents to acknowledge each sibling's uniqueness without losing sight of his or her basic equality to the others. Thus parents can support and encourage differences between their children in ways that contribute to a greater appreciation of one another. Boundaries, of course, exist among individuals within the family, as well as between the family and the external world. Boundary maintenance is required for healthy relationships inside and outside the family. Family dysfunction occurs when boundaries are either too rigid, and thus impenetrable, or too open, leading to symbiosis and loss of identity and control.

Siblings typically fight over issues such as sharing tangible resources and doing chores. Such "realistic" conflict provides a better explanation for normal sibling aggression than does sibling rivalry. Consistent disregard for a sibling's personal and psychological space, however, usually indicates a more serious problem and is often accompanied by emotional abuse. It also may signal a context ripe for sibling assault. One adult participant in our study, who experienced physical and psychological maltreatment by an older sister, described her sibling's gross violation of her boundaries as follows:

> My sister had absolutely no respect for me or my things. It was like I was put on this earth as an object for her to use. I never recall having anything that I could truly call my own until I moved out at sixteen to get away from her. And then it was like . . . I couldn't believe that my things stayed where I left them. No one borrowed my clothes without asking; if I got up from a meal for a second, my food was still there when I got back; and my phone calls were private. I could go on . . . there were just so many things I didn't realize that happened in other families, ways that people respected and treated one another that I had no idea about until I got away from her. It took me a long time to feel that I deserved to be treated with respect after the way she treated me.

Siblinghood is also the first social laboratory for experimentation with peer relationships. The development of autonomy and the ability to share, cooperate, and compete are all practiced first in sibling interactions. Therefore children make contact with their external world with the guidance of an interpersonal template derived from sibling experiences. Children must be encouraged to engage in direct negotiation of rules; this will enable them to reduce conflicts on their own whenever possible. Interpersonal skills achieved within the sibling subsystem are predicated on noninterference by other family members. Unfortunately, however, noninterference in abusive sibling interactions may translate into someone's being seriously hurt.

Ideally, parents learn to create a balance between overinvolvement in siblings' affairs and a lack of protective, competent parenting. Parents in better-functioning families initially intervene more frequently in siblings' fighting, with the goal of gradually teaching children how to resolve conflict autonomously as they mature. Parents must be ready to intervene, however, in the following circumstances:

- When one sibling or more requests their help to resolve a conflict
- When it appears that one sibling is about to be hurt, or is being hurt
- In cases of sibling aggression involving a chronic, identifiable victim and offender

When parental intervention becomes necessary, it is generally best to facilitate a resolution of the conflict rather than protecting or siding with one child, or attempting to halt the argument midstream. This can help to maintain the integrity of the sibling subsystem while simultaneously decreasing the likelihood of underground conflict and retaliation, both of which can be precursors to sibling assault.

Impaired Empathy

Empathy is a critical component of high-quality relationships. Abuse-focused theorists (Herman, 1992; Salter, 1995) observe that adult offenders often demonstrate an impaired capacity to empathize with their victims. The ability to discern other people's emotions and to assume their perspectives is the central cognitive component of empathy (Feschbach, 1975).

Many childhood sibling assault offenders, like their adult counterparts, cannot put themselves in their victims' shoes, and fail to consider injury to others. If a sibling offender has been victimized, it is likely that he has internalized self-statements related to his own perpetrator, which interfere with his ability to imagine how he would feel in the victim's position. Treatment of these issues often requires individual therapy focused on (among other things) the offender's own victimization. In other cases, siblings' empathy development suffers because of extreme deidentification, the process whereby a child rigidly defines himself in direct contradistinction to a brother or sister. This pathological family dynamic, often complicated by deficits in parents' empathy, may cause siblings to feel as if they have little in common with each other.

GENDER DIFFERENCES

Although conflict is inherent in most sibling relationships, distinctions between sibling conflict and assault become critical in studying gender differences in relation to offenders, victims, and traumatic effects. As in the case of sibling incest, assaultive sibling relationships are usually characterized by individual differences in strength, size, developmental sophistication, and power. Whereas nonassaultive, nonvictimized siblings pass through periods of conflict and relative harmony throughout childhood and adolescence, assaultive sibling relationships develop differently. Sibling assault is distinguished by the consolidation of victim and offender roles in which violence, even if it is sometimes reciprocal, becomes an unbalanced clash between nonequals. Under these conditions, males are far more likely to assume offender roles with younger, less mature brothers or sisters.

Power in today's society often appears to be gender-related. Men are more frequently socialized to be in control, and continue to hold authority in the family hierarchy. Conversely, the feeling of powerlessness is often intolerable for many boys and men. The abuse of a younger, more vulnerable sibling gives an older brother a sense (though false) of power and control.

Studies of sibling conflict provide a somewhat mixed view of gender differences. Some researchers measuring sibling conflict through parental report (Felson and Russo, 1988; Roscoe, Goodwin, and Kennedy, 1987) found no significant differences with regard to gender and sibling aggression. Others, however, suggest that parents underreport the incidence of sibling conflict in the home, regardless of the children's gender. Most agree that gender differences become more salient with increasing levels of sibling violence. Studies reveal that boys tend to use more violence and physical force than girls in the sibling relationship. Wiehe (1990), for example, found that most of the sibling physical abuse offenders in his qualitative study were males, and 89 percent of the victims were females.

In an investigation of sibling and nonfamily violence, Mangold and Koski (1990) reported that the boys in their sample were more likely than girls to act aggressively toward a brother, but not toward a sister. They also believed that gender is important in developing sharp differences between siblings in their experience of violence. The authors found that males who act aggressively toward a sister are more likely to be violent outside the home than are females who act aggressively toward a brother or sister. From this finding they conclude that our culture may not contain an experience for females that carries the same meaning as a man committing violence on a woman. Despite somewhat inconclusive research findings, one constant remains: brothers are more often sibling assault offenders in dyads with either male or female victims.

Brother-Sister Assault

Brothers are by far more frequent perpetrators of sibling assault. Among the adult survivors of sibling assault we interviewed, more males reported being assaulted by their brothers (45 percent) than females (30 percent). Yet when we queried survivors of combined sibling assault and incest, proportionately more sisters (61 percent) reported abuse by their brothers (see Appendix A, figure A.2 for complete information). The connection between sibling physical and sexual abuse is still largely unexplored. Also, studies of childhood sibling relationships have not established uniform criteria for, or measurement of, various levels of conflict.

Nevertheless, we agree with others who suggest that differences in gender and birth order are salient in assessing for abusive, violent sibling dyads. One respondent described the combined sibling assault and sexual abuse that she suffered as a child:

> We used to fight all the time, but a couple of things just stand out. He was always real dirty. In fact, his nickname was "Dirty Mick." He was constantly making lewd remarks to me, like, we'd go by a sign that said "Liquor" . . . and he'd say, "Oh, lick her!" Also, he was always trying to look in my room when I was getting dressed, or I'd be taking a shower and he'd walk in on me. Once when my parents were gone and we were out in a tent in the backyard, he took his penis out as if to say, "I'm

ready." When I'd ignore him or say "stop," he would slug me. I don't remember all the details, but he was very mean. I felt constantly under pressure from him. One time he said, "Let's play strip poker" . . . instead of refusing, I tried to play with him. But I must have put ten thousand bobbypins in my hair so that I'd never have to take any clothes off. When he realized what I was doing, he hit me so hard that I was bruised for a week. Then he went outside to the garage, found my favorite kitten, and beat it to death.

Information on gender differences and sibling assault suggests that males and females react differently to conflict and struggle in same-sex peer and sibling relationships. Brothers tend to be comfortable with longer stretches of absence and silence. Wright (1982) found that fewer than half of the men in his sample reported a willingness to talk things out before giving up on a strained same-sex peer relationship. By contrast, more than 80 percent of women said they would try to talk with a same-sex friend before giving up on the relationship. Steinmetz (1981), in a cross-cultural study, also reported that sisters had consistently higher discussion scores than brothers on a questionnaire regarding various types of conflict resolution.

Brother-sister bonds, however, rank in the middle of the sibling "intimacy hierarchy" and may be most challenging to negotiate when there is serious conflict. Research suggests that brothers tend to have a greater psychological impact on their sisters than the reverse (Rosenberg, 1982). Perhaps perceiving their brothers' greater physical and social power and coveting their often more adventurous nature, many women, as girls, desperately wanted to be like their older brothers. One woman, who had been physically abused by her older brother, described her earliest memories of him:

I really looked up to him. At four or five, I remember my mom trying to teach me how to tie my shoes. And I couldn't learn, so my brother stepped in and taught me. He colored half the laces blue and the others orange, and helped me to figure it out. He also taught me how to ride a bicycle. I used to feel the need to impress him or entertain him. . . . It felt really important to gain his approval. He had fingernails, and when we would fight he used to scratch me pretty hard, but I'd always be quick to forgive him.

Sister-Brother Assault

It is widely believed that boys tend to engage in physical fighting, while girls rely more on verbal attacks. The data tend to support this view (Straus, Gelles, and Steinmetz, 1980), but not strongly. Straus, Gelles, and Steinmetz (1980) observed that more boys are severely violent toward their siblings than girls (59 percent versus 46 percent), but "differences are not as great as stereotypes would suggest" (p. 90). Unfortunately, their data was not divided into categories by gender of victim and offender.

Only 10 percent of the participants in our study were men who reported being physically assaulted by an older sister as a child. Yet we believe that here, as among other types of male victims, underreporting is a possibility. As a result, little is known about the unique dynamics of sister-brother assault. In nonclinical families, older sisters typically lavish more attention and nurturing on younger brothers than on younger sisters (Brody, Stoneman, and MacKinnon, 1986). In a seriously disturbed family, an older sister-younger brother link can develop into a highly conflicted, abusive bond:

> One day when he was about eight, which would make me eleven, my brother was teasing our little sister. And I remember I just lost it, and I threw him to the floor. And I beat him until I couldn't beat him anymore. I beat him until I ran out of energy. And he cried, and had bruises on him. I knew he did, but he never showed me. He got up and just crawled away, and left the backyard . . . just curled up in a ball and cried. And he just never spoke to me about it.

Brother-Brother Assault

Physical struggles between brothers are legendary in many of our clinical families who seek treatment. Yet often the violence is not viewed as abusive by the family or even by the siblings. When we learn of an abusive brother-brother interaction, it is usually accidental or the result of direct probing. Mel, a thirty-year-old client, was referred for physically abusing his son and daughter. A routine psychosocial history completed by Child Protective Services ruled out parent-child abuse in the perpetrator's background. The agency required that he enter individual treatment.

The construction of a genogram in the first meeting, and matter-of-fact questions about the quality of Mel's relationship with his younger brother, led to two disclosures. Mel mentioned casually that they had not spoken to each other for several years. Then he explained why:

> I got into some kind of physical battle with my brother every day until we were seventeen or eighteen. He would usually start it by teasing me about my size or something. He was always better with words than me, and he never gave up. Eventually I would get angry to where all that mattered to me was making him stop. And then I would start chasing him because I was stronger and I wasn't afraid of anything. After I caught him, I was out to hurt him and wouldn't stop until he said uncle. He would just curl up and cover his head with his arms while I pounded away at him any way I could . . . with punches, slaps, and kicks. I even threatened him once with a knife. Once my rage was triggered, nothing could stop me.

Mel did not describe this contact with his brother as abusive, even after focusing on it more intensively than ever before. Instead he talked about the more competitive, more conflicted relationships between brothers. He viewed his relationship with his brother much as his parents had seen it, within normal limits of roughhousing and rivalry. Mel perceived that his parents threatened to intervene when they were tired of hearing them fight, not because they were concerned about the boys hurting one another.

Empirical explorations of the frequency of brother-brother assault are inconclusive. According to some researchers, this is the most prevalent type of sibling conflict. Multiple studies (Goodwin and Roscoe, 1990; Roscoe, Goodwin, and Kennedy, 1987) suggest not only that males rely more heavily on physical force than do females to resolve sibling conflict, but also that brothers assault brothers more than they assault sisters (Graham-Bermann, 1994;

Mangold and Koski, 1990). Others (Graham-Bermann et al., 1994; Steinmetz, 1978) assert that although male sibling pairs, as a group, are consistently more violent than female sibling pairs, the dyad most at risk for sibling assault is older brother-younger sister. As we stated earlier, brother-brother assault probably goes unreported much of the time. Our society and many families minimize it as "horseplay" or "roughhousing," and say, "Boys will be boys." In addition, males in our society are rewarded for being emotionally and physically strong and self-reliant, even if at their own expense. Many male victims of sibling assault regard victimization as inconsistent with their male identity. Therefore acknowledging injury or "victim" status generally brings feelings of shame and inadequacy.

Sister-Sister Assault

The incidence of sister-sister assault and its impact on victims remain largely unexplored. Few studies have been conducted, and no reliable estimates exist. We know, however, that the patterns of emotional and physical abuse are somewhat different from those in brother-brother assault. First, chronic physical fighting between sisters is more likely to attract parents' attention because of gender-specific differences in the socialization process. Traditional gender roles for women discourage the use of physical violence. In addition, society's tendency to minimize same-sex female violence indirectly hinders the availability of support for girls who are physically abused by their sisters. Perceptions that girls cannot really "hurt" each other and that their fighting is not to be taken seriously diminish the significance of sister-sister assault and create conditions for underreporting by victims. Thus, even though parents initially may be alarmed by reports of sister-sister assault, they also may minimize its traumatic effects on victims.

When important abuse-related individual and family factors predominate, a female offender may physically abuse her sister over power, territory, and/or possessions, much like her male counterpart. Clinical evidence from the siblings we have treated suggests that although sister-sister assault is much less common than physical violence between brothers or between brothers and sisters, it does occur. Furthermore, female sibling pairs may be more prone to certain forms of verbal aggression (Steinmetz, 1981) and emotional abuse.

For example, fourteen-year-old Sandie was referred for depression. She had made a suicidal gesture, was not eating well, and was preoccupied with her weight. During an initial assessment, she stated that among her family problems, she had an "awful" relationship with her seventeen-year-old sister, Simone, who regularly slapped and punched her hard enough to leave bruises. In addition, said Sandie,

> We argue all the time, and Simone is always cutting me down or dissing me in front of other people. [Simone was the favored child in the family. As Sandie entered adolescence and was becoming more attractive and more popular, the psychological maltreatment escalated.] Like, at school . . . she calls me "funny-looking," or she'll say, "Here comes the hippy." She thinks she's all smart and stuff, 'cause she says that I have fat hips, so she calls me "hippy." She says stuff like that to me at home, too, like, "You can't do anything right" . . . or, "You'd better settle for the first guy who comes around wanting your ass, 'cause with small breasts, big hips, and your ugly mug, you'll be lucky to find anyone."

TRAUMATIC EFFECTS

We can only estimate the extent of sibling assault that occurs in childhood, but the damaging effects are long-lasting (Conn-Caffaro and Caffaro, 1993; Wiehe, 1996). Mounting empirical evidence suggests that children suffer multiple harmful effects from physical abuse by parents; similar data, however, have yet to be collected for sibling assault victims. Studies of family violence frequently fail to identify offenders' family member status; thus it is difficult to determine whether children were physically abused by parents, older siblings, or both. It has been shown, however, that victims of physical child maltreatment suffer varying degrees of medical risk as well as specific physical injury, and their overall daily functioning and health are affected.

Physical aggression and antisocial behavior are among the most prevalent sequelae of child physical abuse (Ammerman, 1989;

Wolfe, 1987). Children suffering severe violence at home also show higher rates of various conduct problems and rule violations including noncompliance and defiance, fighting in and outside the home, property offenses, and even arrests (Gelles and Straus, 1990; Hotaling, Straus, and Lincoln, 1990). Physically maltreated children also appear to be less competent in their social interactions with peers (Howes and Espinosa, 1985). This may be manifested as withdrawal or avoidance (Kaufman and Cicchetti, 1989) or as fear, anger, or aggression (Main and George, 1985).

To our knowledge, no analogous studies have been conducted with childhood victims of sibling assault. Yet the findings, especially with regard to problems in social skills that help to initiate, maintain, and enhance peer interactions, would likely apply to victims of sibling assault as well. Retrospective reports from adult survivors in our study suggest long-lasting effects on their relationship with their offenders. For example, 39 percent of our sibling assault survivors reported feeling emotionally cut off from their offenders in adulthood, a much greater number than is generally reported between siblings from nonclinical families. This impaired connection with a brother or sister seems significant, even after we consider that some proportion of survivors, perhaps after unsuccessful efforts to establish an honest, nonabusive relationship, choose a more distant relationship with their offender. Emotional cutoffs from family members in adulthood have been linked to higher rates of depression, lower adaptability to stress, and greater levels of anxiety (Bray, Williamson, and Malone, 1984).

Family members' general failure to acknowledge the assault only increases the survivor's sense of frustration and hopelessness about having a normal relationship with the offender. In the example cited above, Sandie tried to communicate to her parents how much she was hurt by Simone's verbal assaults. Her parents typically responded by saying that if they did not see it happen, they could not simply take Sandie's word. They advised her to ignore Simone when she said these things, and she would probably stop. This advice minimized Sandie's abuse and left her feeling more frustrated, more helpless, and "stuck" with the problem by herself.

Because the sibling relationship is one template for other, parallel relationships such as those with peers, friends, roommates, and even spouses, we might expect that survivors of sibling assault would have difficulty in these other interpersonal relationships. Indeed, this was true for many of the participants in our study. Molly, an adult survivor of sibling assault, stated:

> I always had trouble in my relationships with men. It seems I just had my antennae out for the ones who would put me down and hit me. After I ended my second marriage, I had to ask myself, "Why did I keep getting mixed up with abusive men?" It finally dawned on me that the thing all of my intimate relationships with men had in common was that they were like my older brothers—the ones who physically abused me . . . almost as if I couldn't make better choices regarding men until I started dealing with what it was they did to me.

Sibling assault survivors are at risk for repeating dysfunctional patterns and roles in other relationships throughout their lives. When trauma related to sibling abuse remains unresolved, the personal costs of dysfunctional marriages, friendships, and other relationships may be significant. The degree to which sibling assault influences a child's expectations for adult relationships with peers, friends, roommates, and lovers remains a rich source for further exploration. According to a recent study (Graham-Bermann et al., 1994), sibling assault affects both perpetrators and victims, but not in the same way:

> Offenders generally exhibit high levels of self esteem mixed with anxiety. Their actions have a self-enhancing effect but there are some emotional costs. Siblings who fight back, exhibit less depression, anxiety and greater self-esteem. Perhaps less guilt or less self-recrimination results when violence is reciprocated. (p. 95)

The authors suggest that a history of sibling violence is also consonant with difficulties in emotional adjustment for college-age women. Women who were the targets of sibling assault in their 1994 study showed increased anxiety on several measures. The authors concluded that the association between sibling violence and negative emotional outcome in young adulthood was stronger for women than for men. Male survivors were less likely to report negative emotional sequelae.

We offer a number of possible explanations for this difference. First, male survivors are less likely to report all forms of abuse, for reasons discussed earlier in this chapter. Gender role socialization may inhibit male survivors' expression of external reactions. Further, men may rely more heavily on denial and rationalization as adaptations to the abuse because of stereotypes and expectations regarding victimization and vulnerability.

Finally, the psychological maltreatment that frequently accompanies sibling assault has far-reaching effects. Although routinely minimized as teasing, persistent harsh emotional abuse can develop quickly into sibling assault if not detected and therefore not addressed by parents or professionals. Victims of sibling psychological maltreatment often internalize the abusive messages received from their brothers or sisters. This outcome has the potential to distort a child's perception of self and of others, and to shape the child's expectations of future intimate relationships.

KEY POINTS

- Sibling assault is by far the most common form of family violence. Researchers agree that it has received less attention than other forms of child abuse trauma, especially in regard to the frequency of occurrence in families. Furthermore, coercion and/or physical violence concomitant with sibling incest warrant further inquiry, given the associated harmful effects.

- Despite high reported rates of sibling assault, underreporting is a major risk. Sibling assault has been linked to violence toward peers and adults, and has been observed most frequently in boy-girl or boy-boy sibling dyads.

- In boys, exposure to spousal abuse during childhood has been associated with later willingness to be violent in relationships. In addition, an association between marital violence and sibling violence was demonstrated among the U.S. participants of a cross-cultural study.

- Some parents also excuse harmful behavior between siblings as the expected effect of sibling rivalry. They may erroneously conclude that sibling abuse is a part of growing up and competing for parental attention. Such minimization encourages offenders' behavior and discourages remorse; as a result, many sibling abuse survivors cannot consider any relationship with their offenders in adulthood.

- Finkelhor and Dziuba-Leatherman (1994) outlined a position for asserting a developmental approach to studying childhood victimization. They group sibling assault behavior into a category that they term *pandemic* because of its frequency in our society. They also observe that sibling assault far outstrips any other type of childhood victimization, and may affect children's lives differently than the other types because it is almost normalized.

- The particular salience of the father's role in forecasting sibling relationships was studied in longitudinal research by Brody, Stoneman, and McCoy (1994). They found that the father's differential negative treatment of siblings was associated with negative dimensions of the quality of the sibling relationship.

- Among the adult survivors of sibling violence we interviewed, more males than females reported being assaulted by their brothers. When we examined survivors of combined sibling assault and incest, however, more sisters reported abuse by their brothers. The connection between sibling physical and sexual abuse remains largely unexplored. In addition, studies of childhood sibling relationships have not established uniform criteria for, or measurement of, various levels of conflict.

- Our complacency regarding sibling assault needs to be shaken. Children are capable of violent, sometimes fatal attacks on their brothers and sisters. Although the actual incidence of sibling homicide appears to be low, Straus and colleagues (1980) suggest that nearly two million children have used a gun or a knife on a sibling at some time in their lives. These figures are almost certainly underestimates.

- Current California law, for example, specifies that child abuse does not include a *mutual affray* between minors. This confuses the reporting procedures for abusive incidents, as well as child protective and treatment protocols for siblings. One obvious consequence is that cases of sibling assault may go unnoticed.

We propose that clear guidelines distinguishing between a mutual affray and assault be incorporated into legal definitions of child abuse.

- The sibling relationship is one template for other, analogous relationships such as those with peers, teammates, roommates, colleagues, and possibly even spouses. Without intervention, survivors and offenders of sibling assault might have difficulty in these other interpersonal arenas. Unfortunately, many survivors of sibling assault never seek treatment or address how abusive sibling relationships influence them in these settings.

PART III:
ASSESSMENT AND INTERVENTION WITH CHILDREN, FAMILIES, AND ADULT SURVIVORS

1.

Chapter 6

Assessment of Sibling Abuse

Accurate assessment of sibling relationships poses unique problems. Family clinicians generally are reluctant to apply formal assessment measures; often the introduction of such measures feels intrusive. In addition, the family assessment literature lacks adequate sibling measures. Family environment instruments generally are developed to measure overall family functioning rather than the perception of events by individual children. Most family therapists acquire information for assessment while simultaneously conducting initial clinical interviews with clients. Yet to treat complex abusive family systems effectively, comprehensive individual and family assessment data are essential.

For a thorough assessment of sibling abuse, it is often necessary to carefully analyze a sibling's behavior under varying forms of separation from his or her offender and parent. The process of interviewing siblings alone without parents is not well established in child or family therapy. Researchers, however, increasingly suggest the efficacy of this approach. In developing a family intervention strategy, it is important to determine if other family members can maintain clear boundaries between the different subsystems. Sometimes, for example, parents may need to distance themselves from the sibling subgroup in order to allow development of productive sibling relationships.

Assessment of sibling abuse can be challenging for other reasons as well. Sibling offenders, unlike their adult counterparts, are more often likely to remain in the same home, school, and community as their victims, even after a child protective report has been filed. Therefore the therapist must make every effort to conduct a thorough family-based risk assessment that can help to determine an appropriate treatment plan, whether to recommend removal of an offender, and, if removal is indicated, how to proceed with reunification. A complete discussion of an offender risk assessment is beyond the scope of this book (for more information see Chaffin and Bonner, 1996). For our purposes, such an assessment minimally would include evaluation of:

- The offender's motivation for the abuse and for treatment
- The offender's ability to accept responsibility for the abuse
- The family's reaction to disclosure of the abuse
- The family's ability to protect the victim
- Sources of support or acknowledgment for the victim
- Evidence of divided loyalties among children and parents

Siblings frequently perceive the same family events differently. In cases of sibling abuse trauma, this developmental truth becomes more significant. Each child's perception of an event may be as clinically significant as the actual event itself in determining where, how, and when to intervene. Areas of strength and vulnerability, both for individuals and throughout the family system, must be identified. Information about interactional patterns and individual personalities, as well as an evolutionary sibling history, is important in arriving at a clear diagnosis and treatment plan.

THE SIBLING ABUSE INTERVIEW

The Sibling Abuse Interview (SAI) explores the history and current status of sibling relationships through a series of questions presented to each member of the family and the relevant subsystem over a series of meetings. (See Appendix B for the complete interview.) Areas of inquiry are arranged in developmental order and address individual, subsystem, and family system functioning from the perspective of abuse trauma. To evaluate safety concerns, the interview highlights sibling and family strengths as well as areas of distress.

For accurate assessment, clinicians must remember that each family relationship is set in a particular cultural context. Differing cultural expectations influence the developmental course of relationships between parents and children, as well as between siblings.

(See the section Cultural Influences in Chapter 7.) The ability to recognize these differences is important when assessing and intervening in sibling incest and assault dyads. In addition, because abuse trauma is likely to involve multiple areas of functioning, sibling assessment must be an ongoing part of treatment rather than a static process that precedes therapy.

Issues to be addressed with sibling abuse families follow, as do questions that serve as guidelines for gathering pertinent information. We also include a brief commentary about what information the questions are intended to elicit, and why. The interview is to be used only for assessment and information gathering, not to determine definitively whether sibling incest and/or assault have occurred. In many circumstances, the SAI also will yield information that provides clarity and direction for future intervention.

Some sections of the SAI will pertain more fully than others to a particular clinical situation. Clinical experience and factors unique to each family should help the therapist to determine which questions are best suited for each client. Therapists should focus on sections of the interview relevant to their clinical needs, interweaving assessment with treatment as indicated in cases of sibling incest and assault.

In addition, the interviewer must be sensitive to family members' varying developmental needs, and must use age-appropriate language as necessary when asking questions. The therapist also must give family members permission to disclose their history from their own perspectives. The therapist's task is to learn how individuals, as well as the entire family, view their experiences cognitively and emotionally.

The structured interview generally begins with an individual assessment of the sibling victim and offender. By obtaining information from individual interviews with siblings before meeting with the family, one often gains an opportunity to establish relationships with the children involved and gathers important individual perspectives on abusive events.

Sometimes the protocol must be modified to allow for each family's characteristics. In some families, for example, it may be more prudent to meet initially with the sibling victim in the context of the family. Consultation with the victim about any meetings with a sibling offender should guide the decision whether to hold such a meeting. Some victims may be opposed to, or upset by, the prospect of their therapist meeting with their offender.

Therapists frequently do not have access to all family members in cases of sibling incest or assault. In this situation it is desirable, if at all possible, to maintain close contact with other clinicians who may be involved in treating other family members, and to coordinate therapeutic efforts accordingly.

Sibling Victim

Fear of the Sibling Offender

- How does your brother or sister react when you've told your parents something that she or he didn't want you to reveal?
- When your siblings get mad at you, what are you most afraid will happen?
- Are you ever afraid that your brothers or sisters might lose control when they are mad at you?
- If your sibling is teasing you, or doing something to you that you don't like, will he/she stop when you ask him or her to?
- Does your brother or sister ever say anything to you that makes you feel uncomfortable about your body?
- Does your brother or sister ever touch you in a way that you don't like, or that makes you feel uncomfortable about your body?

Determining the existence of chronic fear of a brother or sister may support the suspicion of an emotionally abusive relationship, or may be an early indicator (together with other information) of sibling incest or assault. Additional information sometimes can be derived from behavior such as crying when parents plan to leave the child alone with a brother or sister, avoiding contact with a specific sibling, not "tattling" on a particular sibling, difficulty in falling asleep or with bedtime, nightmares, or repeated requests to sleep with parents.

Pam, for example, was often left in the care of her older brother, Jim, when their parents were gone. When Pam did something to anger her brother, he forced her into the bathroom for a spanking. Once inside, while pretending to spank her with a belt, he molested her.

Pam was constantly afraid of being alone with Jim. She avoided him whenever possible, and played instead with her other siblings. She usually did whatever he wanted, and frequently covered for him when he had broken a house rule, hoping to avert further abuse.

Victims and offenders of sibling incest or assault often deny or minimize its harmful effects. In sharp contrast to standard protocols for parent-child abuse, the offender and the victim generally are not separated. As a result, child welfare workers may not become involved, and protective services may be notably absent. When the sibling offender and the victim remain together, attention must be focused on ending the abuse immediately and reducing or eliminating any potential for future harm. This includes an evaluation of individual and family mechanisms for protecting victims, the offender's ability to control the abusive behavior, and community assistance such as additional abuse-specific treatment, self-help groups and/or community agency support, and involvement of church or day treatment programs.

Level of Assertion in the Sibling Relationship

- How do you stand up for yourself when your sister or brother wants you to do something that you don't want to do, or something that you know is wrong?
- Does your sister or brother ask you to keep secrets about things that you know are wrong?
- What is something that your brother or sister has done to you that she or he would never do in front of your parents?

These questions are designed to assess for the victim's ability to protect herself in interaction with her siblings. The victim's ability to assert herself may decrease her vulnerability to revictimization; conversely (in cases where no outside support is forthcoming), it actually may place her in greater danger with an aggressive, sadistic offender. A lack of assertiveness also may indicate fear of a brother or sister.

Lisa, an adult survivor of sibling incest, discussed how she immediately told her mother that her brother Tim was threatening to sell her to his friends (for their sexual gratification) for fifty cents each. Her mother suggested that she watched too much television, and demanded that she stop making up such outrageous stories about her brother.

When Tim later discovered that Lisa had spoken with their mother, he beat her.

Some people who are exposed to family violence seem to have a resilience that makes them less vulnerable to the effects. More research is needed to determine how risk and resiliency factors combine and develop in families. Factors such as the following have been identified as contributing to resilience to family violence:

- Psychological "hardiness."
- Exposure to a greater number of positive behaviors than negative behaviors in the family.
- Development of self-esteem and a sense of self-efficacy.
- Supportive interaction with others in the extended family and the community.
- High maternal empathy and support.
- High internal locus of control. (American Psychological Association, 1996)

Power Differences

- Do boys or girls have the most say in your family?
- If you were to look at your family as being made up of two teams, who would be on each team?
- When you have a fight with your brother or sister, who usually wins?
- Pretend there is something that you and your sibling both really want, and only one of you can have it. Who gets it, and how?

It is often useful to create an enactment or fantasy during the interview to gain direct access to information on power dynamics between siblings. Power imbalances, including those based on gender and birth order, place siblings at risk for assault or incest. The most vulnerable siblings are those whose rigidified victim roles consistently place them on the receiving end of abuse from their brothers or sisters. Gender, birth order, developmental level, and physical size are all important contributors to power differences between siblings.

Assuming Responsibility for Offender's Behavior

- When your brother or sister hits you or touches you in a way that's wrong, whose fault is it?
- When your brother or sister hits you, are you able to go and tell your parents? Will they help you?
- When a sibling shouts at you or teases you, do you believe that it is usually because you've done something to deserve it?

Victims of abuse trauma frequently internalize responsibility for their offenders' abusive thoughts and behavior. These internalizations are associated with an inability to self-soothe and with an increase in self-injurious behavior (Briere, 1992; Herman, 1992; Salter, 1995). Rausch and Knutson (1991) suggest that siblings who feel that they "deserved" punishment, even if it is severe, tend not to perceive it as abusive. This may represent an important factor in the underreporting of sibling abuse, and may pose a significant treatment challenge to clinicians.

Psychological Maltreatment

- How often do you and your brother or sister argue with each other?
- How often does he or she yell at, insult, or criticize you?
- Does your sibling ever embarrass or humiliate you in front of others?
- Do you ever feel like a bad person because of something your brother or sister did or said to you?

Sibling Offender

Acknowledgment of the Abuse

- Do you ever think that you may have a problem with touching or hitting? And if you do, is it something that maybe you might like some help with?
- All brothers and sisters sometimes hurt the other one's feelings. What do you know about the ways your brother or sister has said he or she was hurt by you?

- Tell me how it happens that you might end up

    (a) hitting or kicking your sister/brother too hard;
    (b) touching him or her in private places; or
    (c) hurting your brother or sister by _____ (fill in blank).

- How do you feel about it?
- Whose fault do you think it is?
- How do you think your parents feel about it?

A critical first step is to determine how much responsibility, if any, the sibling offender is willing and able to accept for the abuse. If he or she refuses to accept full responsibility, the offender should be included in sibling or family meetings only at the victim's discretion. In cases involving young victims who are developmentally unable to make this decision, therapists generally should follow guidelines established for instances of parent-child abuse: excluding offenders from conjoint treatment with victims until they are able to accept full responsibility for the abuse and until there are indications that the victim is safe and ready. This is particularly crucial in cases where an older sibling offender serves a pseudoparent role for the victim.

Capacity to Empathize

- How do you feel when your brother or sister feels sad?
- Do you care a lot about what your sibling thinks of you?
- When something positive happens to you, do you ever share it with your sister or brother?
- How do you feel when your parents punish your sister or brother?
- Do you ever take the blame for something that your brother or sister did so that he/she doesn't get into trouble for it?
- What is one of the worst days or experiences that you think your brother/sister ever had, and how do you imagine he/she felt about it?
- What if something strange happened, and you were suddenly transformed into your brother or sister. Knowing how you treat him or her, how would you feel?

Empathy development is a consistent component of clinical and research protocols on sibling offenders (Friedrich, 1988; Graham-Bermann and Cutler, 1994; Schacter, 1985). The sibling offender's ability to empathize with his or her victim is an important prognostic sign. Indeed, several clinical interventions (role reversal, inner dialogues, processing the offender's own victimization) have been adopted to assess and facilitate the development of empathy in sibling incest and assault offenders.

Coercive Behavior

- How are you able to get your sibling to do things that you want him or her to do?
- What's one way that you let your brother or sister know that you don't like what he or she is doing?
- When your brother or sister has something that you want, how do you get it?
- How often do you hurt your sibling's feelings and make him or her cry or get angry? How do you do this?

Some degree of coercion is likely to be present in most cases of sibling incest. Bank and Kahn (1982) report that siblings seldom initiate incest simultaneously. The use of coercion and force is central to behavior resulting in sibling assault. In addition, abundant evidence suggests that incest (both sibling and parent-child) is often accompanied by coercive activity (Laviola, 1992; Salter, 1995).

Coercion and force account for some of the most harmful after-effects for incest trauma survivors. Sometimes the more subtle forms of coercion may be difficult to detect; therefore we believe that a thorough assessment in this area is warranted in each case. A sibling incest or assault victim's so-called "compliance" with the offender is often based on fear. Coercive behavior, however subtle, may lead a victim to blame him or herself for the abuse. The questions above can help clinicians to determine the presence and extent of coercion in a sibling offender's behavior.

To illustrate, one adult client told how she continued an incestuous relationship with her brother into adulthood. She saw herself as a willing participant because she enjoyed the sexual contact and rarely refused her brother's advances. Her self-reproach was all-

encompassing: She made several suicide attempts, and then nego-
tiated a no-suicide agreement in therapy from week to week for
quite some time.

An examination of her other sibling relationships revealed that a
younger sister was born with multiple developmental delays, and
required constant care as a child. During one session, while sharing
memories of caring for this sister, the client suddenly recognized
that she had entered into a grim, unspoken agreement with her
brother: she would allow him sexual access and he would stay away
from her more vulnerable sibling.

Victimization History

- How do you know when people in your family are mad at
  you?
- Brothers and sisters sometimes tease each other in mean ways.
  How do you and your siblings tease each other?
- Who gets teased the most in your family? By whom?
- What is the worst trouble you ever got into and what did your
  parents say and do?
- How often do your parents punish you with spankings or by
  hitting you? How do they do it?
- Has anyone ever touched you in private ways without your
  permission?
- Has anyone inside or outside of your family ever bothered you
  a lot, made you feel real scared, hit you, or hurt you in other
  ways?
- Has your older brother or sister, or anyone else, ever touched
  you in a way that felt uncomfortable?

Information about the sibling offender's abuse history often begins to clarify treatment goals and helps to set priorities for clinical
interventions. A confirmed abuse history can further assist the clinician in conceptualizing family system dynamics. We have found,
for example, that many sibling offenders with histories of physical,
emotional, and/or sexual abuse emerge from families with pseudoparent siblings or peripheral parents. In a widely cited study, Kaufman and Zigler (1987) suggest that about one-third of all individuals with a history of childhood abuse or neglect will mistreat their

own children. Others (e.g., Belsky, 1993), however, suggest that this prediction may be limited by excessive reliance on retrospective reports and by a failure to take into account the developmental status of the children under study. Nonetheless, a history of intrafamilial physical abuse is a consistent finding of sibling incest research with both male and female offenders (Adler and Schutz, 1995; Hunter et al., 1993; O'Brien, 1991).

In addition, although both child and adolescent sibling incest offenders tend to have reported histories of abuse, their motivations for sexual abuse may be quite different. Young children who molest their brothers or sisters are often acting out anger, hurt, or confusion that is likely to be related to their own victimization. Adolescent sibling incest offenders, in contrast, are frequently motivated by desire for orgasm and often require treatment that targets deviant sexual arousal patterns, in addition to other individual and family goals.

Nontargeted Siblings

- Have you seen your brother or sister being touched or fondled on his or her private parts by your mother or father in a way that made you feel uncomfortable?
- By your older sister or brother?
- Has your brother or sister ever told you of this happening?
- Have you ever wondered if this had happened?

Children at home may be traumatized indirectly by witnessing family members' abusive actions. Nontargeted children forced to witness the sexual abuse of a sibling may be confused and upset by the experience. They may experience a combination of guilt and relief at being spared, and powerlessness at their inability to protect their sibling from the incest. In one family, an older sibling who saw her sister being molested by their father misperceived the abuse, believing that her little sister was unfairly receiving preferential treatment. The molestation evoked so much anger and jealousy in the older sister that she began to physically abuse the victim.

In another example, Emily was molested for several years by her father. On one occasion, Emily's younger sister Catherine saw her touching their father's penis in the bathtub; they were joking and laughing. Catherine was so deeply enraged and disgusted that she remained angry with her sister for months, and quit speaking to her after they were placed in separate foster homes. After several years in therapy, Catherine realized that this particular interaction intensified how excluded, unloved, and unimportant she had felt in her family. Subsequently she was able to assign appropriate responsibility to their father, and to begin working toward a reconciliation with her sister.

- Did you ever see your sister or brother being punished by your mom or dad in a way that made you feel sad or afraid?
- Did your brother or sister ever tell you about being punished or physically hurt by someone else in your family?

Questions like these may help nontargeted siblings gain access to feelings of survivor guilt and to the shame connected with viewing the humiliation of their peer.

- When your brother or sister is punished, does it usually seem that he/she deserves it?
- When you are punished, does it usually seem that you deserved it?

Siblings also may blame their victimized brothers or sisters in order to avoid painful feelings associated with witnessing the abuse.

- If you and your brother/sister make the same mistake at home, would you each get punished in the same way?
- Does it usually seem that the punishment "fits the crime" in your family?

According to a growing consensus, witnessing family violence is abusive and may be related to later psychological disturbance (Jaffe, Wolfe, and Wilson, 1990; Rosenberg, 1984). From early on, children are extremely sensitive witnesses to any differences in affection, interest, and discipline on the part of parents or older siblings. This sensitivity is developmentally significant because differences in siblings' experiences with their caretakers are linked to outcome differences in the quality of the sibling relationship.

Sibling Subsystem

The following questions might be addressed to children in the same family. In some situations, the therapist obviously would not meet with a victim and an offender together. Information gathered from individual sibling assessment meetings will provide the data necessary to make this determination. Whether or not the siblings remain in the same household after disclosure will also influence the therapist's work with the sibling subsystem. If they continue to live in the same home, sometimes it may be important to treat them together. In addition, the parents' ability to provide supervision and protection, and to separate siblings if instructed to do so, is crucial. The victim's capacity to protect himself or herself, and the siblings' receptivity to treatment, are also essential considerations. Finally, evaluating the potential for behavior change within the sibling subsystem can often be aided by information gathered from interviews with various other family members.

Strengths

- What are some amusing, interesting experiences that you have gone through together that are unique to your relationship?
- What do you enjoy or like most about each other?
- What are some of the good things and some of the bad things about growing up in this family?

Determining the strengths of the sibling relationship in each family is imperative for accurate diagnostic and clinical planning. It is important to assess the level of identification between siblings, particularly same-sex sibling pairs and those closer in age. Severe deidentification may present as one risk factor for abuse. In addition, stronger sibling ties are generated when children have common interests and maintain respect for each other's differences. The therapist must pay attention to how each sibling responds when the other establishes a boundary (e.g., emotional, physical, with property). If the subsystem is characterized by rigidly defined roles that restrict siblings' behavior, one must assess for how openly the members discuss resentments.

- When you do a good job at something—such as in school, work around the house, or things that your parents ask you to do—what does Dad usually do or say about that?
- What does Mom usually do or say?

- When Mom or Dad say that you will be rewarded for doing something, do you usually get the reward? Give some examples.

Conflict Resolution Skills

- Pretend that this toy or game is one that both of you really want to play with right now. Decide who gets to play with it first.
- How will you decide when it's time to allow your sister or brother to have a turn?

Developing reliable, nonabusive conflict resolution skills is a fundamental task of the sibling subsystem. There are many ways to assess for what skills or deficits currently exist in abusive sibling dyads. We prefer to gather information experientially through role plays, enactments, or drawing exercises designed to elicit useful information while simultaneously providing some intervention possibilities. For example, once a sibling conflict has been described by a child in the traditional fashion, we might ask the following questions:

- Now, take your brother/sister's side in this conflict and pretend that you are speaking as him or her for a moment. How would you respond to what you have just heard?
- Imagine that you and your brother or sister are fighting as characters in your favorite Saturday morning cartoon show. Which character would you each be? What would they be doing?
- How do you and your sibling resemble the characters in the cartoon, and what are the ways that you are different?
- How do the characters usually resolve their fight?

If there are three siblings in the family, we suggest that the evaluation generally focus on the dyad with the most conflict. When possible, the other child can be utilized to verify what goes on, or as a resource for the more conflictual dyad. With four siblings, abuse assessment might easily follow along the lines drawn by the different "teams" in the family. By incorporating discussion about how specific characters or others resolve conflict, the therapist has the opportunity to indirectly or directly teach siblings about boundaries, fair fighting, and conflict resolution.

Communication Skills, Empathy

- Could each of you describe your reaction to an important recent family event? You may choose the same or different events.
- I'd like the rest of you to listen and tell me afterward what new information you learned about your brother or sister.

Assessing for basic listening and responding skills is as vital for therapeutic work with siblings as with couples. The therapist should monitor each child's ability to express his or her feelings and how this behavior is received by the other siblings, with special attention to the nature and frequency of critical responses when different points of view are expressed. By determining how much "air time" siblings allow each other, one can identify key components of symmetrical or asymmetrical interactions. It is also important to listen for, and highlight, ways in which siblings have learned to give and receive mutual support.

- How do you see yourselves as different or alike?
- How do your parents tell you that you are different or alike?
- Do you agree with their perceptions of you?

Sibling identification can be a revealing indicator of a child's capacity to empathize with his brothers or sisters. In addition, comparing the child's perceptions of self and siblings with parents' perspectives may help to determine the relationships between members of the two subsystems. Of course, this process is affected somewhat by developmental realities: the younger the children, the more likely they are to define themselves as viewed by their parents. By preadolescence, however, siblings in better-functioning families generally feel more free to delineate themselves separately from the way their parents perceive them.

Leonard, age twelve, and Kelsie, age ten, had always viewed themselves as very different from one another. When asked if they thought their parents shared their perception of themselves as different, Leonard stated, "Our parents always say they don't know how they got three such different kids" (their fifteen-year-old brother, who physically abused both of them, was not in the session), "but it looks like me and Kelsie think the same way inside about a lot of things that have happened to us."

As children begin to define separate relationships with others and develop a sibling identity, they are less likely to react abusively to differential treatment by parents. They may decide to close ranks with a brother or sister in response to parental conflict and mistreatment. Ariel and her brothers, for example, regularly witnessed their parents' intense and violent conflict. Each parent, in turn, looked to Ariel to support and validate his or her respective position and to help them reconcile. The siblings were not divided by their parents' behavior because they were able to discuss Ariel's role in the family: after each fight she debriefed and consulted with her brothers. By including her brothers in this way, Ariel earned their allegiance and spared them from their parents' collusive attention. Ariel identified herself as a sibling first; this gave her the support she needed to handle her parents.

Parental Favorites

- When something goes wrong at home does anyone get blamed more than the others? If so, how is that for the rest of you?
- How is it for the one who gets blamed more often?
- Does one of you get to do things before the rest of your brothers or sisters?
- Is there someone among you who seems to be Mom or Dad's favorite?

Identifying parental favorites and/or differential treatment of children has important implications for sibling abuse families. A number of studies (Dunn, 1993; Felson and Russo, 1988) have linked differential treatment by parents to the quality of the sibling relationship: siblings engage more often in conflict-laden interactions in an effort to obtain scarce parental support and attention. Children who cannot discuss their rivalrous feelings with each other (in combination with other factors) are at greater risk for maintaining dysfunctional sibling relationships into adulthood.

How Siblings Are Treated in Front of Peers, or When Parents Are Not Present

- Does your brother or sister treat you differently when he or she is with friends? Or when he or she is with friends and your parents aren't around?
- How are you treated by your siblings when you are with your friends?
- Do your siblings ever threaten to hurt you or tease you and try to humiliate you in front of your friends? Or when you are with your friends and your parents are not around?

Parents who are emotionally and physically unavailable may frequently be unaware that sibling physical, sexual, or emotional abuse is occurring in their own homes or neighborhoods. Occasionally the abuse may be context-specific. One adult survivor explained that her brother never sexually abused her himself. Instead he sold her as a sex object to his friends. When in the company of her friends or at school, this brother was frequently helpful and extremely protective.

Siblings' Perceptions of Parental Availability and Discipline

- Is your dad or mom around as much as you would like?
- How much time do you and your brothers and sisters spend at home alone?
- In every family, parents pay more attention to some problems than to others. What are the family problems that your parents attend to most (shoes on the couch, messy rooms, etc.)?
- What are some family problems that they don't pay that much attention to?
- What does your mom do when you fight? What does your dad do?
- Tell me about some times when you have been fighting, and describe how each of your parents have responded.
- Do they discipline you and your siblings in the same ways? If not, how are they different with each of you?

Lack of adequate supervision and parental unavailability are associated with sibling incest and assault in a number of studies (Canavan, Meyer, and Higgs, 1992; Smith and Israel, 1987). Opportunity and access concerns are critical when victims and offenders live in the same household. Research suggests that harsh parent-child discipline also may be implicated in sibling assault and incest (Adler and Schutz, 1995; Duncan, Duncan, and Hops, 1996; O'Brien, 1991). It is important to determine whether all siblings are disciplined equally or whether one child is the scapegoat for particularly harsh mistreatment.

- When Mom and Dad say that you will be punished for something, do they always do what they say they will? Give some examples.
- What are some rules or things your parents expect you to do or not do? Which of these rules or expectations are fair and which are unfair?
- What sorts of things does each of you usually do with Dad during the week? On the weekend?
- How about with Mom? What do you especially enjoy doing with Mom? With Dad?

Siblings' Perceptions of Parental Conflict Resolution

- Who fights more, all of you or your parents?
- What do your parents do when they fight?
- Are you ever afraid your parents will hurt one another, or you, when they fight? Give examples of times you were afraid.

Awareness and Acknowledgment of the Abuse

- During or after an argument or fight between your parents, does your Mom or Dad ever still feel mad and take it out on you? If so, who do they get angry with the most?
- What do the rest of you do when this happens?
- What do you know about your brother or sister's abuse? How do you feel about it?
- Whose fault do you think it is?
- How do you think your parents feel about it?

Determining whether there is another sibling willing to confirm or acknowledge the victim's abuse can be critical in the victim's disclosure and healing process. If possible, this child should be identified in an individual interview before any sibling subsystem meeting. Conversation between the victim and a supportive brother or sister should be encouraged to facilitate:

a. Questions and answers regarding the abuse
b. Shared concerns about any changes in family status that might follow as a result of disclosure
c. Development of additional opportunities for supportive contact outside the therapeutic environment
d. Identification of feelings such as blame, shame, or guilt that a nontargeted sibling may have regarding inability to protect the victim

Sibling and Parental Coalitions or Triangles

- Are there certain personal things, not related to safety (i.e., hurting self or others), that you share with each other and don't tell your parents?
- Do your parents ever talk to any of you about the other, or about their fights?
- Describe the different teams in your family (include extended family members, if relevant).
- When your family disagrees about something, whose side are you usually on?
- Who do your brothers and sisters usually side with?
- Each person in a family has a special role or place that he or she occupies (e.g., the smart one, funny one, the one who is frequently in trouble, etc.). What roles do people have in your family?

These questions attempt to identify cross-generational coalitions and alignments in the family—alignments that may be based on gender, roles, power, age, and physical appearance. Determine whether there is room for everyone in the family, or whether certain children are excluded or scapegoated by parents or siblings, and consequently targeted for abuse, as in the following example.

Sandy, a twenty-five-year-old client and adult survivor of sibling incest and assault, was the only female in a rigidly gendered family with three older brothers. Her father dominated the household and gave what little attention he paid to his three sons. Sandy's mother was seriously mentally ill and was in and out of institutions for most of Sandy's childhood.

Sandy's eldest brother was left in charge when their father was away on business (which was much of the time). Sandy's abuse began when she found herself the object of intense sexualized teasing and humiliation. Her brothers forced her to watch pornographic videos and then threatened to bring their friends to the house and provide them with sexual access to her. Eventually her older brother assumed the role of her protector. He promised her that if she allowed him sexual access, he would keep her safe from the others. The middle brother realized what was happening, and wanted access as well.

Another requisite area for assessment is the integrity of sibling subsystem boundaries. In better-functioning families, as children master developmental tasks, a sibling subsystem evolves that is free from parental intrusion. Parents in sibling incest or assault families are often threatened by close ties between siblings, and simultaneously, are unable to respond effectively when problems between siblings require adult intervention.

- If you ever have children of your own, in what ways will you raise them like your parents have raised you?
- In what ways will you raise them differently?
- If each of you could change anything about your family, what would you like to change? Why?

Individual Parent Interviews

- How do you resolve conflict between the two of you?
- Does either of you ever physically strike the other when you're arguing?
- Do you ever feel frightened or intimidated by your partner?

Ascertaining individual information and perceptions of the couple's ability to resolve conflict is required for a number of reasons. Many spouses are reluctant to disclose evidence of physical or emotional abuse without direct questioning out of their partners' presence. It is imperative to determine a spouse's level of fear, as well as the risk of harm. Immediate referrals should be made, if necessary, to ensure an individual's safety. Social learning theories of aggression demonstrate that spousal violence models assaultive behavior, which may be imitated by children. Parents with serious skill deficits find it difficult to model effective problem-solving behavior.

- Have you ever had, or do you have a current problem with alcohol or drug use?
- If yes, have you received/are you receiving treatment for this problem?

This question should be posed to parents separately as well as conjointly in the parental interview. If either parent answers "yes," the therapist should explore details on the extent of the problem, any efforts to treat the problem, and its effect on parenting functions in the family. Depending on the extent of the parent's use patterns (dependency or abuse), a more complete substance abuse assessment protocol and treatment recommendations may be indicated.

- Do you have any doubts that your son's or daughter's abuse actually took place?

This question has important implications with regard to the parents' providing increased supervision, firmer boundaries, and greater safety for the victim. The clinician must assess the parents' ability to reach an agreement to ensure their children's safety, even if they are not convinced that sibling abuse has occurred. One way to obtain useful information about a parent's reaction to the disclosure of sibling incest or assault is to inquire about relationships in his or her family of origin. This information can be obtained informally through a series of questions or in a more structured way through the construction of a genogram. If an adult has not previously explored abuse-related issues, he or she may be less able, at first, to perceive the child's abuse accurately.

A parent, for example, who disclosed that she had been sexually abused by her father, dismissed her adolescent son's overprotective, manipulative attitude toward his eight-year-old sister as the same kind of "special" relationship she had experienced with her father. One result was that she frequently encouraged her daughter to bathe with her teenage son. When the child disclosed that her brother was forcing her to touch his penis in the bathtub, the mother casually brushed her daughter's concern aside. She suggested that he was showing how much he loved his sister by teaching her about sexual differences between boys and girls.

Some parents may prefer to address abuse-related family-of-origin information individually rather than in a spouse's presence. We respect this option, though sometimes there are obvious advantages to gathering the information with couples together, if at all possible.

In addition, parents may refuse altogether to believe that one of their children was abused by another. Often this refusal is based on the offender's functioning in a critical role in the family and on his or her consequent favored status. Conversely, the sibling victim may be a child who is scapegoated and therefore is less credible to parents. In one such case, a single mother who relied heavily on her teenage son did not believe that he had sexually molested her daughter, despite physical evidence, because her daughter initially did not disclose the abuse to her. She was already angry with her daughter, because she had recently learned that the girl was lying to her about some things. Therefore she believed that she could not trust her. This parent had once told her daughter that if anyone was bothering her, she was to tell her immediately. The fact that her daughter told the school nurse first demonstrated to her mother that her daughter was lying.

- At times in every family, a parent feels closer to one child than another. This may be related to the child's age, personality, physical appearance, or ability. Which of your children do you currently feel more connected to?
- Have you always felt closer to one child in particular?
- Who do your children feel is the "favored" sibling in your family?
- Which child believes that he or she is the "least favored?"

Parental favoritism occurs in all families, but usually it is directed toward different children at different times. These questions are designed to obtain information about each parent's ability to view his or her children as unique and to respect their individual differences. When a parent reveals a clear, exclusive preference for one child, it may suggest the presence of a cross-generational coalition. This hypothesis should be collaborated by collecting information about the adult caretaker's parenting style with this child in contrast to the others. Differential treatment of children and cross-generational coalitions are often associated with highly conflictual sibling relations (Bank and Kahn, 1982; Ross et al., 1994). The child who is left out may become increasingly resentful and aggressive toward the favored sibling. By asking a parent how the children perceive caretaking activity in the family, one gains some sense of the parents' sensitivity to and involvement with each member of the sibling subsystem.

The next three questions should be asked both here and in the interview with the parental subsystem:

- Does your partner ever approach you in a sexual way in front of the children?
- What specific sexual activities, and in what frequencies, are displayed in front of your children?
- Are there sexually explicit materials in the house that might be accessible to your children?

Studies (Canavan, Meyer, and Higgs, 1992; Smith and Israel, 1987) report that a heightened or repressive family sexual environment often accompanies sibling incest behavior. Occasionally a parent responds differently to this series of questions when not in the presence of his or her partner.

- Have you always been faithful to your current partner?

This is another question that can be addressed to parents individually and/or in a conjoint session. First, the clinician must decide whether to believe that the parents will respond honestly to the question in their partner's presence. If the therapist makes the judgment that more accurate information will be obtained in an individual meeting, he or she must make clear to the parents how sensitive information will be handled. Smith and Israel (1987) report a preponderance of secrets and extramarital affairs in sibling incest families. In particular, they suggest that an identification may occur between the parent who is having the affair and the sibling offender; this maintains the family system and ensures that the children will not feel abandoned. From this perspective, the sibling incest can be viewed, at least in part, as a metaphor for the parents' disturbed sexual relationship.

- In every family the members have different roles, such as the smart one, the athletic one, the one who gets in trouble, etc. What roles did you and your siblings occupy in your family of origin?
- What roles do you see yourselves and your children maintaining in your current family?
- Were you abused as a child by a parent or sibling?
- What are your relationships like with each of your siblings now?

In most systemic approaches it is a tenet that parents live through and repeat with spouses and children the unresolved conflicts derived from their families of origin. Specifically, abuse-related problems tend to be repeated from one generation to the next, though not necessarily in the same form. Rosenthal and Doherty (1984) found that significant numbers of abusive preschool siblings' parents were themselves abused as children. Questions about sibling relationships in the parents' original family tend to be overlooked by professionals, who focus on parent-child analogues for transgenerational abuse patterns. Role rigidity has been implicated in sibling assault; therefore information on sibling roles in the family of origin and on the quality of current sibling relationships may have some diagnostic value. In addition, the identification of a positive relationship with an adult sibling may be a source of strength for a distressed family.

Parental Subsystem

Interviews with couples provide opportunities for observing interpersonal interactions and for gathering information, which then can be checked against individual and collective perceptions of the relationship. Frequently this information about the relationship has important clinical implications.

- Do each of you regularly confide in the other when struggling with something difficult, or when in need of love and support?
- If so, does your partner usually make himself/herself available to you when you need him or her?
- If not, do you think that she or he would be available if you needed support or some time together?
- What are some of the ways that your partner lets you know that she or he is not available?

These questions focus on the centrality of the couple relationship in the family. Partners who are emotionally available to each other in times of need model important support functions for children. They also increase the likelihood of being able to operate as an effective coparenting team under stress. Couples in sibling abuse families often cannot communicate their needs effectively, either with each other or in relationships with their children. This heightens the likelihood of establishing cross-generational coalitions, and interferes with a parent's ability to intervene with sibling assault or incest offenders.

- How much time do you spend together, apart from your children?
- What activities do you participate in separately and as a couple?
- How much time does each of you spend with your children?

Studies of sibling incest and assault have in common the finding that parents are often unable or unwilling to provide adequate support, supervision, and structure for their children (Conn-Caffaro and Caffaro, 1993; Reid and Donovan, 1990; Smith and Israel, 1987). The absence of sufficient parental guidance, support, and supervision has direct consequences for siblings in terms of access to victims, the inability to monitor and intervene in abusive sibling interactions, and the installation of an older child to function as a pseudoparent for the younger children. Inconsistent, unreliable, and /or abusive fathering appears to have important implications for sibling incest and assault (Brody et al., 1992; Stocker and McHale,

1992). Simultaneously the development of good relationships between parents and siblings requires the maintenance of boundaries that acknowledge the need for a well-defined adult partnership separate from the children.

- How do you know when each of your children is angry, sad, afraid, happy, etc.?
- How do you know what's going on in your children's lives?
- Who do you talk to or how else do you find out about things in your family?

It is important to assess each parent's ability to be affectively attuned to his or her children and to respond accordingly. This information is critical in evaluating the couple's receptivity to family intervention and in identifying areas for such intervention. The therapist should ask each parent to speak about a time when he or she knew that each child was angry or sad, and should discuss the parent's verbal and nonverbal response. This process will provide data on the couple's emotional availability to their children, their openness to feedback, and their adaptability to stress related to disclosure. For instance, more flexible parents will be able to take in new information and learn from it; that is, they may recall times when they could have been more receptive or less critical toward their children. Areas also may emerge in which parents have different perceptions of their children, as well as ways in which they contribute to siblings' role development (e.g., "She's the happy one . . . always smiling").

- Do your children ever have the advantage of watching the two of you argue, followed by agreement and/or resolution of the conflict?
- What does each of you do when you're angry with each other?
- What do your children do when the two of you have an argument or fight?
- How do they interact with each other both during and immediately following your disagreements/fights?

Various researchers (Brody, Stoneman, and Burke, 1987; Margolin, 1995; Steinmetz, 1981) have studied the effects of conflict-laden couples on the development of assaultive sibling relationships. Although not every study isolated the direction of effects (whether they flow from spousal process to sibling behavior, or vice versa), it seems reasonable to assume that the intergenerational transmission of violence in many families flows from adults to children. In other words, a violent sibling relationship often is a mirror for a high-conflict or abusive marriage. In addition, parents who cannot solve problems between themselves without violence cannot teach their children the benefits of conflict resolution. These questions, or some variation thereof, also may be used by the therapist to ascertain parental values regarding conflict and assaultive behavior. The last two questions cited above are designed to illuminate levels of parents' awareness related to:

a. Each of their children's reaction to their fighting
b. The impact of parents' conflict on the children and on sibling relationships
c. Ways in which the parents may be including or triangulating a child in their conflict
d. Values regarding conflict that the parents are transmitting to their children

• Are you each satisfied with how you resolve your anger with your partner?
• If not, what would you like to do differently?
• What would you like your partner to do differently?

The therapist must help the parents determine what is acceptable and unacceptable behavior for each partner when they are fighting; be alert to any signs that spousal abuse may have occurred or is presently occurring; and, if abuse is evident, pursue this point more directly in an individual session with the partner who gives indications of having been battered.

• How do you show affection for each other in front of the children?
• What are some of the ways that you teach your children about sexuality?
• What are the differences in how you teach your boy and your girl children about sexuality?

• Are there places in your house that are private and off-limits to children?

Some of the above questions should be modified according to the developmental levels of the children in the home. Collectively the questions address modeling positive affect exchange for the children, the restriction or openness of sex-related family discussions relative to the children's developmental levels, gender role differences, setting appropriate boundaries around the couple's private activities, and the sexual climate in the home.

• There are moments when siblings tease each other about their bodies, tickle each other, do things to embarrass one another, and maybe even touch each other sexually in an age-appropriate way (e.g., playing doctor). Describe some of the times you have witnessed or heard about such behavior involving your children, and your response to it.
• What parental sexual attitudes are directly expressed or implied in your family?

One of the goals of this section is to help each parent answer the questions in ways that clarify the differences in their observations, values, styles of parenting, and discipline. The therapist should pay particular attention to the way parents respond to questions about developmentally normal sex play between siblings for evidence of erotophilic (sexually stimulating) or erotophobic (sexually repressed) behavior (Friedrich, 1990). Erotophilic parents create a chronically sexually stimulating family climate through covert and/or overt inappropriate behavior and remarks, and through explicit sexual material; these can mask and normalize sibling incest occurring at home. Erotophobic parents contribute to a sexually repressed family environment by prohibiting open discussion of sexually laden topics (e.g., dating, clothing styles, dancing), concealing any parental display of affection from children, and enforcing stringent codes of behavior regarding the body's natural functions. Such parents may become anxious and excessively punitive with children who display normal curiosity about their sexuality. In addition, the clinician should observe for parental responses that may disregard abusive or sexually inappropriate sibling interaction (e.g., when a brother's tickling of his sister results in torn or removed clothing, when the brother becomes erect, or when the sister's cries for her brother to stop and her calls for parental assistance are ignored).

- What sexual activities are allowed between siblings in the family?
- At what point are sexual boundaries explicitly drawn?
- Describe some of your children's "roughhousing" behavior.
- How do you usually respond?
- Are you ever worried that one sibling will harm another?

How accurately are the parents able to detect sibling assault, and what kind of parental response follows its occurrence? In our clinical experience, parents frequently underestimate the severity of sibling assault behavior. When the assaultive behavior gradually escalates, parents may grow to expect sibling conflict and may not be alarmed when it occurs.

- How do you discipline your children?
- What are the differences between your styles of discipline?
- Do either of you notice ways by which you might favor one child more than the others?
- Which of your children generally "requires" more discipline?
- How is he or she disciplined differently than the others?

Parental guidelines, attitudes, and behavior concerning discipline are crucial for several reasons. First, a structure of accepted and constructive rules guides interactions between family members and provides parents with resources for disciplining children. Families with serious problems of sibling aggression lack such a rule structure and are more likely to punish children physically. Among the adult survivors in our research, 84 percent reported that they were disciplined too harshly. Fifty percent reported harsh discipline either frequently, or all of the time as children. Studies (Adler and Schutz, 1995; Hunter et al., 1993; O'Brien, 1991) of sibling incest offenders also report that a majority were physically abused as children. Parents who consistently favor one child or single out a child for excessively harsh punishment may also inadvertently be creating conditions that (along with other factors) foster the development of abusive sibling behavior.

- What are some of the ways you see your children as being similar to, or different from, each other?
- How would you describe the relationship that each child has with his or her siblings? Explain.

Each parent's perceptions of the children must be determined in relation to the family unit. The therapist should pay particular attention to whether parents emphasize similarities or differences among their children, and to parents' contributions to rigid definition of sibling roles. Schacter's (1985) study of sibling deidentification found that in families exhibiting a pathological deidentification process, the parents behave in conflict-avoidant fashion. They either intervene constantly in their children's struggles or prohibit conflict altogether. Such parental action impedes the siblings' natural development of conflict resolution skills and may lead to rigidifying "good" and "bad" sibling roles in the family. This sets the stage for the escalation of aggressive behavior.

A strong emphasis on siblings' similarities and closeness also may hinder development of conflict resolution skills. Several of the adults reared in abusive families who participated in our study related how their childhood sibling relationships had been shaped by strong parental values of closeness based on unity and loyalty. In adulthood they came to realize that their "close" sibling relationships were viewed by their parents as reflecting positively on their parenting. Several participants discovered that they were ill equipped to resolve disputes in later adolescence and adulthood. As one woman stated,

> It was painful to realize that we weren't as close as I thought we were as children, or as my parents always said we were. I think my parents really needed to see us as being close, so they could tell all their friends and feel like they'd done a good job raising us. Little did they know . . . I spoke more openly and intimately with several of my friends than with my sisters, and yet we were going through hell together. [All three were physically abused by two brothers, and two of the sisters were sexually abused as well.] It was like . . . [in adulthood] we almost had to start all over establishing our relationship again, and do it from scratch. . . . It was real scary the first time I

disagreed with one of them—for both of us. We'd just never learned to do that, and yet we always thought of ourselves as so close. We just stuck together for protection and support, because we absolutely had to, but never really knew where each other was coming from. We never talked about all this stuff until recently.

- What are some sources of stress on you as parents?
- On the family as a whole?
- What sources of outside support do you regularly rely on when family life becomes stressful?

Stress, family resources, social support, and the potential for child abuse are interrelated (Burrell, Thompson, and Sexton, 1994). Stress related to parenting appears to be an especially important correlate of potential for child abuse. The therapist should identify where the adults locate the sources of stress in their functioning as parents and as partners, and should determine the degree to which they have the resources to deal with these stress-related problems, such as child care, after-school activities, parent support groups, in-home support services, or parenting education.

- Do you believe your child who says that he or she was physically or sexually abused by a brother or sister?
- If not, why not?

A parent's or caregiver's acknowledgment of the abuse can be critical in the sibling victim's recovery process. Particular attention should be given to parents' discrepancies in response to this question to determine whether they present unified support for the victim's allegations. Parents in sibling incest and assault families often divide their loyalty between the victim and the offender. If this is the case, the therapist must determine whether loyalty divisions occur along gender, parent-child coalition, or other structural lines (e.g., biological parent-child in stepfamilies).

When parents agree that they do not believe the victim, one must assess what would have to change, or how the couple would be affected, if they were to believe him or her. Also, it is necessary to determine the parents' willingness to behave as if the abuse occurred, such that they would make some changes in the family in response to the "alleged" victim's disclosure and increase his or her feelings of safety (e.g., allowing a lock be placed on the inside of the bedroom door, not leaving the victim and the offender alone together).

Family Interview

Differences exist among parent-child, parent-parent, and sibling relationships in families. Family systems theories frequently are considered important in this regard, and are being explored empirically (Hinde and Stevenson-Hinde, 1988; Kreppner and Lerner, 1989). For example, spousal relationships often influence parent-child relationships in families. It is frequently assumed that these relationships are closely interconnected, especially in light of evidence that poor marital relationships are associated with poor outcomes in children. Hostility between spouses has been related to authoritarian or less effective parenting (de Brock and Vermulst, 1991; Stoneman, Brody, and Burke, 1989). Furthermore, a stressed or unsatisfactory marriage can cause one or both parents to use a child to satisfy an unmet need for love.

The purpose of a family interview is to correct and verify information gathered from previous assessment interviews as well as observe and record patterns of interaction among family members. Once it has been determined that sibling incest or assault is occurring or has occurred, it is crucial to immediately assess for the balance between stressors and supports present in each family, including the following (DePanfilis and Wilson, 1996):

- Victim's safety
- Parent's willingness/ability to protect victim
- Child's ability to protect self
- Mental illness
- Substance abuse
- Family's willingness/ability to support victims
- Strength of religious ties
- Strength of community ties
- Spousal abuse
- Strength of couple dyad
- Family resources
- Family stressors
- Family history of violent behavior
- Interpersonal boundaries
- Sources of acknowledgment for victim
- Extended-family ties

- Beginning with the adults in this family, I'd like each of you to go around and tell me two or three things you really like about each other.
- What are two or three things you really like about your family?
- Every family has some problems from time to time. I'd like to hear what each of you thinks the difficulties are that your family is struggling with now.

Questions such as these are important for a number of reasons. They help to reinforce the importance of the things that are going well for the family and to identify strengths that the family may bring to the current problem. They also can instill hope, and the message (as one family member put it), "Well, at least we are doing some things right." In addition, careful attention to language communicates to the family that difficulties will be addressed in a non-judgmental, nonshaming environment.

- When one of you does not want anyone in your family to use something of yours, are you able to tell them?
- Do they respect your wishes?

The development of good relationships within the family requires boundary maintenance. In abusive sibling relationships, one sibling repeatedly violates another's physical and psychological space.

- If something embarrassing happened to you that you did not want your siblings or parents to share outside your family, would they disclose it anyway to family or friends?
- If a family member started to say something that you wanted to keep private and you asked him or her to stop, would he or she respect your wishes and not do it again?
- Would your other family members also agree to not do this again? Who would agree to maintain your privacy, and who would not?
- If one of you is having private time in your room, bathroom, or somewhere else in your house, does anyone ever intrude?
- How do they intrude, and what happens when you ask them to stop?

This is another section of questions regarding how family members react to another's assertion of his or her individual right to privacy.

Parents model respect for the integrity of a child's personal boundaries. In better-functioning families they exhibit an openness to internal and external feedback. Responses to these questions should not be confused with a dysfunctional family's tendency to operate as a closed system and not seek outside assistance or support for abusive interactions occurring at home.

- What are some of the most important things for us to try to change in your family so that everyone feels better and is safe?

This question helps to define goals for family therapy that incorporate each member's perspective. Eliciting everyone's ideas about how the family might improve sets a precedent for everyone's importance within the family and contributes to a climate of teamwork. Again, these kinds of questions give the therapist opportunities to validate family members and identify family strengths.

KEY POINTS

- Conducting a thorough assessment of sibling incest or assault begins with an acknowledgment that relationships between siblings and within families affect, and are affected by, the society in which they live.
- Each sibling interaction is influenced by the shared history of their relationship. This personal narrative, in turn, is influenced by a wider context, namely the family's relationship to its cultural world.
- Comprehensive evaluation of sibling abuse demands an understanding of a child's behavior, both with and apart from his or her parents. A child's perception and interpretation of incest or assault may be as clinically significant as the event itself. In addition, areas of individual, dyadic, and family strength and vulnerability must be identified.
- The Sibling Abuse Interview (SAI) is a comprehensive family-based interview for assessing dynamics in sibling incest and assault cases. It is designed to evaluate characteristics of individual children, sibling dyads, nontargeted children, parents or adult caregivers, the parental dyad, and the family unit.

Chapter 7

Clinical Considerations
with Children and Families

Psychotherapy with traumatized children and adolescents generally requires an eclectic, family-based approach. Incorporating a sibling perspective into the therapeutic process often proves to be a valuable asset that can be used across modalities and theoretical orientations.

A primary consideration, regardless of orientation, is that treatment maintains a focus on the victim's abuse and safety. The clinician must attend to multiple characteristics of victims and offenders, as well as to the dynamics of the entire family system, that determine the differential selection of sibling abuse victims. One cannot exaggerate the importance of supportive interventions that enhance the family's ability to incorporate change. Including other family members in sibling-based interventions, when indicated, increases the likelihood that these changes will be accepted and integrated into the system. The family configurations described later in this chapter can be used to identify family organization and to suggest directions for change.

In therapy with victims of sibling incest and assault, a variety of subspecialties must be coordinated. A theoretical view that combines principles of abuse-focused therapy with an ecological approach provides an important foundation for treatment. The abuse trauma literature increases our understanding of the traumatic effects of victimization, and of the ways in which these effects shape intimate relationships with others.

Abuse affects each family member differently. Its impact depends on a number of factors including individual personality differences, the victim's age, the extent and duration of the abuse, the victim's role in the family, and the developmental stage of the family system. How children respond to sibling incest or assault also depends on stage-specific capacities and vulnerabilities (Newberger and DeVos, 1988). Outside the child abuse field for example, the literature on the impact of victimization is generally organized around the concept of post-traumatic stress disorder (Foa et al., 1991; Kilpatrick et al., 1989). Some researchers studying victimization in children, however, have felt a strong need to create alternative explanatory models.

Finkelhor (1995) suggests the need to distinguish two types of traumatic effects: *developmental* and *localized*. Localized effects are specific to the trauma experience but do not lead to major developmental ramifications. Examples of localized effects are fearfulness, nightmares, fear of returning to the place where the victimization occurred, and anxiety regarding individuals who resemble the offender. Localized effects generally are short-term and primarily affect behavior associated with the victimization experience.

Developmental effects refer to deeper and generalized types of impact, more specific to children, that result when trauma interferes with developmental tasks. Examples include impaired attachment behavior (Cicchetti and Lynch, 1993), problems with self-esteem (Putnam, 1990), adoption of highly sexualized (Finkelhor and Browne, 1985) or aggressive (Friedrich, Beilke, and Urquiza, 1988) modes of relating, and use of drugs, dissociation, and self-injury to deal with anxiety (Briere, 1992). In many instances, one might hypothesize that because of its often chronic, repetitive nature and its potential to dramatically change the quality of the child's relationship with his or her primary support system, intersibling violence may lead to a mixture of localized and developmental effects.

For example, a primary developmental task for children is establishing and maintaining emotional ties to caregivers. Attachment theorists such as Bowlby (1973) propose that children develop internal representations of relationships derived from interactions with their primary caregivers, which they subsequently employ in maintaining other relationships. Some of our greatest early-life conflicts are threats to these ties, such as separation and abandonment anxieties.

Children severely challenged by an abusive family system often turn to older siblings in an effort to meet needs for nurturance, support, and validation. Simultaneously, parents in these families routinely abdicate caretaking responsibilities to their children. From both sides of the hierarchy, then, older sisters and brothers may become emotional stand-ins for unavailable parents, and important sources of attachment for their younger siblings. When older children become significant caregivers, their influence on a sibling's development increases dramatically. Similarly, their effect on their siblings' internal templates of self and others can be quite enduring. In this context, sibling incest and assault assume even greater developmental significance for children.

CULTURAL INFLUENCES

How we perceive and classify our experience is profoundly affected by our cultural world, and cultural influences are mediated chiefly through differences in relationships. Therefore it follows that an interactive, ecological approach is crucial for understanding how individuals affect, and are affected by, the society in which they live. Each interaction between a child and his or her sister or brother is influenced by the shared history of their relationship. Their sibling connection is also influenced by a wider context, namely the cultural world outside the family. Every family relationship is set in a particular cultural context, and different cultural expectations influence the developmental course of relationships between siblings as well as between parents and children.

Recognizing these differences is an important step in assessing and intervening in abusive sibling dyads. Our measures and descriptive tools must not be based on the assumption that what is "normal" or "best" for siblings is chiefly what our own cultural world views as optimal. Further, each intervention must be guided by its meaning and importance in a larger cultural context. Adopting this perspective entails embracing Belsky's (1980) assertion that to understand individuals we must understand the dynamic system in which they exist.

For couples from diverse racial minority groups, the lack of culturally sensitive health, social, and educational services creates additional burdens when they are raising a family. Childrearing practices are meant to socialize children for effective functioning in their own culture; they are shaped by the specific threats to survival faced by that culture. Minority families are challenged with the task of raising their children to live in their own culture as well as functioning effectively as minority members in a majority culture. Sibling incest and assault between children of color and others outside the majority culture are especially likely to go unreported. Social and economic barriers and inequities have significant effects on the rates of interpersonal violence; yet those barriers also cause fear of reporting and limit access to professional help.

No single entity can be identified as the "Latino family" or the "African-American family." Members of both groups come from many parts of the world; although they may have a common Latin or African heritage, the cultures of each group living in different parts of the world are quite different. Also, of course, significant regional differences exist in African-American and Latino families living in the rural South, the Northeast, the Midwest and the West. Many similarities exist, as well as significant differences. Below we highlight some distinctive characteristics of sibling roles and function, as related to abuse trauma, in Latino and African-American families—the two ethnic minority groups with which we have the most contact in our professional practice, and who were most represented in our research.

Latino Siblings

In the clinical treatment of abusive Latino families, gender segregation and interdependent ties between siblings warrant special attention. Sex differences are also believed to affect the sibling bond in Latino families. In a study based on fieldwork conducted in Sierra Nahuat villages of central Mexico and in the Ca'ceres village of Spain, Taggart (1992) describes the process of gender segregation and its effect on sibling relationships. Although reports from these two communities probably cannot be generalized to the many diverse cultures labeled "Hispanic" that exist in the United States, we find some interesting cultural constructions of sexuality.

Taggart's work consists of inferring differences in sexual beliefs by comparing regional variants of particular stories told frequently in the two cultures. The Ca'ceres and Sierra Nahuat narrators tell many similar stories regarding brothers, but they tell markedly different stories about sisters and brothers. Sierra Nahuat narrators generalize to all gender relations their belief that excessive love will lead to disorder for individuals, families, and even the cosmos. As a result, pronounced gender segregation is practiced for fear of sibling incest. Paredes (1970) and Foster (1945) provide additional evidence that symbolic representation of cross-sibling separation may be widespread in various parts of Mexico.

Many Latinos confront socioeconomic hardships and psychological problems stemming from changes due to acculturation, including the cultural isolation induced by language difficulties. In recent years, they have faced the problem of diminishing access to general health care, which can create even greater stress for families in which sibling abuse occurs. Costantino, Malgady, and Rogler (1994) reported that the literature on service delivery is full of references to the cultural distance between Mexican-American clients and non-Hispanic service providers. This distance creates a barrier to the utilization and effectiveness of mental health services for Latino consumers. In that study, culturally sensitive interventions reduced anxiety symptoms and increased self-esteem, social judgment, and ethnic identity in children and adolescents. According to an investigation by Sontag and Schacht (1994), Mexican-American parents reported a greater need than Caucasian parents for information about how to obtain services. This finding suggests that they are not linked sufficiently to service agencies. Mexican parents also were much less likely than Caucasian parents to feel that they had been told what could be done for their children.

Baruth and Manning (1992) specify key cultural characteristics that must be taken into account in providing culturally sensitive services to Latino children and families. Several Latino cultural tendencies conflict with Anglo-American expectations, making the crisis of abuse trauma within the family even more difficult for Latino children. For example, strong adherence to specific, different male and female sex role behaviors heavily influences who participates in the caregiving tasks necessary for family functioning. Often these responsibilities are assigned to children. Family relationships include greater responsibility and freedom for men than for women. Strict allegiance is given to family loyalty, and the commitment to extended families and siblings offers tremendous support to Latino families. Mental health professionals are very likely to interpret this high degree of family loyalty as overdependence.

Mental illness is a tremendously stigmatized form of social deviance in Latino families. Many Latino families also show an overprotective structure, which entails an extremely strong emphasis on the family's identity as a group rather than as a collection of individuals (Harry, 1992). This orientation toward a group identity may lead to characteristics such as prolonged mother-child interaction, overlapping of nuclear- and extended-family roles, and a perception of illness as a problem that resides in the family rather than in the individual. This situation in turn may explain why many Latino parents feel that their families have been disgraced after their children are labeled mentally ill. To use these signs to judge families as "enmeshed" would be to commit an error of assessment due to ethnocentrism, and to conceptualize as pathological cultural patterns that need to be respected (Falicov and Karrer, 1984).

Cross-cultural research consistently reveals differences between Anglo-Americans and Mexican-Americans with regard to preference for cooperative or competitive outcomes among siblings (Kagan, 1977; McClintock, Bayard, and McClintock, 1979). Research (Knight and Kagan, 1982) suggests that Mexican-American children are more cooperative and more prosocial than Anglo-American siblings regardless of family size and/or birth order. Strong sibling interdependence and the patterns of relationships between family members may result in this relatively prosocial orientation. It is more likely that family size and the children's ordinal positions interact with other factors such as family rules, values, gender roles, the family's style of conflict resolution, and sibling roles in the family.

Abuse may have different effects on relationships between siblings in these families. Both in our clinical work and in the research interviews, we have observed that Latino adult survivors of sibling abuse often go to great lengths to maintain lifelong ties with their brothers and sisters.

African-American Siblings

Cultural differences may strongly influence how family members manage the multiple tasks of caring for a child. Among African-Americans it is common to rely on extended-family members to assist in daily family tasks. The extended family also makes role substitution easier because it makes more members available to share responsibilities (Alston and Turner, 1994).

African-Americans have developed strong family systems that provide informal support for relatives outside the nuclear family. In one study (Horwitz and Reinhard, 1995), interviews with Caucasian and African-American parents and siblings revealed significant differences in caregiving responsibilities and in the burden of care. Although the parents of the two groups did not differ as to caregiving obligations and responsibility, Caucasian parents tended to report more stress or burden than did African-American parents. Angel and Angel (1995) suggest that this may result from African-American parents' greater involvement with intergenerational caregiving for extended-family members. With regard to children, African-American siblings tended to have more caregiver responsibilities than did Caucasian siblings. At equivalent levels of caregiving, however, Caucasian siblings felt the burden of care more strongly.

Role flexibility is another significant characteristic of many African-American families. The elasticity in assigning family roles promotes adaptation to stressful life conditions. The adherence to strict gender roles that exists in many cultures does not usually prevail among African-Americans. Because both men and women traditionally have served as primary providers, role reversals are less threatening to many African-American families than to families of other cultures. This increased role flexibility may be an advantage in dual-earner couples. During economic downturns, for example, one spouse may be unemployed and may be required to attend to domestic activities while the other works. In cultures without such flexibility, men staying at home to raise children and perform domestic functions may be perceived as weak or effeminate. Negative comments from others, including family members, can result in shame and humiliation for the unemployed partner. Financial stressors and their subsequent emotional consequences are known risk factors for increased marital and family discord, and can serve as preconditions for abuse.

Psychological studies of family violence indicate that culture is not significant in predicting or explaining violence (American Psychological Association, 1996). Nevertheless, a child's cultural background may affect his or her experience of sibling abuse. Characteristics of both African-American and Latino families suggest that siblings fulfill roles unique to their respective cultures. One example of role differ-

ences, found in both cultures, is the lifelong, interdependent tie between siblings.

ABUSE TRAUMA

Intrafamilial abuse trauma interferes with the attachment process.
Child victims must maintain needed bonds to caregivers and simultaneously must control painful affects often associated with their abuse.
In one psychological solution to this dilemma, a child assumes internal
command over that which he or she cannot control interpersonally.
That is, the child assumes responsibility for the abuse, believing that he
or she is somehow deficient. This cognitive appraisal inhibits the expression of distressing feelings toward the offender and allows the
victim to maintain a benevolent view of the needed caregiver.

The silent, internal exchange of responsibility allows the abuse
victim's external world to appear safe again. The child pays a price,
however: the victim's fractured perspective supports and maintains
an idealized image of the abuser, and generates both localized and
developmental consequences. Examples of traumatic effects include problems with dissociation, impaired judgment, self-blame,
self-injurious behavior, and low self-worth. In addition, internalized
offender-based distortions frequently serve as templates for future
intimate relationships.

Many victims of parent-child abuse who enter treatment are able
to understand at some point that it was the parent who relinquished
his or her role as protector and caretaker, and who was responsible
for the abuse. Sibling abuse victims, however, often have difficulty
accepting this view. Because no generational boundary was violated, they struggle more often with the idea that they were active
participants, even in cases where the abuse was accompanied by
force or coercion, and was witnessed or experienced by other family members as well. The danger of internalizing responsibility for
abusive experiences is even greater in circumstances where

- The sibling offender did not use force,
- The victim did not resist forcefully at the time, or
- The victim did not consider it abuse when it occurred.

In addition, sibling incest and assault often remain unacknowledged
by family members. Some evidence (Worling, 1995; O'Brien,

1991) suggests that the families of male sibling incest offenders are severely disturbed. Russell (1986) reported that a statistically significant number of sibling incest survivors in her study described an *unsupportive* response to the discovery of the abuse as compared with survivors of parent-child incest. We have observed that this consequence of disclosure is particularly prevalent for victims of stepsibling incest or assault.

FAMILY-BASED APPROACHES

Systemic thinking is compatible with a sibling-informed approach to treatment. It emphasizes each individual's unique position in his or her respective subsystem, as well as his or her place in the larger ecology. We view sibling incest or assault in families from an ecological, interactional perspective, emphasizing the relationships among individual, family, and social support factors (Belsky, 1993). Treatment from this approach seeks to address various child, parent, and family issues, and to enlist the cooperation of all family members by promoting an understanding of coercive and/or incestuous behavior. For example, structural family therapy easily incorporates siblings into decisions about assessment and intervention.

The structural concept of boundary maintenance can be employed to increase the awareness of siblings' functioning. Developing, maintaining, and learning to mutually respect boundaries between oneself and one's siblings is a primary task of childhood, adolescence, and even adulthood. Healthier sibling relationships are characterized by sufficient generational boundaries.

A structural diagram provides a clear picture of present family functioning as well as a visual metaphor for change. The structural model's focus on current interactions, and its basic assumptions that systems strive toward growth and self-regulation, result in a therapy that rests on functionality and family strengths.

A sibling-informed approach also includes the exchange of shared and nonshared experiences in the development of sibling abuse behavior. Nonshared sibling experiences are sometimes overlooked with regard to their impact on individual personality development and relationships between brothers and sisters.

To illustrate, Herlinda was a research participant who revealed how she, her two older brothers, and her mother were victims of physical assault inflicted by her alcoholic father. The youngest sister, Mona, was born when Herlinda was six years old. Herlinda's brothers were nearing adolescence by then, and her father's abusive behavior had decreased. In addition, during times when their father was abusive, the three older children were careful to protect Mona in any way they could; thus she neither witnessed nor experienced any abuse from her father. Ironically, Herlinda's relationship with her youngest sister was conflict-ridden, and as adults they have no contact with each other. Mona's unique relationship with her father isolated her in many ways from her sisters and brothers. Not only was she protected from his abusive behavior, she also could not accept her family's anger and criticism toward him. While her siblings frequently took their mother's side in disputes, Mona defended her father.

CONJOINT THERAPY
WITH NONABUSIVE SIBLINGS

Therapy with siblings is typically conducted as an adjunct to family counseling rather than as an independent treatment modality. Creating flexible but distinct bridges between family-based and individually oriented treatment approaches is a complex but necessary task, especially in treating sibling incest and assault victims. We believe that including nonabusive siblings in the therapeutic process with child victims can enhance positive effects because it incorporates features of both intrapsychic and interactional treatment.

Conjoint therapy with siblings can be productive in unexpected ways. Siblings may be valuable consultants to both the therapist and the victim. Brothers and sisters frequently provide an important perspective on family history. They may be utilized to address the abuse victim's primary problems, or to loosen an anachronistic frozen image of a brother or sister that is interfering with a current relationship. Nonabusive siblings often can facilitate improvement in a brother's or sister's social and coping skills related to their abuse trauma.

For example, seven-and-a-half-year-old Nelly fought constantly with her peers at the group home where she and her twelve-year-old sister Leena lived. According to staff member observations, the fights generally were related to Nelly's defense of her mother. Other children at the group home made fun of their mother on the rare occasions when she visited; she was obese and often made embarrassing comments to her daughters in front of their peers. Leena's reaction was quite different from Nelly's. She was angry with her mother for not believing her when she disclosed that their older brother had molested her. As a result, she sometimes joined the other children when they made cruel jokes about her mother. Nelly, on the other hand, sought love and approval from her mother, and minimized her unavailability, characterized by her frequent absences from home. When her mother was at home, she often retreated to her secured bedroom for the entire day. On those occasions, confident that he would not be caught, her brother locked Nelly in a closet for hours at a time while he molested Leena.

The girls were polarized in their respective positions; thus Nelly had no room to cope with the situation except by strongly defending her mother. Frequently this led to physical violence with the other children. After a few sibling sessions, Leena was able to acknowledge to Nelly that she had more than angry feelings toward their mother. She stated:

> It bothers me that we aren't close like I see other kids be with their moms. Like . . . they all want to go home, and I'm not sure I trust Mom, so I don't know . . . I just don't know if I'm ready to be with her . . . I wish one day we could get along better. But right now, I'm angry and sad, and confused, and . . . it's just all mixed up.

Leena also revealed:

> I feel bad sometimes after when I make fun of Mom with everyone else . . . sometimes I cry at night because I just wish Mom was a different mom, and I feel guilty at myself for making fun of her. . . . I guess I do it because I'm mad and embarrassed, and I think . . . she doesn't act like she loves me, so why should I stick up for her? She likes Troy [older brother]

more than me, and that makes me mad, too . . . because she
believed him and not me.

Leena's candid disclosure freed Nelly to discuss some of the
ways in which she was hurt and a little angry at their mother's
unavailability. Using a puppet to respond to her sister, Nelly stated:

> Well, mostly she misses her Mom when she's not here . . . She
> doesn't like it when you say those things. But sometimes . . .
> when she thinks of before, like when she [Mom] would leave
> and stuff . . . She just wishes she would've stayed at home
> more or not gone to her bedroom sometimes, that's all . . . She
> maybe was a little mad when she left for so long. That's what
> hurt her feelings before.

Ultimately both girls were able to laugh about some of their
mother's embarrassing remarks, as well as join in the pain of her
limitations. Nelly's social relationships improved when her role as
her mother's sole supporter subsided. With the aid of projective
techniques, she was able to express difficult feelings and to acknowledge that she shared them with her sister, rather than behaving in ways that left her on the periphery with Leena and her peers.

A decision to include nonabusive siblings in treatment would
necessarily begin with assessment. Initially, the crucial considerations are to determine levels of shared self-disclosure and the
discussion of feelings among siblings in the family. Research with
nonclinical siblings (Brown and Dunn, 1992) suggests that as early
as preschool, child-sibling interactions (particularly conversations
about feelings) become preeminent over qualitatively similar interactions with mothers. Siblings who regularly have such conversations develop an important forum for learning about others' feelings. In many cases these interactions create the conditions for
empathic connections between brothers and sisters.

Because parent-parent, parent-child, and child-child relationships operate simultaneously in a family system, interactions between any two members of the family can be affected by the behavior of others. Therefore, in examining sibling interactions, it is
useful to consider how other family members affect these relationships.

It is also important to explore the systemic implications for siblings with parents who cannot care for them adequately. Some research suggests that siblings may be a particularly valuable resource for children with such parents. We advise caution, however: parental unavailability usually does not benefit the sibling relationship. Although absent or deficient parenting can promote intensified sibling bonding, this attachment is not always beneficial. As discussed earlier, parents' underinvolvement in the care and supervision of children can lead to increased access and opportunity for siblings; at times this increases the vulnerability for sibling incest or assault. With these cases, sibling sessions can be useful in helping the therapist to assess whether other children in the family have been abused or are at risk.

Certain child characteristics favor the use of siblings as resources in therapy. If a child is timid, for example, a nonabusive sibling may be helpful in modeling alternative behaviors or encouraging the child to be more assertive. Lavigueur (1976) systematically documented the effectiveness of a sibling as a therapeutic agent. In families in which parents are particularly stressed by caretaking responsibilities, older siblings may prove to be important resources by indirectly affecting a younger child's relationship with his or her parents. A nonabusive sibling relationship can provide an important, relatively enduring context for modulating aggression. Baskett and Johnson (1982) suggest that siblings may be more appropriate therapeutic agents than parents for teaching children to achieve a more normal balance of prosocial and coercive behaviors. Conflict resolution skills sometimes can be developed more easily in sibling than in parent-child interactions. Therapists may find it useful to work with nonabusive siblings without parents present, so that conflict issues can be considered without being clouded by parent-child concerns. *Conflict, however, must be distinguished from assault.*

Sometimes nontargeted brothers or sisters may be unaware of the existence or the extent of sibling abuse. If not informed of the abuse in age-appropriate ways, they are vulnerable to assuming responsibility, feeling left out, or blaming the victim for shifts in their family's status. It is not uncommon for siblings to react negatively toward the victim, blaming him or her for abrupt and (from their point of view) unwelcome changes in the family. Under these circumstances, intervention should include individual contact with every sibling. Each child's capacity for support versus blame should be evaluated in order to avoid further trauma to the victim. Where the potential for support is strong, however, conjoint meetings with a victim and his or her nonabusive siblings can facilitate understanding and can provide an opportunity to interrupt a transgenerational cycle of secret keeping and abuse.

In one case, fifteen-year-old Rachel and her twelve-year-old sister Loretta were invited to attend a series of conjoint meetings. Their older brother, Ted, had been removed from the home after Rachel disclosed that he had been molesting her since she was eleven years old. Part of Rachel's motivation for disclosure was her fear that he might begin abusing her sister next. While in treatment at a residential facility, Ted revealed a history of victimization and disclosed the existence of several nonfamily victims in addition to his sister.

Rachel had suspected her brother's abuse history and was informed of the other victims, but her sister Loretta was not. Their parents felt that it was best to protect her from this damaging information about her older brother. As a result, Loretta blamed Rachel for the tremendous upheaval in their family. From her point of view, her older brother was gone, her parents fought constantly (with their mother taking Ted's side and their father favoring Rachel), and school-age peers made embarrassing remarks about how "screwed up" her whole family was.

When, with the parents' consent, the two sisters were allowed to share their different perceptions of events related to Rachel's abuse, they provided missing information and also confirmed each other's reality about key experiences. In one meeting, for example, Loretta accused her sister of turning Ted in to the authorities because of some minor struggle over supervising Loretta while their parents were gone. Rachel was able to place this struggle in context by sharing her heartfelt concern that Loretta might be victimized next by their brother. When Loretta raised questions about her sister's complicity in the abuse, Rachel described the varied ways in which Ted had coerced and threatened her into submission. She also reminded Loretta that sometimes he had manipulated her into doing something she did not want to do (for example, by lying to her about something their parents had said). These exchanges and many others helped the siblings understand their brother's abuse and its influence on their relationship. As a result, they could begin to explore their own unique connection.

Hamlin and Timberlake (1979) suggest that clinicians may be reluctant to work with siblings, and note that the literature over-emphasizes the competitive nature of siblinghood. Therapists also sometimes collude with parents by viewing conjoint sibling therapy as possibly contaminating the "healthy" child. Further, therapists may erroneously assume that working with siblings will be more complicated than other forms of treatment because of the different developmental ages of siblings in the same family. Family-based therapies address this challenge with the following principle: For-mulate therapeutic interventions designed specifically to address the range of developmental levels represented in the family.

Treatment of sibling incest or assault requires sensitivity to other considerations as well. The safety of children in the family is a primary concern. Sibling offenders typically are not removed from the home except in the case of multiple victims, a large age differ-ence between the offender and the victim, or unless parents are willing to support a separation. Unfortunately, little empirical evi-dence exists to suggest how best to integrate treatment of the victim and the offender in these cases. Generally the initial family response is to minimize the assaultive or incestuous behavior and to quietly reprimand the sibling offender. In many cases of older brother-younger sister incest, however, victims have reported that when parents learned of the incest, they accused the victims of lying and were angry at them for "participating." We have observed this dy-namic most often where the offender was the designated family "hero" in a rigidly gendered family, or was joined in a coalition with an authoritarian, abusive parent.

We offer the following key considerations in treating families in which a sibling offender remains in the home postdisclosure:

- Extra precautions to ensure the victim's safety, such as locks on doors, increased adult supervision, and cooperation of par-ents, extended-family members, and the community

- Individual abuse-focused therapy for the victim and the offender, often with different clinicians
- No conjoint sibling or family meetings with the offender until he or she has accepted full responsibility for the abuse, and until the therapist is satisfied that the family can and will protect the victim from further abuse

A nonabusive sibling can be an important source of comfort and acknowledgment to a victim further traumatized by the family's reaction to disclosure. He or she also may be able to validate the victim's perspective of the offender, and perhaps can offer important information about other intergenerational family secrets. In all cases, the family needs information and education about the traumatic effects of sibling incest and assault, and about the importance of the victim's safety—often in addition to individual, group, and family therapy. We strongly recommend intervention and family risk assessment that follow nationally recognized guidelines for child abuse professionals.

A thorough appraisal of the offender's characteristics is also crucial. (Specific precautions related to conducting family meetings with adult sibling offenders present are discussed in Chapter 8.) While some discussion of offender dynamics is presented throughout, a comprehensive assessment of sibling incest or assault offenders is beyond the scope of this book. (For further information see Barbaree, Marshall, and Hudson, 1993; Becker and Kaplan, 1988; Chaffin and Bonner, 1996; O'Brien, 1991.)

Generally, we conduct individual meetings with each child, including the victim and the offender, as well as with each parent. Sometimes extended-family members are involved, and it also may be useful to incorporate them into individual interviews (see Table 7.1). During these individual meetings, the groundwork can be established to (1) support the incest victim with regard to disclosure; (2) prepare parents to hear, validate, and support the victim's disclosure; (3) provide clear messages regarding the responsibility for abuse and the unacceptability of the sibling offender's behavior; and (4) provide the family with hope that problems can be addressed and resolved.

TABLE 7.1. When and When Not to Include Nonabusive Siblings in Treatment

Include Nonabusive Siblings

- When siblings perceive each other in frozen roles or images.

- When it is important for siblings to hear each other's perception of significant events.

- In families where dyadic secret keeping is prominent.

- When an intergenerational pattern of abuse is evident in the family.

- To develop support for disclosure of abuse or for acknowledgment of past abuse.

Do Not Include Nonabusive Siblings

- In families in which intense anger or vindictiveness continues between siblings.

- When a sibling meeting is not in the victim's best interests.

- When it can be determined that a nonabusive sibling is not a source of support or validation for the victim.

KEY POINTS

- Creating flexible, but distinct bridges between family-based and individually oriented treatment approaches is a complex but necessary task in treating sibling abuse victims and their families.
- When siblings become significant caretakers, their influence on a child's development changes dramatically. Their impact on their siblings' internal templates of self and others can be quite enduring.
- Different cultural expectations influence the developmental course of relationships between parents, children, and extended-family members. Understanding and recognizing these differ-

ences is a necessary component of sibling abuse assessment and
intervention.

- Specific benefits can be derived from conducting conjoint
  therapy with child victims and their nonabusive siblings if special attention is given to the victim's safety and readiness. It is
  important to establish guidelines specifying how and when to
  include nonabusive siblings in treatment.
- Unlike many offenders in parent-child maltreatment, sibling
  offenders often remain in the home after disclosure. It is necessary to apply safeguards and procedures unique to treating
  sibling incest or assault when the offender is not removed.

Chapter 8

Specific Intervention Strategies
with Children and Families

SIBLING ABUSE FAMILY CONFIGURATIONS

The family configurations presented throughout this chapter were inspired by Trepper and Barrett's (1989) systemic assessment for parent-child incest. They depict family structural characteristics common in sibling abuse families. Together they reveal family risk patterns which, when coupled with an absence of protective mechanisms, share a heightened structural vulnerability for sibling incest or assault.

The configurations that follow portray traditional nuclear family households. These are simply prototypes and are not meant to exclude alternative gender and cultural parenting alignments such as same-sex couple dyads or extended-family units. The discussion of each family subtype includes a description of family roles, abuse characteristics (boundaries, power alignments, and access considerations), and their specific impact on the sibling relationship. In addition, clinical examples of therapy with siblings and families are provided for several of the configurations.

Families are living, complex systems; therefore great variation exists within and among the six subtypes. These family configurations describe most of the sibling abuse families we have treated. These are not "pure" types, however. A family may resemble some combination of subtypes, or may be organized differently at various developmental life cycle stages. Two families may be similar in structure; yet abuse may occur in only one of these families because of differences in developmental, community, and cultural circumstances.

In addition, children's circumstances within families vary greatly; thus no one-to-one correspondence between family organization and the quality of the children's home environment is intended. Indeed, research findings suggest that the quality of family life, rather than family structure in itself, is associated more consistently with later violence (American Psychological Association, 1996). Therefore, in evaluating for sibling incest and assault, it is important to determine the quality of sibling relations in regard to the individual and family characteristics commonly associated with intersibling abuse (e.g., a child's victimization history, use of force or coercion, compulsive or deviant sexual arousal, parental neglect and/or excessive punishment, spousal violence, parental favoritism, sexualized family climate, rigid sibling gender roles) along with family organization and protective resources.

Sibling abuse has no single cause; rather, the balance of family stressors and supports must be weighed in each case. One must also remember that individuals, not families, abuse children. Nevertheless, in our experience, both colleagues and clients have found the six different family patterns recognizable and useful in making sense of the turmoil that frequently accompanies sibling incest or assault.

PSEUDOCONSENSUAL SIBLING INCEST

Siblings subject to ongoing parental abuse or neglect may turn to each other for validation, support, protection, and nurturance—needs normally met by adult caretakers. High access, coupled with the lack of reliable parental care, can increase sexual tension between siblings and subsequently can lead to incest. A sexually charged climate at home also has been associated with increased sexual tension between siblings who already turn to one another to meet critical emotional needs.

Although many children reared in neglectful families exhibit qualities consistent with this type of family, incestuous sibling interactions seem to actually develop less frequently. When they do so, the incest often overtly resembles noncoercive sex play between children close in age, except that the incestuous behavior may be more intense, more frequent, and longer-lasting. In such families, both children (victim and offender) suffer from an extreme lack of parental guidance and a high level of neglect.

One important difference between pseudoconsensual incest and other forms of sibling incest is that the behavior appears to be motivated primarily by the urge to meet critical emotional needs that are not being met in the family. Coercion between siblings, either in the development or the maintenance of incestuous behavior, can be difficult to detect. In some pseudoconsensual cases, however, overt coercion may be even less apparent in the etiology of the incest. Nevertheless, pseudoconsensual incest can result in traumatic effects for participants. Each individual's perception is important, and harmful aftereffects may be present even in cases in which a child's subjective experience of the incest normalizes the behavior.

Reorganizing the family is a primary systemic goal in cases of pseudoconsensual sibling incest. Although individual sessions may be indicated at times, the structural difficulties that contribute to maintaining pseudoconsensual incest require sibling and family intervention. Specifically, the siblings involved in the incestuous behavior must have the opportunity to learn alternative, more appropriate ways of interacting with one another. Children in such families are often satisfying crucial needs for support, contact, and nurturing in an incestuous sibling relationship because of neglect and/or abandonment by parents or caretakers. Parents must be educated sensitively about the dangers of incestuous interactions between their children. In addition, parents must learn to establish and maintain appropriate individual and generational boundaries; then they can model this behavior for their children. Families can benefit from external support in order to increase the amount of time they spend supervising and nurturing their children. The following abbreviated case example highlights an intervention strategy that addressed several of these issues.

Case Illustration: Elena and Julio

Elena, a six-year-old Mexican child, was removed from her home by Child Protective Services and temporarily placed in a group facility for sexual "acting out" behavior, which led to a suspicion that she had been molested. She was the oldest of five siblings. Early in treatment it was revealed that her uncle, who had lived with the family for a few months earlier that year, had exposed Elena to pornographic materials. In addition, the older children had probably observed their parents having sex on more than one occasion. They lived together in a three-room cottage, where the living room also served as the parents' bedroom.

Elena's father was a migrant worker who was intermittently absent for weeks at a time. When he found work near home, he often worked long hours, six or seven days each week. Elena had a five-year-old brother named Julio and three younger siblings ranging in age from three-and-a-half years to five months.

Consistent with the dynamics of pseudoconsensual cases, Elena's parents were overwhelmed by their parenting and work responsibilities. As a result, they were not reliably available for all of their children. We gathered information about the amount and quality of time that Elena and Julio spent together. A family pattern was solidly established whereby the children automatically sought each other out for comfort and soothing, and shielded the parents from many of their problems. As they grew older, Elena and Julio also used the intense sibling relationship to meet many of their needs for closeness and physical contact.

Elena's parents were proud of the self-sufficiency they had taught their two oldest children. More than a year ago, they had placed them in the same bed, so that when one became afraid or needed something during the night, the other could offer assistance.

After several weeks of play therapy, it was revealed that Elena and Julio had been engaging in mutual and dual masturbation for nearly a year. Their parents were not surprised by the information, and did not understand how it might harm their children's development.

It appeared that there were no other family or nonfamily victims or offenders. Elena's parents underwent a Child Protective Services investigation. The social worker acted to protect the children from additional trauma associated with their neglect, and expressed concern about the parents' inability to establish clear boundaries in the home. They uncovered no additional evidence of sexual abuse. Questions remained, however, about the heightened sexualized climate in the home.

Several characteristics of the sexual interaction between Elena and Julio were consistent with a pseudoconsensual sibling incest pattern. The relevant components were as follows:

- *Frequency and intensity:* Elena and Julio engaged in sexual behavior with one another approximately twice a day: often once in the afternoon and again before falling asleep at night. Their mother estimated that the incest behavior generally continued for thirty to sixty minutes.
- *Duration:* The children had engaged in this behavior for at least a year, according to the mother's memory of when she first noticed their afternoon and bedtime patterns and began to hear particular sounds emerging from their bedroom.
- *Lack of peer relationships:* Elena and Julio rarely played with other children in the neighborhood; generally they preferred to interact with each other. Julio was having difficulty sleeping while Elena was gone, and spent some of his free time making or drawing things to give to her at their next visit.
- *Motivation:* On the basis of information gathered from the family, the incest seemed to be motivated by the children's need to meet critical biopsychosocial requirements that were not being met by their parents.
- *Sexual activity:* Elena and Julio (according to Elena's self-report, and as confirmed by Julio) engaged in closed-mouth kissing and holding each other, touching (both over clothing and when undressed), and mutual and dual masturbation. In addition, Elena masturbated in the evening before going to sleep (occasionally whispering and crying for Julio, as one might expect another child to do for his or her mother or father), and also sometimes during the day. Elena's physical examination at the group home revealed findings consistent with frequent, abrasive touching: she was developing a callus on the external area of her vagina.
- *Developmental inappropriateness of sexual activity:* Although children's sexual behavior generally increases between ages four and six, Elena and Julio's sexual activity would not be considered as within normal exploratory limits for children in their age group. On the other hand, individual and conjoint interviews with the children and various family members determined that no apparent force or coercion accompanied the incest.

Interventions

A treatment challenge unique to pseudoconsensual incest cases is how to reorganize the family so that the incestuous behavior no longer occurs, without inducing shame or guilt. This is especially critical when the siblings involved are younger-age peers, such as Elena and Julio. Further, the incest behavior evolves gradually in the interest of self-preservation, given the parents' caretaking deficits. The siblings must learn other coping skills without being shamed for those that they have developed to meet critical survival needs. One must take care to avoid shaming parents as well; such care, in turn, decreases the likelihood that shameful feelings will be expressed or projected onto the children.

Establishing a Framework for Change

It was important to employ interventions consistent with the cultural context of Elena's family. Both of her parents were raised in a small rural town in Mexico. They were not well educated and had not been exposed to contemporary information about childrearing or sex education. Early conversations with Elena's parents were used to establish a framework for change by stating certain assumptions. The therapist emphasized how the children were already trying to incorporate the parents' values, and thus how effective the parents had been so far in helping to instill them. This was obvious to the therapist because of Julio's and Elena's efforts to be loyal and respect their parents' wishes. They demonstrated this by learning to be self-sufficient, as opposed to burdensome, because both parents were extremely busy and therefore were unavailable to meet Elena's and Julio's basic emotional and psychological needs. This framework included a paradox for the parents because one of their strong cultural values was closeness and community.

The therapist planted an additional seed by establishing that the children were attempting to meet their normal developmental needs elsewhere in an effort to avoid burdening their parents—as if they felt that giving a little more love and attention would be a burden for the parents. The word *burden* was used to take this concept to an extreme, with the hope that the parents would move toward the desired goal by responding that showing more love and attention to their children would not be a burden. The therapist reminded the parents, however, that Elena and Julio had the judgment of children. They could not possibly know, in ways that adults could, about the problems that might follow from the mutual sexual touching. Their strong desire to respect and obey their parents provided the context in which the touching took place.

Addressing Parental Neglect

The therapist then continued: "If we were to assign a numerical value to hugs for younger children, we all would know and agree that a hug from a parent is worth ten points, while a hug from a sibling is worth only one point. Therefore, in a desperate effort to meet their needs for parental attention, validation, and contact, the children were having lots more touching between them." The therapist also explained that Elena and Julio were obviously very strong and determined. They probably felt a great deal of inner pain about their infrequent contact with their parents; yet they continued to respect their parents' wishes and remain self-sufficient. We now know, the therapist informed the parents, that the children on their own can never fill the void of not having more parental love and attention.

As one step toward increasing the father's involvement, he was labeled the family teacher of how brothers are supposed to treat sisters. He was given brief assignments that initially were discussed and practiced in the office. For example, he and Julio, along with the next oldest boy, were to watch a television commercial or look at a magazine and discuss any messages they found about how boys treated girls. The father was also asked to review various alternatives with his sons, emphasizing appropriate and positive ways of treating girls. The three-and-a-half-year-old was included primarily to generalize the lessons and to prevent Julio from feeling as if he had done something wrong. Special conversations exclusively between the father and Julio were also scheduled, with the understanding that this was to be done because Julio was older and therefore ready for more advanced material than his younger brother.

Once this exercise became easier, another element was added. The therapist asked Julio and his father to review the advertisements from the perspective of a brother or a sister. Throughout the course of these assignments, Julio's father asked some previously agreed-to questions, some of which underscored differences in the ways brothers and sisters relate, such as, "Would a brother look like that at his sister? Would he touch her in that way? Why or why not? When would a brother and sister hug? When would they hold hands, or look at each other like that? What are the ways only adults look at, and touch, each other?" The father was coached not to include additional information about sexual behavior—only to clarify with Julio the kinds of behaviors he had already learned. Simultaneously, Elena and her mother worked on a similar assignment designed to establish and teach guidelines for physical contact between sisters and brothers. Additional questions and exercises were included, which emphasized the delineation of boundaries and the identification of feelings, encouraged empathy development, and invited the children to play at creating stories or contexts around the ads and commercials (e.g., change people in the ads to cartoon characters, reverse their gender).

Elena and Julio were encouraged by way of homework assignments to devote more time to activities with peers. This gradually increased their time spent apart and helped to develop their social skills. Previously they had shared a bed. Now, arrangements were made for them to share beds with their same-sex younger siblings when Elena returned home. Parental supervision practices were adjusted to minimize their unsupervised time together and to monitor their interactions with their younger siblings. Sibling play therapy meetings were organized to review their separate parent-child assignments and to strengthen their learning about appropriate versus inappropriate touching between adults, children, and family members.

By all reports, the family was able to maintain changes related to ending the sibling incest. This appeared to have a positive effect on overall family functioning. For example, progress in the nurturing connections the parents developed with Elena and Julio simultaneously influenced their interactions with their younger children. The result was an increase in the amount of caring interaction and in feedback exchange between children and parents. This increased the likelihood that their parenting styles would be more responsive to future developmental changes in the children.

One important responsibility with clinical and safety implications was to determine whether any coercion or force accompanied the pseudoconsensual incest in this case, and whether the incest was initiated and maintained by both children or introduced by Elena. Cases of mutually initiated sibling incest are uncommon in our clinical experience (again, possibly because of underreporting), but they do occur. Particularly in pseudoconsensual sibling dyads, where coercion may be subtle and covert, extra effort must be made to evaluate each child for evidence of offender behavior. Furthermore, pseudoconsensual sibling incest is accompanied by neglect on the part of adult caretakers. Clinicians must be aware of the long-term traumatic effects of neglect on children, and whenever possible must emphasize treatment that addresses and reverses such effects.

Sibling incest between age peers traditionally has been viewed in the literature as harmless, exploratory behavior. Recent research and clinical observation, however, suggest that sometimes this is not the case. What appears to be mutual sexual exploratory behavior may actually be pseudoconsensual incest. Such behavior usually requires individual and family intervention to address the incest, the serious neglect, and the dysfunctional relationships associated with this type of sibling abuse.

PERIPHERAL-PARENT SIBLING ABUSE

Specific Considerations

- Determine whether either parent is abusive to spouse or to children.
- If not, then increase the peripheral parent's involvement in the family or with the children, if possible. Determine whether the nonperipheral parent encourages his or her involvement.
- Decide whether there is a child who metaphorically represents the peripheral parent in the family, and how this affects his or her sibling relationships.

In peripheral-parent families, one parent maintains a role exterior to the others. In many cases, he or she re-enters the family system in an authoritative or abusive manner. (We consider this to be one family subtype, regardless of which parent resides on the periphery.) The parent who is more available in the family may be nurturing, but unable to protect himself or herself and the children when the peripheral parent becomes abusive.

Conversely, the nonperipheral parent may be the one who abuses the children. One mother, Noreen, acknowledged physically abusing her children due to resentment related to her role as primary caretaker, anger at her peripheral husband for frequent extended absences, and frustration over learning of his recent extramarital affair. Another client was the victim of domestic violence by a peripheral-parent husband who was also physically abusive to both of their children. Janice felt overwhelmed whether her husband was home, or out of town on business. She realized that she was also occasionally abusive to her son, whom her husband favored.

One parent might be on the periphery of the family for a variety of reasons. This family organization is prominent, for example, in military families, in families characterized by separation, mental illness, substance abuse, or domestic violence, or in families in which, out of economic necessity, someone is required to remain out of the home for long periods.

An absence of parental contact and support renders children vulnerable to sibling abuse for a number of reasons. Children in peripheral-parent homes may feel that there is not enough love, attention, or support for everyone. These feelings can create adversarial relationships among siblings who are attempting to meet their needs in a family with limited resources. In addition, sibling interaction often is not supervised adequately; this situation creates structural deficits, and a lack of nourishment in the family. Parents must be present to intervene when one child is abusing another. When adult caretakers are not available to facilitate problem solving, siblings are left to resolve conflicts using their own inadequate (albeit developing) skills. Thus the benefits of learning effective communication, sharing, and natural and logical consequences are not integrated readily into their abilities to resolve problems.

Sibling violence in peripheral-parent families sometimes may be understood as a metaphor for spousal distress. One parent inadvertently may encourage the other's "favorite" child to be abused by children at home. The risk of sibling assault increases dramatically when parents encourage divided loyalties among their children:

siblings are drawn into each parent's different plight. If one child is aligned with the abusive peripheral parent, he or she may be scapegoated and abused by brothers or sisters, especially in that parent's absence. Under these conditions, the father's presence and availability are important factors in understanding sibling abuse. Researchers suggest that children who have a warm relationship with their father, in which he treats them with relative equality, have lower levels of sibling conflict.

In certain peripheral-mother families, the victim of father-daughter incest is groomed to act both as a surrogate spouse and as a caretaker for other siblings. A peripheral mother may be unable to provide protection and support for her abused daughter, and may also expect younger children in the family to care for her. In this case, her behavior can be viewed as an attempt to meet her own needs for support, attention, and value as a parent through her children. Puzzled by the reversal in hierarchies and boundaries, an older sibling may begin to imitate aspects of the parent-child abuse with a younger brother or sister.

Tabatha, age fifteen, had been molested by her father since she was twelve years old. Her mother's drinking problem had grown worse at about that time, and she was progressively more unavailable to Tabatha and her two younger brothers. What little time she shared with her children, especially the two younger boys, she spent asking them to massage her feet, back, and head, to fix her something to eat, or to meet her emotional needs by telling her how much they loved her. Tabatha was expected to care for her two younger brothers, maintain the household, and attend to her mother's basic needs—in addition to meeting her father's emotional and sexual demands.

In treatment, Tabatha struggled with issues related to her mother's unavailability and lack of protection. Her sadness and frustration were complicated by a perception that the incest was the only parental nurturing she received in her family.

Just before the planned termination of therapy, Tabatha revealed what she described as "the worst thing of all." For much of the therapy hour she tried to express what she wanted to say, and finally was able to explain herself by writing it down. Here are some excerpts from Tabatha's letter, reprinted with permission:

Something I don't think I can ever forgive myself for . . . the one thing that still makes me think of killing myself . . . I couldn't tell you when you asked before because I was trying to make excuses for myself, like . . . that it happened to me so that's why I did it . . . that it wouldn't hurt them that much and anyways they're young and would just probably forget it . . . and I thought I could get over it, but I can't stop thinking about it. I don't know what to do because it makes me feel sick to my stomach whenever I see them or think about it . . . I can't stop seeing you right now because I have to face up to what I did to my brothers . . . I did some of the same things to them that my dad did to me. I can't believe I'm telling you this. Please don't hate me or say you won't work with me anymore . . . I hate myself for doing this . . . I know it's not totally her fault, but I sometimes blame my mom . . . . Why couldn't she have just taken care of them, then none of this would've ever happened.

Case Illustration: The Carlson Family

The Carlson family entered therapy primarily concerned that Amber, their fifteen-year-old daughter, was depressed (father's complaint) and that there was serious ongoing conflict between Amber and her twelve-year-old sister Tanya (mother's complaint). Although they came together for the initial therapy session, Ron and Rosalie Carlson had divorced approximately nine months earlier. Mr. Carlson had custody of the two children, though Rosalie made unannounced visits to the home to see them several times a week. Mrs. Carlson behaved as if she could not accept the reality of her divorce, particularly the lack of regular contact with her family. The therapist also understood the mother's behavior in the context of the family's current development challenge: Amber was an adolescent, and Tanya was not far behind. The entire family was "launching" in different directions. This probably intensified Mrs. Carlson's difficulty in accepting the divorce.

Amber's abusive behavior consisted of slapping Tanya and occasionally leaving red marks or welts on her face. She also punched her (which once resulted in a black eye, and another time in a swollen lip) and threw things. Amber had kicked and scratched her sister hard enough to leave bruises on her body. She acknowledged her behavior but argued adamantly that her parents did not observe what Tanya brought to their conflict.

Family Assessment

The therapist viewed the sibling violence in this family as occurring in the midst of unresolved conflict between their divorced parents, who thus far had neither separated successfully nor redefined their relationship to reflect the recent divorce. The fact that problematic interactions between the sisters had increased dramatically over the previous nine months also supported this view. In treatment it became clear that Tanya and Amber held opposing "good" and "bad" sibling roles in the family; furthermore, two distinct parent-child coalitions existed. Ron and Amber (the stronger team) were aligned against Rosalie and Tanya. The adults competed overtly for who would be viewed as the better parent—a process paralleling their daughters' rivalry. The net effect was the creation of two teams in the Carlson family, which metaphorically reflected the unresolved conflict between the parents.

Rosalie did not want the divorce, and continued to make her presence felt in the family. She wanted to avoid the pain she would experience if Ron were to "move on with his life," as she put it. Ron, for his part, was uncomfortable in stating his needs directly, especially to women. Thus he quietly collaborated with his ex-wife's wish to postpone their emotional separation. Now, however, Ron was trying to establish clearer boundaries. His current girlfriend, Autumn, did not want to spend time at his house for fear that Rosalie would drop in—an uncomfortable situation for everyone. Ron's primary strategy for handling this situation was avoidance. He planned weekends away with his girlfriend and left his daughters largely alone to fend for themselves.

Addressing Tanya's Safety

The therapist obviously needed the cooperation of both parents, as well as the children, to put an immediate end to the sibling abuse. To accomplish this, she developed an intervention strategy based on her assessment of the following family characteristics: (1) Ron had custody of the girls and thus held more power in relation to their ongoing treatment; (2) Ron did not view the sibling violence as problematic, much less abusive, although he was concerned about Amber's depression; (3) Rosalie had a clearer understanding of the sibling abuse, but the therapist had to be careful not to be perceived as favoring one team in this divided family.

The therapist told the family how common it was for depressed children and adolescents to express their despair by becoming irritable and aggressive, even to the point of being physically assaultive, as Amber had done. Amber's increasingly serious symptoms (poor school performance, increased violence) suggested that her abusive behavior was linked to a serious increase in her depression—which, of course, required immediate attention. Whenever she hurt Tanya, the abuse increased her feelings of guilt, low self-worth, shame, and ultimately depression. Amber was caught in a rapidly downward-moving spiral.

The therapist assumed that Ron and Rosalie cared deeply for Amber and did not want this situation to continue. She suggested that Amber's aggression was a concrete problem which, once under her control, might begin to provide some immediate relief for her depression. In closing, the therapist wondered if the family might put their heads together and determine how to end something that was seriously hurting Tanya and increasing Amber's depression.

The family began to develop alternative supervision plans. They reached a compromise decision to ask Ron's mother to come and monitor the children three days a week after school. On alternate days, the children were to spend after-school hours at their mother's home. Ron also agreed that the girls could spend every other weekend with their mother and that he would arrange his out-of-town trips accordingly. He promised to eliminate any unsupervised time for the girls until their relationship improved and the abuse was eliminated.

These agreements also addressed the family's struggle to move toward a postdivorce, binuclear (Ahrons, 1979) family, in which the adults relinquish their spousal relationship and continue to share parenting responsibilities for their children. The mother's peripheral-parent role was recognized as contributing to the family's overall developmental dissonance. She was entering the father's home and behaving in an authoritarian manner, which helped to maintain their rigid roles and conflict. In peripheral-parent families, the peripheral parent should be encouraged to maintain contact with his or her children whenever it is safe to do so. In this case, however, it was felt that contact with Mrs. Carlson would be less confusing, and actually would facilitate the family's progress, if it occurred at her home. Mrs. Carlson was also provided with a group therapy referral for divorced parents as a way of increasing support for her apart from the family.

Decreasing Role Rigidity

Several family meetings were held to reinforce provisions for Tanya's safety, to resolve developmental impasses, and to diminish the role rigidity prevalent in the family. Ron's mother, whose husband had died recently, was included in several sessions as an expert in grief and loss. Her presence was utilized to facilitate the expression of loss that the family members experienced as a result of significant developmental transitions. The grandmother also was coached on her role as monitor for Amber's depression while the girls were under her supervision. The family agreed that Tanya would inform her whenever Amber was verbally or physically abusive. The therapist also helped the family to outline what the grandmother was to do, on behalf of both children, in the event of further abuse. The safety plan included calling the parents or the therapist, Tanya or Amber staying at the grandmother's home for a couple of days, and holding a family therapy meeting to address concerns and assess whether additional steps were necessary to monitor Amber's depression or to ensure Tanya's safety.

Mr. and Mrs. Carlson's polarized relationship—Ron wanting the divorce and Rosalie feeling victimized by it—also had to change to allow for shifts in the parent-child and the sibling relationships. During one session, the therapist instructed Amber (solidly in a coalition with her father) to role-play her mother. Tanya was asked to role-play her father. Then the girls were assigned the task of reenacting a parental conflict about the divorce until they reached a resolution. Tanya and her sister seized the opportunity to recreate a parental struggle; they had witnessed the real thing countless times.

This intervention heightened Ron's and Rosalie's awareness of their roles in the divorce. It also led them to recognize the numerous ways in which their unresolved conflict influenced their daughters' relationship. The enactment increased Tanya's awareness of her father's view of the conflict and Amber's view of her mother's. Finally, the siblings recognized how their own relationship had become polarized because of their parents' conflict, which actually had little or nothing to do with them. As a result of this intervention, Ron and Rosalie worked harder to establish clear boundaries concerning their role as coparents. They gradually established a coparenting contract specifying how to address expectations, support, and disagreements about disciplining the children.

Decreasing Sibling Deidentification

Tanya and her sister had been close at one time. Their difficulties and Tanya's abuse coincided with their parents' marital problems and ultimate divorce. The therapist therefore began to prepare Amber for conjoint meetings with her sister in which she would take full responsibility for her hurtful actions, apologize, and initiate steps to improve their relationship. In an early session, Amber expressed some understanding of her sister's victimization and began to apologize. She quickly offered to make up for the abuse by allowing Tanya to wear her favorite dress or bring her pager to school.

The therapist suggested that perhaps it was premature to decide how to make amends, and asked that they give it some thought for later discussion. Instead she asked them to identify previous times or activities when they were on better terms. The siblings were encouraged to state two or three qualities they liked about each other, and were asked about their similarities and strengths. This naturally evolved into a discussion of their reactions to the divorce.

Through the process of sharing individual perceptions of their parents' marital problems, Amber and Tanya began to develop a sense of sibling unity. (This later served as support for a more significant breaking of their respective alliances with each parent.) Amber, for the first time, gave her sister some details of her abuse by their mother. She also brought Tanya up to date on her recent, productive mother-daughter therapy meeting. Each girl demonstrated increased empathy for the other's feelings about having been abused. In turn, Amber's ability to feel more closely connected with their mother created the space for Tanya to develop a closer relationship with their father.

The therapist intervened to solidify changes that would diminish the likelihood of subsequent abuse, once the sibling relationship was stabilized. Amber valued her artistic and creative qualities. In a meeting with Mrs. Carlson and the siblings, the therapist (with the mother's permission) outlined the mother's reasons for abusing Amber as a child: her sense of powerlessness and her feeling that she lacked the creativity to generate safe, alternative options for responding to her daughter.

The therapist framed Amber's abusive behavior toward Tanya as reflective of a similar problem: a lack of creativity on her part, which was likely related to her depression. Amber was challenged to perfect her artistic style by generating ways to negotiate with her sister in satisfactory, safe ways instead of hurting her, which called for little or no creative energy. Amber was instructed that whenever she used physical force against her sister, she was stating, "I am weak. I am not a creative person." She agreed to maintain a log in which she recorded the various creative solutions she developed. She was taught that the truly difficult problems or struggles in life would always require the most creative solutions. By challenging herself to see whether she was really creative, she would also be teaching her younger sister about being artistic and cool—a worthy side benefit because Amber did not want a sister who was not viewed as cool by others. Tanya greatly welcomed some direction from her older sister in this area.

This discussion elicited Tanya's sadness at feeling abandoned by her older sister. She revealed that her anger and hurt about feeling ignored were often the stimulus for her cruel verbal instigation. When Tanya was angry, she knew how to provoke a response from Amber, and then enjoyed watching her get into trouble. The girls made agreements with one another about ways to express their feelings constructively. Tanya actually was better at this than Amber, and could help her to develop this skill. In turn, Amber agreed to spend time each week giving Tanya fashion and makeup tips.

Incorporating Sibling Changes into the Family System

The therapist arranged separate meetings with each parent and the children to further support the family's separation into two distinct minifamilies. During these meetings, Amber and her sister shared new insights about their relationship. They were able to negotiate verbal agreements with each parent for support during difficult times, and safe behavior contracts with each other. They organized several in-session family enactments to practice new sibling conflict resolution skills and parent-child behavior patterns.

At the conclusion of therapy, the role rigidity between Tanya and Amber had decreased significantly, and the Carlsons no longer resembled a family with two distinct parent-child teams. Amber was able to maintain the changes initiated early in treatment; she had not been physically abusive toward Tanya for several months. The siblings remained vulnerable to intense verbal battles, especially when their parents reverted to taking sides in their struggle. Now, however, they all recognized signs of impending trouble and had the resources to interrupt the fighting before it escalated into abuse.

PSEUDOPARENT SIBLING ABUSE
(TWO-PARENT FAMILY)

Specific Considerations

- Complete an intergenerational abuse assessment.
- Determine whether the sibling incest or assault mimics parent-child abuse.
- Look for presence of parent-child coalitions that exacerbate the sibling abuse.
- Assess the quality of each parent's relationship with the younger children. Determine whether the children feel supported and empowered by parents.
- Determine whether the parents are able to delegate responsibility to the eldest sibling, yet maintain appropriate control of establishing rewards, consequences, and limit setting in the family.

This is a family configuration increasingly common in our society. A caretaking role for siblings has become a viable alternative for many families across cultures, ethnic groups, and economic levels in this country. Siblings often serve as surrogate parents, baby-sitters, and (in some homes) income providers because of the rising number of dual-income families and the lack of adequate, affordable child care alternatives. Parents delegate caretaking responsibilities for other siblings to a pseudoparent sibling, who is often the most capable eldest child in the family.

In pseudoparent sibling families in which abuse occurs, typically neither parent is reliably available. This leads to the development of an additional generational boundary between the parental and the sibling subsystems, which further isolates the pseudoparent sibling. The child becomes a highly relied-upon family member, but simultaneously cannot fully join or maintain membership in either the sibling or the parental generation.

Knowledge of cultural norms and differences is particularly important here because of the widespread presence of pseudoparent siblings in some cultures. Many well-functioning families include children in pseudoparent sibling roles because of economic necessity or cultural heritage. One method of determining dysfunction in such families is to assess (1) the parents' ability to provide adequate caretaking for their pseudoparent child and (2) the presence of chronic and persistent caretaking of one or both of the parents by the pseudoparent sibling in addition to his or her role as caretaker for younger children in the home.

In dysfunctional families, the pseudoparent sibling becomes a primary caretaker for the younger children. This role can increase the child's experience of responsibility and isolation. One of our respondents, for example, has several siblings, but was unable to develop an egalitarian relationship with any of them because of the demands placed upon her from an early age. Each Mother's Day she receives a card from one of her younger sisters. In the following excerpt she describes her relationship as a "mother" to her siblings:

> I was the third parent in a very active sense, including washing clothes, doing homework, saying their prayers with them at night, tucking them in. My mother went to work—part-time when I was nine and full-time when I was eleven. . . . At night, when they got scared, they came to my bed. I changed their sheets; I covered for two brothers and sisters who had bedwetting, serious bedwetting, through their teens. I took the sheets off and put them in the washer, and tried to cover because my dad would really beat up, verbally or physically, either one of them if they did that. So I covered for them.

A child in the pseudoparent role is often isolated from friends, and is kept from utilizing other support networks because of the demands of the family role. Such children are not allowed the luxury of fulfilling their own needs for nurturance and caretaking. In multiproblem families with co-occurring partner and parent-child abuse, younger siblings may be at greater risk of incest and/or assault by an older sibling in the pseudoparent role. When siblings assume responsibility for younger children in such families, adult caregiving patterns are often mirrored; this can result in excessive authoritarianism. Older sisters or brothers may tyrannize, sexually harass, and threaten their siblings. Younger children also may be abused by siblings who are not necessarily caretakers but are them-selves abused by older brothers or sisters. Overindulgence or ne-glect by older siblings in caregiving roles can also lead to abusive interactions with other children in the family.

Sibling assault is more likely to occur when inappropriate expec-tations are placed on the eldest children by unavailable parents who either disregard or remain ignorant of developmentally appropriate and inappropriate behavior. Maltreated children constrained by the pseudoparent role usually have limited options for functioning ade-quately as primary caretakers. Generally they lack insight or under-standing of how to set limits and distribute consequences; instead they resort to coercion or even assault as a means to resolve a sibling dispute. Parents can intensify sibling violence through fur-ther abuse or inappropriate intervention.

The family may respond in various ways to a child in the pseudo-parent sibling role. Each child may feel very differently toward his or her older brother or sister, depending on the nature and extent of abuse that characterizes the sibling relationship. On the one hand, sisters and brothers nurtured and abused by an older sibling in this role frequently develop strong ties with those siblings, which mimic parent-child relationships. In many instances, pseudoparent siblings offer protection from abusive parents, as in the example of the sister who covered for her younger siblings' bedwetting for years to keep them from being beaten by their father. These close ties between siblings may continue into adolescence and adulthood; they may be challenged only when and if the younger sibling begins to deal with issues related to the abuse, and to voice dissatisfaction with the care-taking elements of the relationship.

At the other extreme are younger siblings who dislike the power inherent in their pseudoparent sibling's role, especially when that brother or sister flagrantly misuses the power. This can easily lead to struggles for control, and to efforts by younger children to create problems requiring parental intervention. In one case, eight-year-old Summer fought regularly with Marie, her older sister. After most scuffles, she scratched herself and ran to her parents in tears, stating that her sister Marie had hurt her. Summer resented her sister's authority and tried to equalize the power difference between them whenever possible. Marie had little interest in her younger sister, and was often cruel to her in an attempt to "get her out of my hair."

The following case example illustrates dynamics in a family in which intervention simultaneously addressed parent-child physical abuse and sibling assault. Early multilevel intervention with a motivated and resourceful family created possibilities for individual and systemic change in an intergenerational pattern of male sibling violence.

Case Illustration: Samuel

This African-American family consisted of Kenneth and Sharon Green, nine-year-old Samuel, seven-year-old Charles, six-year-old Ericka, and five-year-old Afeni. The family had recently relocated to Southern California from the Philadelphia area. A Child Protective Services (CPS) referral for family therapy was initiated when it was discovered that Mr. Green had been physically abusing Samuel for approximately the past one-and-a-half years. For the past few months, Samuel had had problems with aggressive behavior at school. An evaluation by the school psychologist found no evidence of organicity or learning disabilities.

Kenneth Green had been underemployed for the last two years, and had become increasingly depressed and withdrawn from his family. Sharon Green was working overtime whenever possible to try to increase the family's income. As a result, her efforts to discipline Samuel were increasingly ineffective and inconsistent. After drinking, Kenneth frequently hit, pushed, or grabbed Samuel by his arms while shaking and shouting at him. The family had entered into a six-month voluntary contract with CPS for services. The children were to remain in the home with their mother, and Kenneth went to live temporarily with a friend.

Family Abuse Assessment

At first, each member of the Green family was interviewed individually. Afeni wanted her sister to be present, so the two girls were seen together. The therapist listened to the different perceptions of the family environment, and gradually a consensus emerged about their current struggles. Kenneth was no longer able to adequately supervise the children after school because of his deteriorating condition. As a result, Sharon began to rely on Samuel to care for his younger siblings. He was expected to attend to his younger siblings after school and then to complete his own chores and homework, and frequently help out with dinner. Thus Samuel was left with very little time for himself. He was beginning to behave angrily toward his brother and sisters. When they were asked for examples of his angry behavior, they complained that he was often mean and "he always bosses us and tells us what to do."

The initial assessment supported the view that the physical abuse which had recently emerged in the Green family was a symptom of underlying family dynamics. Samuel was overburdened with responsibility for the younger children and for the family as a whole. He and his father had had decreasing positive contact over the past few years. To complicate matters, as Samuel assumed more and more family responsibility, he began to lose respect for his father and was less willing to follow his rules at home. Kenneth, through an accumulation of increased stress from being out of work and feeling that he was a failure to his family, began to drink more heavily, and physically abused Samuel when he did not comply with his instructions. In addition, since their relocation to the West Coast, the family had become more and more socially isolated from extended-family and community sources of support.

Various responses to questions made it clear that they were a close-knit group with many internal strengths. Though the family currently was not functioning well, they had a history of communicating openly with each other, resolving past problems, and engaging in family activities, and they shared a willingness to face and resolve their current difficulties. In the first meeting with the entire family, minus the father, the therapist cited to them the many strengths they possessed with which to face this crisis. She also outlined a treatment plan offering individual sessions to Samuel to address abuse-related issues, in addition to couple, family, and individual meetings with Sharon and Kenneth, as needed.

The therapist recognized that one immediate concern facing the family was the need for supervised after-school care of the children. This was important because it would be a first step toward decreasing Samuel's responsibility for his siblings. African-American siblings tend to have more caregiving responsibilities than Caucasian children (Horwitz and Reinhard, 1995), and it is not unusual for oldest children to participate in childrearing. In functional families, however, parents or caretakers delegate certain responsibilities to the eldest child when they are not at home. The boundaries between siblings' and parents' responsibility for caretaking remain clearly defined. In the Green family, Samuel was forced to assume unreasonable responsibility for the well-being of both his parents and his younger siblings. Further, it was determined that his role was being maintained at the expense of normal, age-appropriate development and interaction with peers.

Sharon agreed that after-school child care was a high priority. The therapist therefore helped to establish the children in an after-school program through a local Boys and Girls Club. This intervention built some trust, which helped the family begin to invest in the process of therapy.

Disclosure of Sibling Abuse

During an early family meeting with Sharon and the children, Sharon requested some individual time and reported that Samuel was becoming increasingly aggressive toward his siblings. When asked what she meant by "increasingly aggressive," she stated that he was still attempting to control their behavior both at home and at the Boys and Girls Club. He frequently made derogatory, shaming comments, and threatened his siblings with physical harm when they would not listen. Sharon observed him hitting Charles on several occasions. The Boys and Girls Club staff reported similar incidents.

After speaking with Sharon, the therapist conducted an abuse assessment by interviewing Samuel, each of the other children, and personnel at the school and the Boys and Girls Club. She determined that Samuel's verbal aggression had been escalating for some time, but he had only recently started to hit other children. Indications that Samuel's behavior had developed beyond normative sibling conflict with Charles included (1) role rigidity, whereby Charles was always on the receiving end of the hitting; (2) Charles's report to the therapist that he was being hurt unfairly and repeatedly, and was unable to stop his brother's abuse; (3) Charles's sudden request that his mother intervene; and (4) Samuel's rapidly deteriorating peer relationships. Samuel was also developing a reputation for bullying others and being in trouble at school. In the past week he had returned home with a bruised eye, the result of picking a fight with someone at school two years older than himself. Samuel's behavior was rapidly escalating out of control.

Interventions

Family Meetings (without Father)

The therapist collaborated with the school counselor and the Boys and Girls Club staff to establish plans to temporarily keep Samuel and Charles in separate activities, and to monitor Samuel's aggressive behavior. She also helped Sharon become more proactive and more effective in establishing alternative strategies for handling Samuel's aggression. This was important for maintaining Charles's safety and for reinstating her strength and executive function with the children. In this way Sharon reminded the children that she was strong enough to administer consequences, keep them safe, and establish limits on Samuel's behavior when necessary. Sharon and the therapist collaborated to establish behavioral charts to reward Samuel for any positive contact he made with his younger siblings. The charts also delineated age-appropriate responsibilities, rewards, and consequences (administered by his mother or father) for each of the other children in order to lighten Samuel's burden and restructure the siblings' interactions regarding household activities.

In subsequent family meetings, Sharon was encouraged to validate Samuel for taking steps to secure help for the family during their current crisis. She in turn, praised Charles for disclosing Samuel's abusive behavior. The therapist wanted to help Sharon communicate to the family that it was all right to get help when there were serious family problems. She also wanted to decrease Samuel's vulnerability to being treated as a family scapegoat, particularly with his siblings—because his efforts on the family's behalf had led to Kenneth's temporary removal from the home. It was equally important that Sharon give the children permission to discuss Samuel's aggressive behavior openly.

Individual Meetings with Kenneth

In his individual and group work with another therapist, Kenneth was making good progress in maintaining his sobriety and commitment to an anger management program. Collateral contact with his therapist revealed that he was developing insight about his vulnerability to various stressors and acquiring new skills for handling tension and anxiety. Therefore a time-limited contract with Kenneth was established to address issues related to Samuel's abuse, so that his therapeutic gains could be incorporated into the family treatment. The construction of a family genogram provided a window into his background, which had connections to his current abusive behavior.

Kenneth's older brother, Michael, had the responsibility for raising Kenneth after their father died. Kenneth had always been his dad's favorite, and he was devastated by his death. When Michael began to order his younger brother around and then to mistreat him, Kenneth initially fought back. With no one to set strong limits on their behavior, however, the fighting quickly escalated. Kenneth was repeatedly humiliated and physically abused by his older brother. He never told his mother, believing that this would be a sign of weakness. As soon as he completed high school, he joined the Navy and never returned to his childhood home. His relationship with Michael remained distant. They rarely saw each other; in fact, his children had never met their uncle.

Kenneth spoke about his victimization in a reporting tone of voice, devoid of any affect. He had not processed his feelings about events related to his own abuse. As a result, when Kenneth observed Samuel gradually assuming increased responsibility for his

younger siblings, particularly his brother Charles, issues associated
with his earlier physical abuse were activated: he became short-
tempered with Samuel and felt that he must control him at any cost.
Losing control of Samuel represented danger. Kenneth and his oldest son initially had been close, but he began to see more reflections
of himself in his second-born son, Charles, as Charles matured. The
two also had an obvious physical and temperamental resemblance.
Consequently Kenneth began spending less time with Samuel. He
now recognized that this was due in part, to an unconscious association between Samuel and Michael, his abusive older brother. Samuel's role in the family, in combination with present stressors,
worked together to trigger Kenneth's abuse-related shame and humiliation. His abuse of Samuel could be viewed, in part, as a mis-
guided effort to master his own childhood sibling trauma through
identification with the aggressor.

The therapist worked intensively with Kenneth on his strong
reactions to Samuel, helping him to sort out feelings and thoughts
about his own victimization from his feelings for his son. As Kenneth began to redirect his anger toward his brother Michael and to
recall some positive interactions with him as a child, the power of
his anger lessened. These feelings were replaced by sadness about
the helplessness and isolation he had felt while he was being
abused. Eventually he was able to acknowledge anger and disappointment toward his mother for not providing him with adequate
protection from his brother.

Individual Meetings with Sharon

Evaluating Sharon's ability to protect and care for her children
was also crucial. The therapist met with her individually to give her
the opportunity to discuss any issues that she might not want to
raise in front of her children. For example, Sharon's role in not
protecting Samuel was important in maintaining the status quo. Not
surprisingly, she revealed an abusive family history in which she, as
the oldest child, felt unable to protect herself or her younger siblings from their father's rage. Thus she learned to be compliant at an
early age. Sharon expressed guilt and remorse for not doing more to
protect Samuel from his father's abuse. She recognized her part in
minimizing the danger to Samuel's welfare.

Individual meetings also focused on reinforcing alternative strategies, previously agreed to in family meetings, for protecting the children in the future. These included developing ways to assume a more egalitarian position with her husband and strengthening her increased willingness to trust and make use of outside resources when appropriate.

Couple Sessions

Couple sessions were interspersed with the family meetings to help reduce any denial still present in one or both of the parents and to address coparenting issues related to Samuel's abuse. The Greens also used these meetings to renegotiate expectations of each other as spouses and as parents.

The conjoint therapy had systemic value as well; it was another step toward the reunification of the family. Each spouse shared insights with the other from his or her respective work on family of origin issues. This helped strengthen them as a marital and parental team—one committed to heightened levels of supervision, nurturing, boundaries, and support for their children.

Processing Samuel's Abuse Trauma

After considerable time was spent in establishing safety and trust in individual therapy with Samuel, the focus turned to identifying trauma-related triggers (e.g., current experiences that activated responses associated with being physically abused by his father). These triggers, in turn, were linked to Samuel's abusive behavior toward others. For example, Samuel reported that he was often verbally or physically hurtful to others who touched him (intentionally or not), especially when the touch was linked to something that someone did or said that made Samuel feel bad about himself. Samuel felt even worse after hitting someone; this only reinforced the negative sequence of events. Samuel's individual treatment involved a variety of interventions: building self-soothing skills, processing thoughts and feelings associated with his abuse, projective drawings, and in-session enactments of traumatic events.

The first stage of treatment was to teach Samuel self-control, or "cool down" skills. He particularly enjoyed a "slinky" visualization and an exercise in creating a safe place (flying in a spaceship). After several in-session and homework practices, he moved on to playing a game that eventually would help him to identify triggers and process the feelings associated with them. He titled it the "get hot and blow-up, or space out and cool-down game" (referring to his relaxation exercise of flying in a spaceship). Samuel generated three categories based on his love for Mexican salsa: mild, medium, and hot. Each corresponded to the intensity level of a trigger that Samuel identified. The therapist suggested that they create a picture which would serve as a visual anchor for his experiences. Samuel drew a large volcano with three sections. He labeled the bottom as the mild section, the middle as medium, and top as hot. Within each section, Samuel listed one or two events or memories that were mildly, moderately, or very distressing for him.

Once Samuel felt confident about his ability to use his self-control tools, they moved on to explore the contents of the volcano. Samuel was asked to choose one of his mild triggers and to talk about it. He was encouraged to stay a little longer with a mild memory or experience by stating two feelings he had about it or two details that he remembered. Next he was asked to "space out," i.e., go for a visual ride in his spaceship. The relaxation exercise was designed to heighten Samuel's ability to focus on associated thoughts and feelings with the goal of developing greater tolerance for them. Initially he chose to leave his difficult feelings far behind. The entire exercise was framed as Samuel's way of taking care of himself when he was not quite sure what else he could do, or how else he might handle a stressful situation.

After Samuel completed several successful trials of associating the "space out" response with thinking of each of his mild triggers, they celebrated by having a play-only session. Throughout this process, Samuel was assigned to practice handling his triggers in this way at home, at school, and at the Boys and Girls club. On several occasions he returned to therapy with examples of new methods he had used to respond in a safe way to triggers in his environment. These were added to the list of cool-down activities at his disposal in the volcano.

In subsequent sessions, Samuel practiced this activity with only the mild triggers until he was able to talk about thoughts, feelings, and perceptions associated with the mild trigger and to adequately practice alternatives to aggressive behavior when faced with similar triggers outside therapy. Similarly, when he reviewed his medium triggers, he was instructed to practice "spacing out" or to use a cool-down/self-control tool, if necessary, before or after talking about traumatic events. At this stage, Samuel allowed his difficult feelings to travel with him on the spaceship as long as they were sealed in a box.

By the time he processed the hot triggers, Samuel had developed so much experience with self-soothing tools that he was able to productively explore more abuse-related material. This was viewed as a sign that he had established some tolerance for feelings associated with his abuse. Further, he routinely employed safe alternatives to aggression to deal with unpleasant thoughts or feelings.

In a meeting that focused on hot triggers, the theme of responsibility for Kenneth's abuse of Samuel emerged. This process worked as follows.

Samuel's hot trigger section included the item "When my dad looks at me with that face he gets right before he hits me." When asked about two feelings accompanying this memory, Samuel stated, "I get scared. Then I feel like I did something wrong and I'm gonna get it." "And then what happens?" asked the therapist. "I get a little mad, too," he replied. They discussed each of these feelings, locating where in his body (stomach, heart, and arms/fists) he felt afraid and mad. Then Samuel practiced a cool-down activity of his choice.

Later the therapist asked Samuel to think of a detail he had not yet told her about this trigger. "Well, when my dad is coming after me, I start to . . . um, well, I don't really cry, but sometimes tears just come, like . . . you know, I'm not really crying but they just come anyway." The therapist asked Samuel to draw a picture of the tears that just emerge on their own. When he was finished, they created a puppet from his drawing. "What would the tearful puppet like to say about your father hitting you?" the therapist asked. He answered, "'I'm sad your dad is hitting you, but if you could only do what he says and be a better son, all these bad things wouldn't have happened'."

"So the tears really believe it is your fault when your father loses his temper and hits you," she replied. "Yeah, I guess they do," he said. "What do you think about that, Samuel?" "Oh, of course they're right, 'cause they saw everything that happened, too. Can we do something else now?" The therapist noted the good work Samuel had done on a difficult topic. The experience of being able to manage his thoughts and feelings about the abuse seemed to be empowering. He did another brief cool-down exercise and engaged in an activity of his choice for the remainder of this meeting.

Alternate sessions focused on projective techniques to help Samuel process his trauma. He was asked to draw an animal that was being hit and hurt by another animal. Samuel chose to draw a lizard: ever vigilant for danger, and able to speed away at a moment's notice. He drew a tiger as the aggressor. He kept the drawings in the therapist's office; over time, he created dialogues between them to explore means of resolving trauma-related material, achieve conflict resolution, and reach peaceful agreements. For example, after much processing had been done between the lizard and the tiger, the therapist asked the lizard if it wanted to give the tiger an opportunity to atone for his mistakes. The lizard appeared to be interested because he and the tiger had been friends before the hurting began. But he also felt that the lizard was bad for making the tiger angry. It seemed that Samuel was still suffering from shame and guilt related to feeling responsible for his abuse.

The therapist used this opportunity to explore with Samuel the many ways he believed he was the cause of his father's abusive behavior toward him. She also explored whether Samuel viewed his siblings as responsible for the emotional abuse by their father. Samuel did not think they were to blame; yet he held himself to a higher standard. He had made great strides in developing ways to handle his anger safely, and was no longer abusing his brother Charles. Thus, the therapist noted Samuel's inner strength: a truly strong person doesn't need to flaunt his or her power, and knows when to use it (for example, in sports, or if he's actually in danger). The therapist commented on his maturity. Samuel was now committed to maintaining safe interactions with peers, even during disagreements, and creative enough to develop ways to be strong with words instead of using his fists. Then, paradoxically, she reported feeling sad that Samuel was so certain his father had none of the qualities necessary to change his behavior in order to prevent him from hitting one or more of his children again.

Samuel became quiet and began to cry. "If it wasn't my fault, then why did he do it? . . . Why did my dad hit me all of those times?" Together they agreed that he might feel ready to ask his father about this in the near future. For now, Samuel wanted the lizard to talk with the tiger about it. Samuel (as the lizard) asked the tiger why he had hurt him. Samuel tried to speak for the tiger, but got stuck and requested help.

> **Therapist** (as the tiger): I made some mistakes with how I handled my anger, and one of the biggest ones is that I took it out on you. In my therapy and classes, I'm learning some of the same things you are about solving problems without hitting. I want you to know it was my mistake, not yours, and that I love you very much.
>
> **Samuel:** If you love me, how come you hit me? How come you're always mad at me?
>
> **Therapist** (as the tiger): It sounds like you're upset with me, which of course I understand, since I didn't always treat you kindly, and I hurt you at times. [Samuel nods.] I made some mistakes, and I took my anger at other things out on you sometimes. I really was mad at myself for not being a better father, and I should have been changing how I was as a father instead of yelling at you or hitting you. [Samuel nods again.] I'm very sorry I did that to you—I feel bad about it. I do love you, even though I haven't always acted like it. You have really learned how to tell me about your angry feelings—I'm happy you can be so honest with me.

This dialogue continued until Samuel had expressed or asked all that he needed at this time. "I wonder if there is something more you want from the tiger right now," the therapist said. Samuel replied, "I wish you would spend more time with me."

Samuel had successfully integrated a new view of his more difficult feelings (i.e., that they operated somewhat like the warning lights on a spaceship, to tell the pilot when something needed immediate attention). At this point, during his "space-out" exercises, he granted his feelings "second pilot" status, as he was now more aware of the benefit of paying attention to his internal "warning" signs.

Toward the end of the meeting, after his "space out" activity, the therapist asked Samuel how he was feeling about that day's conversation between the lizard and the tiger. He replied, "Pretty good. Do you think sometime me and my dad could talk about this stuff? We have a lot of things to iron out between us."

The enactment using the animals set the stage for similar work with Samuel related to the sibling abuse. The therapist asked Samuel to draw a picture of an animal that reminded him of his brother Charles when Samuel was hitting him. He drew a frightened zebra (Charles's favorite animal), and drew himself as a cheetah. Again, a dialogue between the two animals was facilitated, much as with the earlier enactment.

Working in tandem in this way, Samuel identified parallels between how he felt when he was abused by his father and how Charles must have felt as the victim of his abuse. He began to be sad about hurting his brother and wanted to see if there was a way he could resolve things with Charles, much as the animals had done in fantasy. The therapist thought this might be a good time to move toward conjoint sessions between the two brothers.

Conjoint Sibling Meetings

One technique utilized in the sibling meetings was the Sibling Comic Strip exercise. Each child was given some paper and crayons and was asked to divide his paper into a comic strip with five boxes. (The therapist showed them a blank comic strip to illustrate the format.) Then they were instructed to draw a comic strip describing a recent time in their past when Samuel had grown angry with Charles and was still resolving conflicts in an abusive manner. They agreed on a specific incident. The actual conflict was drawn in the center comic strip frame; they could draw themselves and the action any way they liked.

The two boys took turns describing their pictures and then discussed them. As is often the case, they drew different versions of the conflict. The therapist slowed this process down, and they discussed each version and explored the differences in perspective. Later they were asked to draw the actions leading up to their conflict in the first two frames. Again, the therapist slowed down their conflict to explore each frame in turn.

Gradually, the boys discovered something about the sequence of events that typically preceded their fighting. For example, Charles did not like it when his brother took the video game control out of his hands without asking, as he did frequently. Charles usually tried to grab it back, pushing Samuel in the process. Samuel, who viewed his brother as selfish and unwilling to share, then struck him with his fists or whatever was available, sometimes hurting Charles physically.

Next, in the two boxes following the center frame, they were asked to draw what happened afterward. From the drawings it was painfully evident that both lacked adequate skills to resolve their conflict. Samuel might respond with verbal criticism but was more impulsive when frustrated. Confident of his physical superiority, he usually chased Charles with intent to harm.

At this point, Charles often ran to a room in the house with a lock on the door to protect himself from further injury. Samuel then threatened to hurt Charles when he came out. The fighting eventually diminished, sometimes as a result of parental intervention, and they each went off to separate activities. The conflict remained unresolved, however, and the cycle of events repeated itself (see Figure 8.1).

The therapist suggested that they slow down the sequence and attend to the moment when Samuel took the video control out of his brother's hands without asking:

> **Therapist:** Samuel, I want you to see yourself in that picture. [Points to his comic strip.] What are you thinking and feeling at that moment?
> **Samuel:** I'm thinking he's not going to share it with me, and it's my turn.
> **Therapist:** OK, and what are you feeling?
> **Samuel:** It makes me angry. I'm older and he should respect me more.
> **Charles:** That sounds like what our dad says.
> **Therapist:** Is that right? [They both nod.] OK [to Charles], what happens next?

FIGURE 8.1. Artist Rendering of Sibling Comic Strip

Adapted from Benson, Schindler-Zimmerman, and Martin (1991)

Charles: I grab it back.

Samuel (to Charles): Yeah, but not without pushing me first!

Charles: But I don't hurt you, I just want it back!

Therapist: OK, Samuel, so what happens inside when Charles pushes you?

Samuel: I think, "He's pushing me just to start a fight. I can't let him get away with this. I have to teach him respect."

Therapist: Yes, and what are you feeling?

Samuel: I feel mad inside.

Therapist: OK, good. Pay attention to that feeling. Where do you feel it in your body?

Samuel: In my stomach, hands, and arms.

Therapist: Good, now I want you to take a deep breath—you know, like we've done before—and pay attention to the feeling in your arms. Excellent. Now think about Charles pushing you, and tell me what you are feeling.

Samuel: It feels sort of like when my dad grabs me, like I want to stop him . . . or punch him back, but I can't. I think our dad must like him better 'cause he doesn't hit Charles. And that's another thing I don't like at all. I guess it's like I feel mad at Charles like I do about my dad, and about Charles pushing me, too, so I hit him.

Therapist: Those are two very important things you just let us in on that we'll talk more about, Samuel. The first is that you think your father likes Charles better than he does you, and the second is that when Charles pushes you, it makes you feel angry, like you felt when your father was hitting you or shaking you. Charles, did you know that your brother thinks that your dad likes you better?

Charles: No.

Therapist (to Charles): What do you think about that?

Charles: Well, I know our dad doesn't hit me, but he lets Samuel get away with lots of things that I get in trouble for . . . so I don't know.

Therapist: Oh. So each of you sort of feels like the other one gets special things from your father that you don't get, and that maybe your dad likes the other one more?

[Charles and Samuel nod in agreement.]

Therapist: Charles, did you know that sometimes when Samuel hits you, that he's also saying how very angry he is at your father for hitting him?

Charles: No. But I get pretty mad at Samuel for hitting me, so I think I should know how it feels.

Therapist: Yes. That's something you both have in common—you feel badly and get angry when someone hits you. I think most people feel the same way.

Samuel: At first, I feel better after I hit Charles, because I think he deserved what was coming to him for acting like he did. But then I feel worse because I feel bad that I hit him. And believe me, I know how bad it feels to be hit, especially by your own dad.

Therapist (to Samuel): Could you say more to your brother about how you feel badly after you hit him?

Samuel (to Charles): It's like . . . I do feel bad after I hit you. That's why I don't want to play or anything later on after we fight, because I'm too angry . . . but then I feel bad, and sorry about when I made you cry.

Charles: How do you think I feel? Everything's messed up, then I have to play by myself.

Therapist: It sounds like you'd both like to get along with each other better. Charles, what do you think about what Samuel just said to you?

Charles: Well . . . it's OK. It's good. I mean, he's my brother. Of course I don't want to always fight with him.

Samuel: Well, I'm sorry that I hit you so hard sometimes. I don't really want to fight anymore, either, you know. I've had enough of fighting, if you know what I mean.

After this interaction, the brothers were ready to begin generating mutual agreements for ways to handle fights differently. Then they practiced these in the office. They agreed that if Charles did not want to share the video control immediately, that Samuel could use it in a reasonable, predetermined amount of time. Samuel recognized how he had borrowed his father's words, "I need to teach him respect," and used them to justify hitting Charles. The therapist suggested that there was no better way to teach Charles respect than by modeling it in his interactions with his brother. To balance the intervention, Charles's cooperation was framed as giving his older brother the opportunity to practice these skills so that Samuel's relationships with friends could also improve.

The brothers later discussed similarities and differences related to their feelings about their father's temporarily moving out of the home. To decrease the role rigidity and the power difference between them, it was important to highlight the qualities that Charles brought to their relationship which Samuel enjoyed. For example, Samuel loved his brother's sense of humor and fun. Their ability to be playful together increased as the angry interactions diminished. Charles was also adept at playing several computer games that both boys enjoyed. At one point, Samuel asked Charles to teach him how to play some of the newer games that he had not yet learned. Interactions such as this reestablished and enhanced their sibling connection.

Addressing the Parent-Child Physical Abuse

Meetings between Samuel and his father were arranged to facilitate and solidify changes in their relationship. Kenneth apologized to Samuel for threatening and physically hurting him. He assumed full accountability for the abuse and told Samuel how proud he was of him for being able so quickly to change his behavior toward his brother and sisters. In a tender and sincere manner, he thanked Samuel for enabling the family to get the help they needed. Samuel was relieved to discover that his secret belief that he was a bad kid, and the cause of all the trouble in the family, was not confirmed.

Kenneth also shared what he had learned in the parent-focused programs about dealing with his angry feelings and about alternatives to hurting his children again. He then discussed his own history of sibling abuse. Samuel was fascinated by his father's story. Both Samuel and his father were supported for being strong enough to alter their family legacy. The unity they experienced as a result of working to overcome their abusive behavior led to the development of a much stronger connection between them. Their dialogue ended with Kenneth's agreement to a no-violence contract. Samuel spontaneously decided that he would generate a similar agreement with his siblings.

The next several meetings were arranged so that Kenneth and his son were required to interact with each other for most of the session in some activity of Samuel's choosing. In initial sessions Kenneth was coached to practice specific communication skills likely to facilitate positive exchanges between father and son. He was also acknowledged for Samuel's positive qualities, which helped him to see his success as a parent. He was encouraged to attend to, and offer praise for, his son's positive behavior. This improved their previously strained relationship. During this period, Samuel also was coached to use words to express his feelings, and to practice his assertiveness skills when interacting with his father.

Later in treatment, it was important to address a problematic interaction specific to their father-son relationship. Kenneth was helped to practice setting positive limits on Samuel's tendency to curse when he was frustrated, and to make constructive use of time-out procedures when Samuel required a little extra help in regaining self-control. Instead of labeling Samuel as "no good" for using negative language, Kenneth was encouraged to produce a list of alternative words, such as "creative" or "passionate," for his son's behavior. This enabled him to help Samuel redirect his frustration through more positive and productive interactions.

Kenneth was also supported for teaching Samuel how to make amends when he made mistakes. One intervention related to this goal was to assign both Kenneth and Samuel the task of pretending to make two mistakes during the therapy hour to give each the opportunity to acknowledge, apologize, or make amends for them. They were encouraged to practice outside therapy and to discuss their mistakes with each other in the following session.

At the end of four productive meetings, the therapist assigned homework to Kenneth: to spend some time playing with his family during supervised visits, and to allow the children to take turns coming up with games to teach him. Once he completed his court-ordered treatment program, he began unsupervised visits and gradually moved back home.

Family Reunification

Several meetings were held with the entire Green family to develop a reabuse prevention plan and to incorporate structural changes initiated with various family members into the entire family system. The family configuration that corresponded most closely to theirs (i.e., the "pseudoparent sibling" in a two-parent family) was reviewed, and the changes they had made were discussed and reinforced. The therapist actively supported the parents' heightened awareness of their role as the responsible adults in the family. It was also noted that they had delegated a few selected age-appropriate responsibilities to Samuel, which would enhance his role as the oldest sibling but would not interfere with developmentally normal activity. Samuel's improvement in school performance was also recognized at this time.

Kenneth and Sharon were increasingly spending positive time with their children. Many of the family's therapeutic goals had been reached, and there were no observable signs of continued abuse. After reunification, Child Protective Services closed the case. The family continued in treatment for several months to facilitate Kenneth's smooth transition back into the home.

PSEUDOPARENT SIBLING ABUSE (SINGLE-PARENT FAMILY)

No conclusive evidence exists to suggest that single-parent families in general pose a greater danger for sibling incest or assault unless other risk factors, combined with a lack of protective mechanisms, are also present. Kubo (1959), however, observed that most of the thirteen cases of brother-sister incest in his study occurred in fatherless homes, where an older brother offender had been elevated to a fatherly role and thus exercised considerable power in the family. In these families, the child in the pseudoparent sibling role is vulnerable to elevation into the parental hierarchy and to remaining there, misplaced as a chronic surrogate parent. This child generally has more power and authority than the sibling who occupies the same role in a two-parent family. In one respondent's family, his pseudoparent role began at the time of his parents' divorce, when his father left the home: "My dad said, 'Andy, you're the head of the household now. Take over.' My mom checked out emotionally through the divorce because she had no idea it was coming."

After a divorce, a single-parent family generally evolves into a temporary environment of decreased limit setting, increased democracy, and greater likelihood that parents and children will nurture, support, and stabilize one another. This creates a heightened likelihood that the eldest sibling will be elevated into the parental subsystem. This sibling also may attend, to some degree, to the single parent's needs as well as those of the other children. Statistics suggest that one-quarter of the children in this country currently live in single-parent families.

One respondent from a single-parent family described how her mother's coalition with her brother was a factor in the abuse that she and her siblings endured:

> **Respondent:** [A]s for my relationship with my mom, it was very emotionally abusive; she was very controlling and manipulative while I was growing up. She was always, "Do, do, do, do"; not a lot of love and affection. She didn't show that to any of us [younger children]. . . my oldest brother was a mama's boy, and he still is. He was always mama's little boy, and she'd do anything for him, and anytime he got in trouble, she'd let it go.
> **Interviewer:** This was Elliott?
> **Respondent:** Uh-huh.
> **Interviewer:** Is Elliott the brother who abused you?
> **Respondent:** Yes, he was the one that abused all of us. Like, constantly, when he was in charge of us, and the things that he would do, physical abuse, or sexual abuse, or whatever it was . . . . My mom didn't know anything about the sexual abuse, but the physical abuse—she never did anything about it. . . . It was just like she had these blinders on with my oldest brother, that he could do no wrong.

A potentially important protective factor in single-parent families is the presence of another adult in the household. Several studies showed that some children who live with a single parent exhibit fewer problems if an additional adult resides in the household, especially if that person is a grandparent (Dornbusch et al., 1985; Stolba and Amato, 1993). Residential grandparents can promote children's development by providing emotional support, assisting the parent with supervision and discipline, and assuming child care responsibilities when the parent is overburdened. This situation simultaneously relieves the eldest child of many of the obligations that otherwise would have been delegated to him or her.

For example, twelve-year-old Joi was hospitalized briefly for a suicide attempt. While in the hospital, she disclosed to her social worker that her older brother Ben was physically abusive when their mother was out of the house. Ben admitted that in trying to make Joi do what she was supposed to do, he sometimes hurt her physically. Joi's mother was a single parent; she often left Joi home alone with her brother for a few hours after school until she returned from work.

During her stay in the hospital, the social worker met with the family and discovered that Joi's widowed grandfather was a potential resource for watching the siblings while the mother was at work. He became involved in family meetings and agreed to stay with the children each afternoon after Joi was discharged from the hospital. The grandfather's influence with the children, coupled with his support for Joi's mother, gradually brought the sibling abuse to a halt. His presence was such a positive experience for all that he ultimately moved in with his daughter and her family.

PSEUDOPARENT SIBLING ABUSE (STEPFAMILY)

The structure of the American family is changing dramatically. The number of remarried families has increased sharply, and it is projected that by 2000, one-third of the siblings in the United States will live in a stepfamily. Stepsibling conflict is a frequently cited complaint among families seeking professional help. Until recently, however, minimal attention was paid to the distinctive dynamics of stepsiblings, especially in regard to abuse trauma.

Stepsibling relationships are characterized by a number of important factors; some of these apparently are related to the development of abusive interactions. First, stepsibling relationships are often formed instantaneously, so that children have no time to adapt and accommodate to each other. Further, because of the lack of a shared family history, stepsiblings espouse different values, customs, and family styles, all of which require increased tolerance and accommodation. Stepsiblings have in common the loss of their original families; often they struggle with feelings about the past, both real and idealized. Each child's experience of loss is unique, however, and must be addressed according to the individual's current subjective and objective needs.

Stepsiblings usually are torn between at least three families: the original family, the stepsibling's original family, and the remarried family. Conflicting loyalties frequently result as children attempt to make room for each other's links to past as well as present caregivers. Family ties outside the immediate household also have the potential to attract stepsiblings' loyalty. Fluid boundaries are more the norm in stepfamilies than in first-time nuclear families because household membership shifts frequently. Stepsiblings may have custody and/or visitation arrangements that result in a large number of exits and entrances.

In addition, shifts in siblings' position, role, and function generally are inherent in the formation of a stepfamily. For example, children may be confronted with a new gender ratio or ordinal position in the stepsibling subgroup. A sibling may no longer be the only or eldest child. A sibling comfortable with a parentified role in a divorced single-parent family may suddenly be replaced in that role. Remarriage also entails an abrupt change in family size, and consolidation of economic and emotional resources. When siblings make the transition into a reconstituted family, the two eldest may jockey for the most powerful position. Younger siblings may become victims of abuse when an eldest exerts power and control in a new and unsettling situation. Sometimes a pseudoparent sibling in a stepfamily may react to an abusive stepparent by identifying with the abuser and victimizing younger siblings. Abrupt family upheavals demand even greater flexibility from siblings, who are acutely sensitive to issues of power, favoritism, and fairness.

Gender also plays a critical role in determining stepsibling relationships. Same-sex siblings tend to be rivals; they may compete for resources as well as parental attention. Parents are often surprised to learn that treating stepsiblings equally is not a satisfactory solution for their biological children, who interpret equality as a step down from a previous exalted position in the family. Opposite-sex stepsiblings present an even more complex set of circumstances, primarily because of the potential for erotic attractions. Unrelated opposite-sex adolescents are the combination most likely to stir up sexual conflicts in the stepfamily. The incest taboo in first-time families more clearly serves the function of directing siblings outside the family in the search for a sexual partner. In stepfamilies, however, the boundaries between kin and nonfamily members are less clear; thus rules regarding incestuous behavior are often considerably weaker.

This situation has a paradoxical element: society does not uniformly regard stepsiblings' sexual relations as incestuous. Yet the family's everyday stability requires the prohibition of sex because it interferes with normal development. The stepfamily must manufacture its own stepsibling incest taboo in the absence of a societal one. Individual and systemic characteristics usually determine stepfamily members' degree of success at accomplishing this complex task.

In the following example, we present segments of individual therapy with an eight-year-old child to highlight the importance of treating the harmful effects of coercion frequently associated with sibling incest. Family therapy with this stepfamily was less successful because both parents had difficulty in acknowledging the effects of the incest on themselves and their daughter.

Case Illustration: Emma

Eight-year-old Emma was brought to therapy by her parents after the disclosure that her fifteen-year-old half brother Ian had been molesting her. Mr. and Mrs. Browning refused to discuss the incest in any depth, but were angry at Ian. They also implied to Emma that she was responsible for her abuse, asking, "Why didn't you tell us sooner? How could you let him do that to you?"

A Child Protective Services investigation was made and a report was filed with the police. The Brownings refused to press charges. The authorities said that Ian had to be removed from the home; otherwise they would assume custody of Emma. As a result, Ian went to live with an uncle and participated in an outpatient program for juvenile sexual offenders. He was required to attend weekly individual, group, and family therapy for one year. Child Protective Services closed the case after Ian moved out of the home.

The Brownings did not think it was necessary for Emma to receive treatment; they believed that her symptoms (nightmares, fearfulness, enuresis, and regressed behavior) would subside, now that her brother was out of the home. Child Protective Services warned them, however, that if Emma was not in treatment, they would intervene and might remove her from their care. They also strongly encouraged the family to seek community support services (e.g., Parents and Daughters United) for child incest victims and their families.

Family History

The following information was gathered from a CPS psychosocial family history, the police investigation, collateral contact with Ian's individual therapist, and initial assessment interviews with Mr. and Mrs. Browning and with Emma. At no time during these initial meetings did Mr. and Mrs. Browning express concern about the impact of the incest on Emma.

Emma's father was an officer in the Marine Corps who was periodically absent for several weeks or months at a time. When he returned from duty, he reassumed his position as the head of the family. He was often verbally abusive and sadistic toward his stepson Ian; sometimes he struck him for minor infractions at home. Ian was Mrs. Browning's biological son from a previous marriage. She had learned only recently that her husband, Emma's father, was having an extramarital affair. In combination, these events gradually increased their marital conflict.

Emma's parents held a number of values and beliefs that contributed to a family environment vulnerable to the development of sibling incest. Mr. Browning's attitudes about sex, gender, and violence reflected the hypermasculine, hierarchical culture in which he worked and had spent most of his adulthood. He applied very different standards to men and to women in regard to sexual activity; he was critical of violence against women, but nonetheless tacitly accepted it.

Mr. Browning found it very difficult to be a parent to Ian. He struggled with his stepson over issues related to normal stepfamily development. For example, Ian did not share many of his stepfather's interests, yet Mr. Browning required Ian to spend their time together his way. Ian also disliked calling him "Dad." Mr. Browning viewed this as disrespectful, and refused to accept alternative titles. Furthermore, Mr. Browning was critical of what he termed "provocative" clothing worn by his wife or daughter; he made remarks to his wife such as "Where did you get that? Are you trying to turn my daughter into a slut?" At the same time, he forbade any discussion of sex in the home, and the children received no sex education at all. When the incest was disclosed, Mr. Browning stated that he did not want to see Ian because he was afraid of what he might do to him. He then turned to his wife and said, "What kind of a sick kid do you have?"

Mrs. Browning disclosed a history of spousal abuse by her ex-husband, including a rape that Ian had witnessed as a child. Interactions between Ian and his mother revealed a rapport that was more like that of peers than of parent and child. It was also evident that she had not resolved her trauma from the previous victimizations. Consequently, she sent Ian harsh signals about sex and violence, stating that "All men are animals, and don't you grow up to be one of them."

Mrs. Browning tolerated considerable emotional abuse from her husband. He often restricted her activities outside the home, and was severely critical of her parenting of the children. She projected many of the unresolved angry feelings about both her former and her current husbands onto Ian. In the assessment meeting, she stated, "I know where he got it . . . from these so-called male role models in his life. They don't have respect for anybody, and don't need anybody. You know—real loner types. And boy, do they have short fuses. Ian is exactly the same way." Mrs. Browning was also aware that she felt closer to her daughter and openly favored Emma at home.

Mrs. Browning's unresolved traumatization likewise influenced her treatment of Emma. She frequently told Emma how beautiful she was, and that she had better watch out for the boys, who would want only one thing (sex) because of her appearance—but that once they got it, they would never respect her again. Once, for example, while taking a drawing class, she had Emma, then six years old, pose nude on a living room chair every day for a week. Mrs. Browning's own mother was an artist who sometimes photographed her daughter while nude, and included some of these pictures in her exhibits. Mrs. Browning also enjoyed "dressing up" Emma, especially when Mr. Browning was gone, in reaction to his control.

When the incest was disclosed, Mrs. Browning's initial response to her son was "Don't do that again!" She then turned to Emma and said, "What were you thinking! Why didn't you tell me?"

Ian had begun molesting Emma about two years earlier, when she was six years old. According to independent conversations with Emma and with the therapist working with her brother at the day treatment program, the sexual abuse developed gradually over time, like many incest cases. Initially Emma looked up to her big brother. He taught her how to ride a bike and tie her shoes, and served as her companion and protector. When he got angry, however, Ian could be very cruel to Emma. He criticized her and called her stupid, stating that she was "only good for one thing." He also used coercion and threats to intimidate her. Once, after an argument, he pulled the heads off her dolls and placed them in her school backpack. Sometimes he used physical force and the threat of violence to ensure his dominance and keep her quiet so that he would avoid punishment.

One evening while he was alone with her in the house, he threatened to destroy one of her dolls because she wouldn't go downstairs and bring him something to eat. He later apologized. Emma stopped crying and decided to take a bath so she could watch television before going to bed. Ian sweet-talked his way into the bathroom, and under the guise of making up for his mean behavior, began to soothe her by rubbing her back. He then began to rub her genital area; apparently this is how the sexual abuse began. It progressed over time to include the use of explicit pornography, talking dirty, and masturbating in front of her while she used the bathroom or sat in the tub. More recently he had forced her to perform fellatio, and he had attempted intercourse with her.

Ian generally isolated himself from peers and had few friends his age. On one occasion, however, he introduced Emma to some neighborhood children. They held down a younger boy, and made Emma take off her clothes and dance over him like a stripper, while Ian and his friends laughed and cheered.

The abusive experiences were more confusing for Emma because Ian also offered her protection at times. For example, when one of these neighborhood boys alluded to wanting sexual access to Emma, Ian became enraged and gave him a beating. He then told his sister how much he loved her and that he would always take care of her.

Interventions

Couple Sessions

Mr. and Mrs. Browning were confused by Emma's condition. They did not understand how Ian could make Emma participate in the incest, and why she could not refuse. They were upset about CPS intervention and about the family disruption following Ian's removal from the home. They did not want to participate in treatment but also did not want their daughter removed from their care.

The therapist underscored the parallels between these two experiences of feeling out of control. The Brownings felt that they had been forced into a position where they had to do something they absolutely did not want to do. They were attending therapy out of fear of the consequences. Perhaps, the therapist suggested, Emma felt something similar in relation to the sibling incest.

The couple's extreme difficulty in communicating with each other and their reluctance to explore the incest were the most striking aspects of their behavior during the early meetings. The therapist held individual meetings with Emma's father and mother to explore their respective families of origin and their experiences of being hurt or abused in previous relationships. Mrs. Browning's victimization in her former marriage was explored at some length, first in individual meetings and then in conjoint sessions with her husband, in an attempt to build empathy and understanding for Emma. They were informed that Emma probably felt compelled to keep all of her feelings inside while the abuse was active, and that she was in constant danger. It was predicted that when she began to feel safe again, her previously suppressed feelings might be quite intense for a while. This was framed as an indication of progress, a sign of increasing trust in her parents, and an early, necessary step toward healing.

Addressing Trauma-Related Effects
of Coercion

Emma had a high need for control in our individual meetings and preferred to engage in structured activities of her design. She also vacillated between regressed and pseudomature behavior during her therapeutic activity in the office. Sometimes she enjoyed puppet play; this frequently provided a window into some of the developmental effects of her trauma, such as low self-esteem and deficits in relational skills. At other times she behaved more like a young adolescent, discussing family problems or current events as if she were much older. Emma's variable presentation, particularly in the early phase of treatment, gave the therapist an important challenge: she had to monitor her own desire to gently encourage Emma to resolve abuse-related issues before she was ready, thereby creating another coercive experience.

The excerpt below, carefully reconstructed from notes, illustrates one way in which this issue was addressed in treatment. This particular session followed one in which the therapist recognized that she had inadvertently pressed Emma to explore something that was beyond her current capability. She had asked her to reflect on, and describe, her internal experience following a puppet show. Emma responded by quietly withdrawing from the exchange and coloring by herself for the remainder of the meeting. The therapist commented indirectly by speaking through a puppet. She acknowledged her premature curiosity, and reinforced Emma for letting the therapist know that she had asked too big a question. Emma was also validated for being able to clearly communicate the wish for some quiet time when she felt the need for it.

Our therapy office has a large trunk containing numerous toys, games, and play activities that children can chose from. Among its contents are small and large lamb puppets. Emma identified one as "Baby" and the other as "Mama." She liked to play with them when she was feeling safe enough to explore some of her thoughts and feelings related to current situations as well as to the incest trauma. In the session described below, she chose to play with Mama and Baby Lamb, and designated two other puppets to be the police officers who had come to school to ask her questions about "stuff."

This was stuff that Baby did not want to talk about, but she had to, "cuz they were the police."

> **Therapist:** So Baby really didn't like answering those questions when she didn't want to.
> **Emma** (Holding and stroking Baby)**:** Nope. She simply didn't like it at all!
> **Therapist:** Well, I can totally understand that. Emma, I've been thinking . . . you know Baby a lot better than I do. I know that I ask Baby questions in here sometimes, and I wonder if I've ever asked her a question she that didn't want to answer, but felt she should. Would you mind asking her that, and letting me know?
> **Emma:** Okay. I'll ask her. But you have to go sit over there so she can tell me in private.
> **Therapist:** Fine. I'll go wait over there. I'm sure glad you told me about this being private, so I could give Baby her space.
> [Emma pretends that she and Baby are talking to one another.]
> **Emma:** All right, I can tell you now. You can come back [pointing to the chair across from her]. Sit right here and I'll tell you.
> **Therapist:** OK. Thank you for asking her, because it's really important to me that I don't push Baby to talk about things before she's ready.
> **Emma:** Well . . . Baby said that she couldn't remember exactly, but that she did sometimes feel like that. Like, maybe once or twice she didn't really want to talk about something you asked her about but it's not that much.
> **Therapist:** I'm so glad Baby was able to tell you that. You really are a good friend to her, someone she can talk to about things like this. I don't ever want to make Baby feel that she has to talk about things she's not ready to talk about in here. I want her to know that she has the final say with what we talk about. Emma, do you have any ideas for how Baby and I could work this out?
> **Emma:** Well, she wouldn't want to hurt your feelings, she told me that before. But maybe . . . well, I'm not really sure about that.

Therapist: I wonder if you think she might make a deal with me about this. You're very creative. Would you help Baby make up a signal or a way to tell me whenever I do that? This way I'll know to put that topic on our "things to talk about another time" list. Then I'll know when I make that mistake of bringing up things she's not ready to talk about, and making her feel bad.

Emma: Just let me discuss it with Baby for a minute. [Pause] She said that she would tell you. I told her what signal to use, and how she'll do it is this: Every time you ask her something she doesn't like, she'll go like this. [Emma scrunches Baby's eyes closed tightly, then lets Baby fall to the ground with a noise.] She'll close her eyes tight, then she'll faint.

Therapist: OK. And that will be her way of telling me, "No, I would prefer to not talk about that right now."

Emma: Exactamundo!

Therapist: It's a deal, then. That's great. Thank you for all your help, Emma. You know, now I'm wondering if I might ask Baby a question.

Emma: Go ahead.

Therapist: Baby, this might be a private thing between you and Emma, and if that's the case, I'll understand. Just tell me. I am wondering, has Emma ever shared with you that she feels that same way sometimes, too? Like, that I bring things up in here before she's ready to talk about them?

Emma (as Baby): She didn't tell me.

Therapist: Do you think she would mind if you asked her?

Emma (as Baby): Well, I could try, and see what she says. You go sit over there again until I come and get you.

Therapist: OK. And thank you for trying, because it's very important to me that Emma and I work out a deal like the one that you and I made so she can tell me, too, in case I'm making the same kind of mistake with her sometimes.

[Emma and Baby talk.]

Emma (as Baby): Well, she said almost the same thing as me.

Therapist: Oh, I'm so happy she was able to tell you! All right, then, did she tell you how she might want to let me know the next time I do that same mistake?

Emma (as Baby): Yes she did. She won't say a thing . . . she'll just go and get the list for things to talk about later, and tell you to write it down.

Therapist: That's a terrific plan! And that will mean no discussion of that topic until Emma is more ready.

Emma (as Baby): That's right.

Therapist: What if Emma feels shy about telling me, or is afraid to hurt my feelings, Baby? Do you think she'll *really* know that it's OK to tell me?

Emma (as Baby): Well, you already told her it was all right, didn't you?

Therapist: Yes.

Emma (as Baby): Then I think she can tell you the next time.

Therapist: That's great. And would you be willing to help her the first time or so, in case it's a little hard?

Emma (as Baby): Oh yes. I will help her.

Therapist: Do you agree, Emma, with the deal Baby set up between you and me?

Emma: Yes.

Therapist: Good. And like I told you before, for my part, I will do my best to not bring up hard things to talk about too soon. It won't hurt my feelings when you use your right to not talk about something in here, or to tell me "No." In fact, I am happy to know that we can work this out together in case I make a mistake.

This exchange was an important step toward creating a safe therapeutic environment where Emma could begin to feel that her needs would be respected. She was given permission to practice asserting herself without negative repercussions, and her feelings and personal boundaries were treated as important. In addition, the therapist was modeling the point that making and acknowledging mistakes could be addressed without serving as proof that one is a bad person, and that misunderstandings could be resolved. In subsequent meetings with Mr. and Mrs. Browning, room was created for incorporating these new behaviors into the family system so that Emma could continue to develop them outside therapy in a similarly supportive environment.

Another abuse-related theme was addressed in a much later individual session. Emma was given an opportunity to process the traumatic effects of coercion suffered as a part of her sexual abuse. She was discussing how a friend at school was trying to get her to do something she did not want to do, and that she knew was wrong. The conversation led directly to puppet play thematically associated with the way Ian had coerced her into doing things that she knew were wrong. This topic was difficult to discuss directly; Emma created a way to incorporate Baby, Mama Lamb, and an imaginary uncle into the conversation, thereby giving herself some needed emotional distance. By using the puppets to process her trauma, Emma had a means to regulate the intensity of her affect and to increase her ability to tolerate difficult feelings.

> **Therapist:** I'm sorry you were treated this way at school today. And I'm glad you shared it with me because I can see that it has really upset you. Are there other times that someone has tried to make you do something you didn't want to do that also made you feel bad like this?
> **Emma:** All the times Ian made me do things . . . but that's on the list [of things to talk about at a later time].
> **Therapist:** Yes, that's on the list. I wonder if we could talk about just one of the times when Ian made you do something you didn't want to do, or should we keep it on the list for now?
> **Emma:** Which thing?
> **Therapist:** That would be up to you. Lots of brothers and sisters know how to get each other to do things they don't want to do. Sometimes these things feel OK, sometimes they feel kind of bad, and other times they feel really bad. Maybe you could talk about one or two ways that Ian got you to do something that felt a little bad, and talk about the things that made you feel really bad another time.

With Emma's agreement, we then moved into the following area of work. She wanted to use the puppets to talk about this, and she decided to be Mama Lamb, telling me about what had happened to her child (herself), Baby Lamb.

Therapist: So, Mama Lamb, Emma told me that you know of one or two ways that Ian got her to do some things that made her feel bad.

Emma (as Mama Lamb): I know lots of things about that, because they're the same things that Baby Lamb's big brother, no, I mean . . . her uncle, . . . things her uncle did to her a long time ago.

Therapist: Oh, I didn't know that Baby Lamb's uncle hurt her, too. I'm very sorry to hear that.

Emma: Here [handing a puppet to the therapist]. You be Mrs. Chick-Chick, and the two mothers can be gossiping.

Therapist: OK. I'll be Mrs. Chick-Chick, gossiping to my friend Mama Lamb about our children.

Emma: No, it's "Mrs. Lamb" to you.

Therapist (as Mrs. Chick-Chick): Oh, OK. Now I've got it. You were saying something, Mrs. Lamb, about how Baby Lamb's uncle had made her do some things she didn't want to do . . . ?

Emma (as Mrs. L): Well yes . . . he did. He's a lot bigger than her, you know.

Therapist (as Mrs. C-C): I didn't know that . . . so her uncle is bigger than her. That could have made it easier for him to force his niece Baby Lamb to do things she didn't want to do.

Emma (as Mrs. L): Exactly my point.

Therapist (as Mrs. C-C): So how did Baby Lamb's uncle make her do things?

Emma (as Mrs. L): Well, Baby Lamb always wanted to play with her uncle because there weren't any friends that lived by us for her to play with. So whenever he said, "Do this, and then I'll play a game with you," Baby Lamb would feel happy because she would have someone to play with, but . . . then he usually never would.

Therapist (as Mrs. C-C): So, like most nieces, Baby Lamb trusted what her uncle said, and he got her to do things because he knew she trusted him so much. That must have been hard for Baby when he didn't play with her after she did what he wanted her to.

Emma (as Mrs. L): Well, of course she didn't like it.

Therapist (as Mrs. C-C): Hmm . . . I wonder how Baby Lamb felt at those times.

Emma (as Mrs. L): It just breaks my heart to know this, as her mother and all, but she felt so sad and all alone . . . all alone. [Emma's eyes become teary.] Because she couldn't tell anybody, not even me. And like, oh, he was just lying to her like that.

Therapist (as Mrs. C-C): That is not a good thing for an uncle to do to his niece. You look sad about that, Mrs. Lamb.

Emma (as Mrs. L): Yes, I am sad. My poor Baby. [Emma made Mrs. Lamb cuddle and stroke the Baby Lamb puppet.] How would you feel if your daughter was hurt by her own uncle . . . and before that, she trusted him and everything?

Therapist (as Mrs. C-C): I am sure I would also feel very sad . . . very sad . . . probably much like you are feeling now.

Emma (as Mrs. L): And you know what? I'm also a little angry about that, as her mother, you know.

Therapist (as Mrs. C-C): What exactly are you a little bit angry about, Mrs. Lamb?

Emma (as Mrs. L): I'm angry at him . . . well she couldn't tell me, because he made her afraid.

Therapist (as Mrs. C-C): What did Baby's uncle do to let her know he didn't want her to tell anyone about these things?

Emma (as Mrs. L): That's the scariest part. She told me, you know. He told her if she told anybody, that her parents—me and Mr. Lamb—would get sent to jail, or she would get taken away from the family forever, or she might have to go to jail. So she just couldn't tell now, could she? Do you think she could have told?

Therapist (as Mrs. C-C): I don't think Baby Lamb could have told even one minute before she did—she was trying too hard to protect her parents and herself. She must have been very scared to even tell at all.

Emma (as Mrs. L): Oh, she was scared, all right. She wanted to tell the whole time. . . . She wanted it to never happen at all, is what she wanted.

Therapist (as Mrs. C-C): Yes. What was the scariest part for Baby Lamb?

Emma (as Mrs. L): She was extremely, very scared, probably the most scared, when the police came to school, because she thought they would arrest her and take her to jail like her uncle said!

Therapist (as Mrs. C-C): Did the police let Baby know that neither she, you, nor Mr. Lamb would have to go to jail?

Emma (as Mrs. L): Oh yes. They told her about that. They said that they just wanted to make her safe so she didn't get hurt anymore. . . . . but they asked her lots of questions about stuff. He[her uncle] used to say he didn't want her to get hurt, and then he protected her sometimes, too.

Therapist (as Mrs. C-C): Mrs. Lamb, we've been talking for a little while about some things that I know, as Baby Lamb's mother, are difficult to discuss. One of the things Emma does to help with hard feelings is to take a relax break. I'm sure she'd be willing to help you with one if you want to take a little break or anything.

Emma (as Mrs. L): Oh, well, as you know, it isn't pleasant talking about my daughter's . . . what has happened to her and everything. But no, . . . if we don't take a relax break for five more minutes, then can we play a game?

Therapist (as Mrs. C-C): Yes. As long as we can agree that you'll let me know if you would like a break before five minutes is up, how about if we go on? [Emma has Mrs. Lamb nod.] Would you tell me about a time that Baby Lamb's uncle protected her?

Emma (as Mrs. L): Um . . . like the time over at Andy's house, the boys were teasing her and playing "keep away" with her Baby doll. But then her uncle told them "no" and they got mad because they said, "Well why can't we, what do you care?"

Therapist (as Mrs. C-C): So he protected her from those boys.

Emma (as Mrs. L): Yeah, Baby told me that he took her out of there. They did bad things, those boys. I want to go back there and tell those kids' moms so they get in *big* trouble. They're bad!

Therapist (as Mrs. C-C): Yes, that does sound like bad behavior. Those big kids probably hurt Baby's feelings and scared her. Mrs. Lamb, as an adult, you know that when uncles who hurt their nieces offer protection, they sometimes expect their nieces to do something to pay them back for that protection. Was there anything Baby's uncle pushed her to do to pay him back for protecting her from the boys at Andy's house?

Emma (as Mrs. L): Well, as you know . . . she had to . . . well, you know about it, don't you? Well . . . mostly she had to do stuff with her uncle. Can we play a game now?

Therapist: Sounds good to me. We talked about some scary things that happened to your daughter, Baby Lamb, for quite a long time, and you're ready to stop; so we'll play a game now. You did a good job of telling me you want to stop.

Emma made steady progress in therapy through the graduated processing of traumatic material, using puppet and play therapy over time. Her fearfulness and nightmares lessened, and eventually she became less anxious and more able to express a wider range of feelings and behavior in therapy. Yet she continued to suffer from developmental effects of the abuse, including difficulty trusting others and increased sexualized behavior.

Family therapy was problematic. Her parents' commitment to treatment wavered, and they never overcame their reluctance to openly discuss the incest and its impact on each of them. Satisfied that Emma's condition had improved, they ultimately decided to end therapy after seven months. Once again they were strongly encouraged to seek community sources of support for children and families with incest-related concerns, as well as continuing in family treatment with Ian through his offense-specific offender treatment program.

THE DISORGANIZED FAMILY

Specific Considerations

- Which parent has the greater potential for being appropriately in charge, thus increasing stability within the family system and protecting children from abuse?
- Evaluate sibling contact with nonfamily children or adults for signs of abuse.

- What are the family's primary needs for services that might increase stability (e.g., in-home support services, mental health referral, financial need/employment agencies)?

Disorganized families move from crisis to crisis with little or no leadership, nurturing, or stability. These are often highly defensive, transient, and chaotic families that rely on social service and child welfare agencies for external support. Poor boundaries and a lack of parental supervision increase the vulnerability to multiple forms of child maltreatment, including sibling abuse. No one family member is consistently in charge and a primary caretaker may be suffering from a mental illness. One research participant from a disorganized family recalled her parents as follows: "I have no memory of anybody seeming like a parent to me. I remember feeling like I made a lot of decisions on my own . . . feeling like I wasn't getting much guidance from anybody. So . . . there wasn't even a sense for me, growing up, that they were parenting me. We were just all these people living in a house."

Many of the participants in our study who grew up in disorganized families have not maintained contact with their siblings into adulthood. In not sustaining relationships with adult siblings, they often echoed earlier patterns of interaction. One participant described herself and her siblings as "each one of us out for ourselves. We were on our own on the streets when we were little, and we're still on our own as far as any relationship is concerned." Another respondent described her disconnection with her abusive brother in this way: "I've heard from people in our old neighborhood that he's been into drugs, and has been in and out of jail a couple of times, but I have no idea where he is now. And I don't want to know. To me, he is just bad memories and trouble." Some siblings attempted to reestablish their relationships only after years of severed contact. Adult survivors of abuse typically had few positive memories of childhood sibling interactions, and many had no wish to reestablish ties with their sibling offenders.

Another characteristic of disorganized family functioning is that caregivers are emotionally unavailable, and sometimes are physically absent from the family for long periods. Usually neither parent is able to provide adequate or consistent financial support, so the family may be forced to rely on outside assistance. In disorganized families, the parents may use available resources to support a drug or alcohol addiction. Children are frequently neglected, with young siblings left responsible for toddlers or infants. In short, these are multiproblem, crisis-prone families.

Parents able to secure supervision may lack good judgment regarding appropriate caretakers. Sometimes they entrust the children to persons ill-equipped to assure their safety and well-being. In Ellen's family, while at work her mother had been sending an older sister to a neighbor's home to do housekeeping for money. Suddenly her sister refused go back. In response, her mother sent Ellen, whom this neighbor then molested as well.

Nearly all aspects of family functioning are strained beyond the available resources in disorganized families. As a result, the level of neglect in these families is often so severe that even in the absence of parental physical or sexual abuse, siblings generally have extremely limited skills for caring for younger brothers and sisters. Limits, boundaries, and models for healthy interaction may be severely inadequate or altogether missing. School often is the first stable environment for young children reared in disorganized families. The inherent lack of family stability, however, results in frequent school dislocations and disruptions in attendance.

Because no one family member is consistently in charge, the potential for multiple abusive interactions within the family increases. Children in disorganized families are frequently at risk for parental abuse; because of the family deficits typically present, children also can be vulnerable to abuse by older siblings or nonfamily acquaintances. It is relatively uncommon for a disorganized family to enter treatment voluntarily. Basic survival takes precedence over emotional or psychological needs, and families resist forming therapeutic alliances with mistrusted professionals.

Chapter 9

Psychotherapy with Adult Survivors of Sibling Incest or Assault

I feel like I had this rearview mirror, which helped me to see things and know who I could trust, and he adjusted it to his view—not mine. I still don't have it back.

Jackie, age twenty-nine

Many intervention principles fundamental to treating adult survivors of parent-child abuse can be applied to therapy with survivors of sibling abuse. For example, our approach in treating adult sibling abuse survivors is based on a phenomenological perspective in which an individual's development unfolds from moment to moment. Clinical events are understood in terms of self-experience, and experience emerges from interactions between the therapist and the client. The client's behavior and experience can be understood only in the context of that interactive field. As a result, the client's subjective experience, including his or her perceptions and personal experiences, are important determinants of therapeutic actions. Indeed, this therapeutic position leads to an emphasis on the client's subjective experience itself, rather than on the interpretation of that experience.

For example, one clinician might interpret a survivor's idealizing and pleasing behavior as an attempt to act out seductive and dependent feelings toward the therapist. Another clinician, however, taking a phenomenological approach, might investigate directly why the client engages in such behavior and what about the therapist elicits or supports this reaction. The therapist's experience therefore is also important. The clinician must be able to receive and rever-

berate with whatever is going on between himself or herself and the
client. In this way, the therapist becomes not only a responder and a
giver of feedback, but also a participant in the therapeutic process.

An emphasis on experience minimizes the hierarchical nature of
therapy, which assumes that one person (the therapist) knows more
than another (the client) and is able to apply his or her meaning to
the client's life events. We have observed that this is an important
component of therapy with adult survivors, given the peer-oriented
nature of sibling abuse trauma. A phenomenological orientation is
necessarily empathic because one of the therapist's most powerful
tools becomes his or her ability to partially inhabit the survivor's
inner world and to perceive indirectly what the survivor perceives
(Briere, 1992).

The ability to view an event from the client's perspective also
diminishes the likelihood that the therapist will form value judg-
ments. Empathy on the part of the therapist enables the survivor to
incrementally build the emotional skills necessary for self-regulation. In feeling understood, the survivor receives the support necessary for an increasingly self-reflective attitude toward his or her
feelings and behavior. This curiosity often leads to an awareness of
internal strengths and resources that formerly may have been ignored or diminished.

In keeping with this process-oriented approach, the psychotherapist focuses on what is *actually and presently* happening in therapy.
Paradoxically, accepting and identifying with what is occurring
supports change and growth. As with clients in general, building
safety and providing support are paramount to establishing a therapeutic alliance and productive treatment. Regarding process issues
in treatment, much has been written about viewing an abuse survivor's "resistance" as a mechanism of communication or feedback to
the therapist (Briere, 1992; Herman, 1992; Salter, 1995). Resistance, however, also can be viewed as a protection against injury
while one pursues development during actual interpersonal events
in therapy (Stolorow, Brandchaft, and Atwood, 1987). For example,
one adult client who was physically assaulted by his brother
throughout childhood could recount detailed descriptions of events
surrounding the trauma. Yet because his brother beat him harder at
the first sign of tears, the client still could not allow himself to

experience any feelings connected to his abuse. Once he felt that he was understood and accepted for his present way of dealing with these issues in therapy, tears gradually followed.

Establishing clear therapeutic contracts for change and determining a proper sequence of treatment goals are also critical aspects of therapy with abuse survivors. A primary objective in treatment is to facilitate a balance of environmental and self-support. This can be achieved in a variety of ways. Survivors may feel empowered by the normalization of their subjective experience in treatment. Opportunities for this type of acknowledgment previously were available for survivors of parent-child abuse, and more recently have been available for sibling abuse survivors as well. Because adults abused as children sometimes depend heavily on their therapists, clinicians must respond to these needs to facilitate self-responsibility. The therapeutic interaction gives clients an opportunity to experiment with new ways of experiencing themselves, which then may be generalized in other relationships.

An important component of treatment emphasizes boundary confusion and relationship dynamics because sibling abuse survivors typically have endured interpersonal boundary violations that caused them great difficulty. The absence of a generational boundary violation in sibling incest cases poses additional therapeutic challenges. For example, siblings may believe more readily that they were active participants in the abuse and could have put a stop to it. Survivors may be even more ambivalent about responsibility for the abuse when adopted or stepsiblings are involved. Furthermore, they may blame themselves for childhood traumatic attachments to their sibling offender, which they formed as a result of parental abuse or neglect.

Another important task is the development of a therapeutic context in which the client is challenged sufficiently by the risks inherent in growth, and supported adequately in efforts to change. A climate offering support and risk in the proper balance must exist if survivors are to achieve and maintain treatment gains. This therapeutic climate, although often elusive, facilitates the development of self-support for new experiences and increases a client's range of support for an expanded sense of self. According to Briere (1992):

A major goal of therapy with abuse trauma survivors is the desensitization and integration of painful states and memories by utilizing self-regulation tools for balancing cognitive and affective fluctuations. This usually entails client self exposure to manageable quantities of abuse-related distress. The therapeutic process must be monitored closely, however, for insufficient processing of traumatic experience will accomplish little, while too much exposure may flood the survivor with painful affect. Titrated exposure can provide the survivor with opportunities to learn how to tolerate tolerable pain, rather than reflexively turning to dissociation or tension reduction. (p. 121)

Therefore a rhythm between the exploration of abuse-related material and consolidation is fundamental to good progress in treatment. Psychotherapy is essentially a relationship—it is hoped, one of wisdom and empowerment. Its power is connected inextricably to the present, and the primacy of present events in therapy is a central fact. Present-centered interaction is modeled initially by the therapist; gradually its benefits also become obvious to clients. During such interactions, symptoms are relieved and new learning occurs. This task is deceptively complex for both client and therapist.

An eclectic, multidimensional therapeutic approach includes challenging the adult survivor's abuse-related cognitive appraisals about him- or herself and the world. This point is especially relevant in light of the frozen images (of self and of offenders) often maintained rigidly by sibling abuse survivors, which then serve as templates for other intimate adult relationships. Cognitively oriented interventions can help the survivor to develop a more accurate self-image and a more realistic view of relationships with others. Therapy also must focus on helping the adult survivor to identify and express his or her feelings. Finally, skills and behaviors needed for competent, effective day-to-day living are sometimes an important component of treatment. Therapy frequently can provide opportunities for experimentation with a variety of behaviors that one may not yet be ready to practice in everyday life.

Jay, for example, a survivor of sibling assault and incest, was reluctant to assert himself; he believed his brother Earle was aggressive enough for the two of them. As a result, he frequently settled for less than satisfying contact with others. Labeling Earle as the "aggressive" sibling had other consequences as well. Jay secretly feared that if he were to begin asserting his own needs, he would become more like his abusive older brother. When he admitted to having homicidal fantasies about Earle as a child, his anxiety was only reinforced. By facing his fears through practicing healthy self-assertion via contained exercises in therapy, Jay had the opportunity to experience a wider range of feelings and behavior. As a result, he was supported in developing a more inclusive, more accepting attitude toward himself.

Another primary task of therapy with survivors is to locate sources of acknowledgment of the abuse within the family whenever possible. Clients need assistance as they progress through their unique mourning process concerning the abuse, and they need aid in the recovery of self-functions. Family-of-origin members who are available and willing to offer support can help to stabilize, facilitate, and expedite a survivor's healing process. Larger families often contain at least one sibling who is able to participate to some extent in the survivor's treatment, from letters and phone calls to conjoint sessions. Unique concerns related to treating clients who are both sibling abuse survivors and offenders also must be addressed. Determining whether meetings between survivors and their sibling offenders are in the client's best interests is an important decision, which generally is faced at some point in therapy.

One essential component of establishing a therapeutic context for change is creating a safe, supportive environment. Clinicians can begin by immediately honoring the client's need to reestablish safety in relationships. A certain amount of therapeutic structure serves as a basis for the creation of limits and boundaries. Therapy often proceeds more smoothly when one can view a client's *resistance* as creative adaptation, or as a statement to the therapist about the timing or competence of an intervention. Communications both during and after sessions are often best understood as the client's efforts to teach the clinician about some aspect of the reaction to his or her trauma.

For example, after some limit setting regarding nonurgent calls to the office, Jay canceled his next appointment and considered not returning to therapy. When this was processed in a later session, he revealed that he disliked the control exerted over his behavior by the therapist. Further exploration led to the disclosure of important traumatic material associated with cruel and unfair treatment by his brother, and to the expectation that the therapist would behave similarly. Once the therapist was able to convey the uniformity of his phone call policy and demonstrate respect for Jay's behavior, Jay continued to make progress in treatment. Initially this consisted of struggling with reactivated feelings of helplessness and outrage, partially in response to the therapist's efforts to set clear therapeutic boundaries. Later, Jay's hard work caused him to feel more fully in charge of certain elements of his therapy, and signaled a turning point in treatment. By expressing frustration with the course of therapy thus far, he was asserting himself in a highly productive manner and revealing the centrality of his need for control in interpersonal relationships. His willingness to display such behavior was directly associated with increased self-support and trust in the therapeutic process.

It is also important to thoroughly assess the effects of trauma and its impact on the development of faulty identifications. Adults abused as children are not necessarily prone to repeating their victimization in the same form. Careful attention to a client's potential for revictimization in therapy or in outside relationships is crucial.

Finally, understanding developmental differences between siblings in terms of their reactions to abuse, the increased risk of abuse at various ages, and the impact of abuse trauma on nonabused children in the family contributes to more effective treatment of sibling abuse survivors.

Psychotherapy has no tradition for conducting sibling meetings nor for utilizing sibling-oriented interventions. Our clinical and research experience, however, along with the accumulated knowledge of others (Dunn and Plomin, 1990; Lewis, 1988), suggests their value, particularly in cases of sibling abuse trauma. Professionals' lack of a focus on siblings also has ramifications for parents. For example, caretakers often become desensitized to escalating sibling conflict, and thus overlook abuse that occurs at home. Clinicians inadvertently may neglect traumatic interactions by failing to screen for sibling abuse, even in families where other abusive interactions have been acknowledged. Evidence also suggests a link between sibling assault and socializing children toward later violence. The following clinical example is illustrative in this regard.

CASE ILLUSTRATIONS

Steve

Steve's social worker referred him for issues related to anger management. Allegedly, he had punched his eight-month-old son Anthony, knocking him out of his high chair. When Steve arrived for treatment, the therapist initially was curious about the absence of any intergenerational parent-child struggles in the Child Protective Services investigative report. Therefore Steve and the therapist began therapy by constructing a genogram to obtain more information on his family-of-origin and his current living situation. This intervention revealed that he had been living with Nicky, Anthony's cocaine-using mother, for about six months. They fought regularly about Anthony. Steve complained that his girlfriend clearly favored their son, and at the same time he accused her of neglecting the child's basic needs.

Steve also disclosed that his parents had divorced when he was sixteen. Since age seven he had felt emotionally distant from his father, whom he believed favored his younger brother Paul. His relationship with his mother was more complex. He felt close to her but was conflicted about their emotional interdependence. When the therapist inquired about Steve's relationship with his brother, he stated that it was strained, though slightly improved from years before. When pressed for details, Steve confided, "I pretty much beat up my brother regularly throughout our teenage years."

Developing a Context for Change

Early treatment goals focused on developing self-monitoring anger management tools. Anthony was already in protective custody. Part of Steve's motivation in treatment was to have regular supervised visits with his son, whom he loved very much. His relationship with his girlfriend, Nicky, had ended, but his connection to his son seemed strong. He began to keep a journal of his angry thoughts and feelings, and to learn alternative ways to handle his anger in stressful situations through role plays and cognitively oriented sessions. Steve was deeply ashamed of his behavior toward his son. His violence with Anthony was framed as a metaphor for his violence with his brother Paul in his family-of-origin. This explanation allowed Steve to explore parallels between the jealousy and competitiveness that he felt toward his son, Anthony, for monopolizing Nicky's attention, and toward his brother, Paul, for having a favored relationship with their father. The sibling framework also supported Steve as he explored and uncovered layers of feelings related to his responsibility as an offender.

Addressing Steve's Accountability

A simultaneous focus on Steve's relationship with his brother and on his father directed his trauma-related boundary problems back to their origin. This approach had the advantage of containing both intrapsychic and interactional components. It was jointly decided to eventually hold individual and conjoint sibling meetings with Steve, age twenty-four, and his brother Paul, now twenty-one.

Individual sessions with Steve were focused on specific details related to his abuse of Paul. His accountability for the abuse was explored in a variety of ways. The following exchange represents one therapeutic dialogue:

> **Steve:** Paul would always get to go places with our dad when he was still around. And then when [Dad] left, Paul got invited over to his house more often. No matter how hard I tried, I never seemed to be able to get my father's attention except in a negative way.
> **Therapist:** It sounds like you really missed having more of a connection with your dad as a child.
> **Steve:** Well, [Paul] wouldn't hesitate to let me know that he was Dad's favorite or whatever . . . sometimes he'd get dropped off after a weekend visit with Dad and I'd see a smug look on his face, like he'd won or something. Then, before you

know it, we would be at each other with the insults—and then most of the time, I'd wind up hitting him just to shut him up.

Therapist: So you and Paul were in competition for your father's attention. I'll bet you still feel angry and hurt when you think about those times.

Steve: Yeah, I guess.

Therapist: If you could imagine for a moment that your father is here in the office with us, what might you want him to know about your anger?

Steve: My father wouldn't ever be here. He thinks that therapy is for crazy people!

Therapist: Sounds like another example of feeling abandoned by him.

Steve: Well, he wouldn't come!

Therapist: OK, you may be right. You certainly know your dad better than I do. But this is for you, and it doesn't matter whether or not it could ever really happen. I'd like you to pretend that he's here in the room so that you can get more in touch with your feelings about him. And I understand that it's an unusual thing to ask, so don't feel that you have to do it.

Steve: Well, I don't exactly know how.

Therapist: Let me see if I can help. Just close your eyes, and go inside your head for a minute and make a picture of your father. Maybe you can describe the picture out loud.

Steve: I can see him yelling at me for something.

Therapist: Great, just keep looking and describe what you else you see.

Steve: Well, now I see us all getting mad at each other, and then he goes off somewhere with my brother.

Therapist: OK, as he's leaving with your brother, pay attention and listen for a voice inside your head. Is there anything you want to say to your dad? You don't have to say it out loud. Just quietly to yourself—tell him how you feel about seeing him walk off with Paul.

[Steve looks visibly uncomfortable, and shifts in his chair.]

Therapist: Could you say what's going on right now?

Steve: I don't know. I'm really confused. You said to speak to my father, but I keep thinking about my brother and how angry I am at him for screwing things up for me.

Therapist: Say more about that.

Steve: Sometimes I wish my brother were just dead. If it weren't for him, me and my dad could go fishing or hunting. When we'd be fighting sometimes, I just would really lose it—like I'd forget he's even my brother. I've never felt so mad in my life.

Therapist: Yes, it sounds like you really were fighting over something very important with your brother.

Steve (quietly)**:** You mean, like for my dad's love.

Therapist: You look sad, like you have a lot of feelings about this.

Steve (begins to cry)**:** Well, he just never spent any time with me. I hated always being left out. I'm the oldest—I was here first, but my brother still got more.

Therapist: I wonder if it's easier to feel angry with your brother, your rival, than it is to be angry with your father, since he's the one you wanted to have notice and love you.

Steve (while sobbing)**:** He was always leaving. It seems like my dad never wanted to be around me even when I was a kid.

Therapist: What do you remember telling yourself about that?

Steve: I just figured that he didn't like me for some reason. And then when he started to spend more time with Paul, I thought, well, he obviously likes Paul better.

Therapist: So, at least some of your anger and hurt sounds like it belongs to your relationship with your dad. Since you didn't feel that you could safely let your dad know how you felt, maybe you took your anger out on your brother.

Steve: Well, he was around all the time. Besides, Paul could really provoke me. He was often the one who started things by taunting and embarrassing me in front of others. He was better at arguing than me and knew how to push all of my buttons.

Therapist: Nonetheless, you were physically stronger and more mature than Paul. That suggests that you were responsible for setting the limits on the fighting.

Steve: Well, my parents certainly didn't teach us much about how to solve our problems. They either left us to fend for ourselves, or made things worse by fighting in front of us and saying that we were the reason that they were getting divorced. And sometimes my dad would stop the fighting and then stick up for Paul . . . which only made it worse in the end.

Therapist: You know, you have a lot of insight and a mature view of your parents' role in escalating the conflict with your brother.

Steve: A lot of good it does me.

Therapist: Well, I'll bet Paul would benefit from hearing your perspective on things. Both of you suffered from your parents' limitations—and Steve, I can understand your feeling angry and upset by this fact.

Steve: Thanks, I feel better now that I got those feelings off my chest.

Therapist: With such a clear understanding of your original family, you now have the opportunity to accomplish two things that your father was unable to do. First, take responsibility for your hurtful behavior toward both your brother Paul and your son Anthony. Also, you can work to repair these relationships so that you don't continue to behave in ways that hurt your brother or your son—something that your father lost out on because he was unable to do this with you.

Steve was more willing to acknowledge and explore his shame and regret after several more thorough reviews of his history as an offender with Paul. He also agreed to continue to work on improving their relationship. For the first time he was able to express feelings of inadequacy at not being his father's favorite. Siblings routinely compare the amount of love and attention they receive from each parent. The perception that one is loved less is especially difficult to bear, and is associated with higher rates of sibling conflict.

Sometime before the first scheduled conjoint sibling meeting, Steve began to express remorse for abusing his brother. His willingness and ability to apologize had been set as a prerequisite for their first meeting. After several individual sessions focusing on Steve's remorse and on plans for the sibling sessions, the decision was made to invite Paul into the treatment process. Toward the middle of the initial conjoint meeting, Steve apologized to Paul for the abuse, and shared his regret and pain for victimizing his younger brother during their childhood years.

Conjoint Sibling Meetings

Siblings, much like couples, are unique in that their relationships contain both complementary and reciprocal features. Therefore it is very important to maintain a balance of power between participants. The therapist made sure to provide equal attention and time for both voices. After allowing ample opportunity to understand Paul and his perspective, the therapist invited the brothers to work on solving some of the problems in their relationship. These skill-building sessions included basic speaking and listening exercises, teaching conflict resolution tools, and learning to listen for solutions.

The brothers' competitiveness for the therapist's attention and favor was observed firsthand and addressed throughout this process. Further exploration revealed that Steve often spoke for his mother in disagreements, and Paul assumed his father's voice. The brothers agreed that they generally felt like opponents: sibling stand-ins for either Mom's or Dad's side. Although their polarized sibling roles served the systemic function of stabilizing their parents' chronic disputes, they also set Steve and Paul on a collision course. Therapeutic interventions therefore were provided within the frame of the sibling *team effort* required to survive such an abusive family environment. For example, they had split up to allow for closer connections with one parent or the other. The notion of this pattern as part of a larger, more collaborative system provided the siblings with therapeutic support to evaluate the current benefits and drawbacks of maintaining this mode of interaction. One result was that they began to assume more responsibility and initiative for their unique relationship, separate from their parents.

In one conjoint meeting, Paul requested some individual time with the therapist to explore his feelings around the victimization he had experienced as a child. This was discussed and agreed to by all parties. However, in light of issues such as fairness and competition between the siblings, it was decided that Paul's individual sessions would be limited to addressing his victimization as it related to his wish for an improved relationship with his brother. The individual meetings also provided Paul with an opportunity to feel on more "even ground" with the therapist, who had already established a good working alliance with Steve. A good deal of Paul's individual treatment was focused on helping him reconcile his brother's violent behavior with the nurturing that Steve had also provided at times. They had grown up in a family where their father was peripheral and their mother was financially and emotionally overburdened by the responsibility of raising two boys on her own. Through their early school years, Steve frequently was left to care for his younger brother.

As the siblings took part in their final conjoint meetings, the therapist asked Paul to remind Steve of his earlier caretaking role. Steve was obviously moved by his brother's comments, and they exchanged childhood memories of good times together. Their interaction gradually led to shifts in each sibling's perception of images of the other, which had been frozen since childhood. As a direct result of the conjoint sessions, Steve gradually began to access and accept his nurturing qualities, which would be valuable in his new role as a father.

Making Intergenerational Connections

Steve began to make intergenerational associations between his abuse of Anthony and his role as a sibling offender in his family-of-origin. His girlfriend preferred Anthony to him; she tried to win her son's favor by degrading Steve in his presence and making it difficult for Steve to maintain anything more than a peripheral role in parenting his son. Steve resorted to a familiar pattern of violence to deal with his feelings of rejection and inadequacy. A major goal of treatment was working with him to accept full responsibility for his abusive behavior. This was accomplished in a series of steps. Initially Steve acknowledged responsibility for abusing his brother; then he gradually accepted full accountability for assaulting his son.

Sometimes it is useful to view generational hierarchies as reversed in abusive families. That is, parents who resort to violence to discipline children relinquish a certain amount of control, along with their role as the adults in the family. Steve's childhood abuse of his younger brother Paul represented a similar betrayal of caregiving responsibility. Steve frequently was left to supervise Paul; in addition to offering protection and nurturing, he caused significant harm to his brother. The therapist adopted an analogous perspective with regard to Steve and his son; this was built on therapeutic gains regarding his accountability as a sibling offender, and the subsequent development of empathy for his brother.

Steve was invited to create an internal image of his son and to conduct an imaginary dialogue with him in the office. It was suggested that he use Anthony as a consultant to aid in improving his parenting skills. Speaking as Anthony in the guided fantasy, Steve suggested that he could spend more time with his son and play with him more. He also recognized that Anthony was totally dependent on him for his well-being, and he felt a deep connection with this profound responsibility for his young son's welfare. This awareness facilitated the beginning of an empathic connection between Steve and Anthony. Steve made steady, regular progress after that point, and eventually began supervised visits with his son.

Adult survivors who assume responsibility for their own abuse suffer both short- and long-term emotional consequences. Survivors of sexual abuse often report difficulties in developing and sustaining intimate relationships (Briere, 1992; Courtois, 1989; Finkelhor et al., 1989). Indeed, survivors frequently find it difficult to trust important individuals in their lives. Therefore one of the most powerful effects of successful treatment is the realization that close human relationships are not inevitably dangerous (Briere, 1992). Adults abused as children also regularly have trouble negotiating boundaries, sexual issues, and interdependency in relationships. The developing alliance between the clinician and the client can be especially helpful in revealing specific issues related to these concerns.

For instance, the therapeutic alliance sometimes evokes self-protective defenses. These may arise when the survivor is afraid of being hurt by the therapist in the same ways he or she has been hurt in the past. The client's fear may be especially prominent during moments when he or she dares to reveal aspects of the self to others. This "dread to repeat" (Stolorow, Brandchaft, and Atwood 1987) is usually triggered by an interpersonal event in the therapy. It may seem insignificant to the therapist, but the meaning ascribed to the event by the client endows it with significance.

Therapy with adult survivors also focuses frequently on ways to counter thinking errors. In the following example, the therapist facilitates the client's process of challenging offender-based distortions. The client is encouraged to differentiate between, and give voice to, disowned aspects of self. The full expression in therapy, through either fantasy or action, of otherwise discredited behavior often dissolves anachronistic feelings and beliefs about oneself. This approach allows for empowering dialogue and contact between internal aspects of self, rather than between therapist and client. For some clients, internal imagery is less threatening and can be equally effective in confronting an internal critic or other offender-based introject. The therapist also can assume a more active role through repeated, supportive rejection of a client's self-critical thoughts, therapeutically reframing abuse-related symptoms as logical responses to trauma, and introducing the client to books or tapes that affirm survivors' struggles and stress the offender's responsibility for the abuse.

The psychotherapist is a continuous indirect influence through his attitude and position toward each client. A focus on present interactions in treatment is essential for identifying and processing abuse-related distortions. In the following extended example we illustrate several components of a multidimensional approach to therapy with an adult survivor of sibling incest and assault: the importance of setting clear boundaries, amplification of the client's attention to in-session behavior, processing a survivor's self-protective adaptations in the therapeutic relationship, and challenging cognitive distortions and frozen images of self in relation to siblings. This particular clinical example also highlights the importance of a supportive and validating family member in helping a survivor of sibling abuse to address trauma.

Cathie

Cathie, thirty-one years old, requested therapy for difficulties related to childhood abuse. These difficulties were beginning to surface in a long-distance intimate relationship. She and her boyfriend were fighting a great deal over everything, from what to do on the weekends they spent together to eating food off each other's plate at restaurants.

Cathie recognized a pattern of not standing up for herself in these disagreements. She characterized her relationships with men as "I can't live with them or without them." Her major struggle was that she often went along with her boyfriend's direction, even though she objected inwardly. Her boyfriend's authoritative style made it more difficult for her to assert herself. According to Cathie, he believed that he was right most of the time and that he knew what was best for them as a couple.

The therapist asked whether her boyfriend would participate in conjoint therapy; he explained the benefits to them as a couple and the risks of leaving him out. Cathie agreed. She planned to eventually bring him in, but first she wanted to examine her role in their struggles as it related to her abuse. Besides, because her boyfriend currently viewed therapy as a waste of time, it might take some time to get him involved.

Family History

In the first few meetings, Cathie dutifully recounted her childhood history. One of the therapist's early tasks was making sure she did not disclose more information than she was able to process in each session. Cathie was raised in a family of some prominence. Her father was a respected physician, and her mother was an attractive, socially conscious volunteer for those less fortunate. Cathie was born twelve years after her only brother, Scott. Although she had fond memories of her older brother caring for her as a small child, she also spent very little time with him. By the time she turned six, he had already left home for college.

Shortly after Scott's departure, Cathie's parents adopted two children. One day, as Cathie remembers it, two siblings, Michael and Monica, began living with her family. Cathie had no time to accommodate to the loss of her exclusive relationship with her brother, nor to make the transition from being a youngest sibling to an only child, and then back to being the youngest with two strangers four and five years older than herself.

Cathie tried her best to adapt to her new situation, but it was difficult from the start. She felt abandoned by her brother and her parents, who now had three children to care for. To make matters worse, she was unable to form a strong alliance with either of her new siblings. Cathie had had limited contact with other children until her adopted siblings arrived; her world had consisted largely of adults. She was eager to please her new brother and sister, identifying with her parents' wish that they care for those less fortunate than themselves and become one happy family.

In this case, the result was devastating. From ages seven to eleven, Cathie was sadistically abused by Michael and Monica. Her parents, blinded by their image of the picture-perfect family, offered no protection. In the interest of family harmony, and because of her desperate need for acceptance, Cathie attempted to trust her new siblings but was victimized repeatedly.

Early stages of therapy focused on providing Cathie with reliable and context-appropriate support, and building safety and trust. For example, her anger at her mother's nonprotective stance was framed as courageous, given Cathie's experience that support from her mother was not forthcoming whenever she was vulnerable. The therapist also began inviting her to pay closer attention to the way she desensitized herself to feelings that arose during the therapy hour or between sessions, but without any requirement to change or to disclose details of her trauma. Generally an important therapeutic intervention with abused clients is to help them gain greater awareness and control of the methods used to desensitize themselves. Cathie was empowered by the process of beginning to identify and regulate her internal experience in therapy. She was also keeping a journal and practicing internal self-soothing techniques introduced in therapy during this time (e.g., mental imagery, creating a safe place, and positive self-talk).

Paying Attention to Trauma-Related Adaptations

During one session, while Cathie was telling how her mother did not provide much nurturing but how her adoptive sister (who also had abused her) did, she became quiet. The therapist wondered aloud what was going on, but Cathie appeared to be confused by the question. Then he noticed that she was repeatedly looking up and to the right toward a wall hanging in the office, and asked her about this. She replied that she just enjoyed looking at the decoration, and denied that there was any significance to her behavior. The therapist suggested that she continue to look toward the wall and focus in on her present experience of looking away. Suddenly she acknowledged that she was disappearing in the room, and realized that the distraction was a way to ground herself.

This awareness in therapy had genuine value for Cathie. She recognized the meaning of her behavior in treatment, and of the way she typically regulated painful feelings by keeping busy and distracting herself whenever possible. She stated, "If I am looking at you, it's harder for me to talk about this. It's like . . . as you become more real to me, I have to block you out; otherwise it's not safe." The therapist asked if she could say more about not feeling safe. Cathie replied, "It sounds kind of silly, but my fear is that you could hurt me in some way." Cathie revealed that it actually felt more as if she could not trust herself to express strong feelings in therapy. She began to cry. She then glanced reflexively at her wrists and made a reference to wanting to hurt herself in the past (she had made several suicide attempts as a young adult). The therapist inquired about present suicidal feelings and/or self-destructive impulses and was able to determine that Cathie was not in any current danger of harming herself. They devoted the remainder of the hour to making sense of connections between her abuse and her present feelings. The therapist, aware of her increased vulnerability in the session, normalized her reactions and supported her growing strength.

Examining Offender-Based Distortions

Cathie began to talk more specifically about her childhood victimization after an experience with her boyfriend that triggered memories of her abuse. She arrived for her session agitated; she had just spent the weekend with him. After completing a previously rehearsed grounding exercise, she seemed ready to continue. While being intimate with her boyfriend, she had had a troubling experience. When they were in bed, he asked Cathie to touch him. Cathie became very anxious. The therapist asked, "What happened next?" She reported that she visualized her adopted brother making her touch his penis. The next thing she remembered was the sight of her boyfriend's penis after making love. It looked small—about the same size as her offender's, she speculated. This was all she could recall about the sexual experience over the weekend.

Cathie was beginning to look and feel uncomfortable. The therapist acknowledged her discomfort and suggested that she pay attention to familiar ways in which she could ground herself in the present. She was gently guided to orient herself to familiar surroundings in the office. She sat with her feet planted on the floor, took a few deep breaths, and repeated positive, soothing self-talk. In a supportive climate, with the therapist remaining present and available, Cathie signaled her readiness to continue.

The therapist wondered what more she wanted to say about her experience over the weekend. Cathie wanted to talk about the abuse experiences triggered by the weekend events. She described how her adopted siblings sometimes tickled her so furiously that she could not breathe. "Did you ever feel afraid that you might die?" the therapist asked. Cathie sobbed quietly and nodded yes. She said that her siblings would take her down into a crawlspace under the house, tie her up, and blindfold her. They then placed various objects in her hands and made her guess what they were. Once Michael had placed one of her hands in hot water, and forced the other around his penis. Another time they forced Cathie to suck her sister's nipples while her brother made humiliating comments. Cathie looked anxious and began to breathe more rapidly. The therapist intervened and led Cathie through a grounding exercise. He asked if she wanted to continue processing these events now. Cathie again nodded yes. She was reminded that she was free to end their current discussion or take a break whenever she wanted.

Cathie related most of her memories as if the abuse were somehow her fault. She stated, "I don't remember liking it, but I must have." The therapist suggested that Cathie say more about the part of her that "must have liked it." She paused and asked, "How would that help?" She was embarrassed by the statement. The therapist told her that he knew that it was an unusual thing to ask, but thought she might feel differently after a full hearing from both sides of her internal conflict. Cathie began hesitantly, "I have mixed feelings about all of this. Maybe I'm making too much of a few incidents. After all, I never told them to stop when they did all these mean things to me." The therapist suggested that she switch and speak about the part that did not like being hurt by them. Cathie continued, "Well, the things they did to me did hurt. Besides, I couldn't tell them to stop . . . I was just a kid, and I wanted them to like me so much . . . and I still have trouble with saying no to this day, but that doesn't mean I like the things to happen that I can't say no to." The therapist directed her to respond from the other side. She replied, "You are just playing the victim, wanting people to feel sorry for you. I wish you would just grow up and get over it already." He motioned for her to continue the dialogue.

Cathie looked uneasy. She was reoriented to her present surroundings in the office, and then was asked to pay attention to what she had just said. She stated that this was what she had heard all of her life—from her parents, her boyfriends, everyone. The lack of support from others made it difficult to dismiss these thoughts and feelings. Her abusers' sadistic nature added to her confusion: Cathie recalled that her siblings did not look angry while they did cruel things to her. The therapist suggested that she might want to address each of them in fantasy at some point in treatment. Now, however, could she focus on the part that "wished she would get over it," and respond? She took a deep breath and replied, "I want to get over it, too. But I know now that in order to do that I have to face what happened, not pretend it was OK or my fault."

Cathie paused and then cried, "I wasn't too small!" "What do you mean?" asked the therapist. She continued, "Michael used to tease me by saying that I was too small for him to, you know . . . Then he would regularly attempt intercourse to see if I was big enough for him to enter me. For years, I thought there was something wrong with me. Now, I realize, believing that only caused me to feel responsible for the abuse. I grew up believing that he kept hurting me because I was too small, not because he was sick. For the first time ever, I'm starting to believe that I'm fine the way I am."

Cathie was empowered by her growing capacity to tolerate feelings associated with her abuse. She had also challenged a powerful negative cognition related to her victimization. She could now begin the process of discriminating between offender-based internalizations and her current perceptions of herself.

Processing Boundary Violations

During a therapy meeting several months later, Cathie abruptly ended her session with several minutes to spare. She was out the door before the therapist realized what had happened and was able to intervene. The following week he mentioned her premature exit and wondered if she had any thoughts or feelings about it. Cathie revealed that she kept an eye on the clock and worried about going over her allotted time. This led to a productive discussion about her fear of being rejected as a child and her subsequent tendency to take care of others. When asked about specifics, she cited multiple examples of meeting her adopted sister's need for a companion, and her adopted brother's need for a confidante, to gain their acceptance and approval. The therapist acknowledged Cathie's growing self-support, as well as her ability to rely appropriately on him for support in the therapy hour.

After she received assurance that the therapist indeed was responsible for monitoring their in-session time together, Cathie spontaneously began to discuss her previous therapy. She revealed that her previous therapist had borrowed books from her and never returned them. Cathie had made one request for the books six months before entering her current treatment, but had not received a response. She wanted the books returned, but was confused. She was angry at her previous therapist but also thought that perhaps she was making a big deal out of nothing. She also considered replacing the books herself many times, but it was now two years later and she had not taken any action. Cathie was ashamed about this, and expressed relief at being able to speak about it with someone else, particularly another therapist.

Further discussion revealed that Cathie knew intimate details of her previous therapist's private life, including specifics regarding a troubled relationship. Apparently her previous therapist had gradually spent more and more of Cathie's therapy focused on her own personal issues. Cathie recognized the continuation of an interpersonal pattern set in childhood: she had been groomed to take emotional care of both of her adopted siblings. Her previous therapist assumed a self-serving stance whereby Cathie was able to reenact her caretaking role. She felt some comfort and familiarity in relating in this way, but also felt that she was being interpersonally exploited once again. This discussion was followed by a great deal of active listening and reality checking from a position of therapeutic neutrality about a clinician's responsibility for setting appropriate boundaries in therapy. Cathie seemed relieved when her experience and intuitions were validated, and created a plan for obtaining her books.

Addressing Frozen Sibling Images

At another point in treatment, a change in Cathie's schedule necessitated a change in her appointment time. She went from an early morning appointment, when she arrived and left without ever seeing anyone else in the office, to a busy afternoon time scheduled between other patients. This change had unexpected consequences for Cathie's therapy. During one session she seemed to have trouble getting started and began to speak about her dislike for the new appointment time. When encouraged to elaborate on her complaint, she mentioned that she did not like sitting in the waiting room and watching someone else leave shortly before her scheduled time. The therapist asked, "What about that bothers you?" Cathie recalled that she wanted all of her parents' attention as a child and could not tolerate sharing them with her siblings. She stated that she did not like sharing the therapist either; maybe this was related. When asked for some examples, she remembered that she had to compete with her adopted siblings for clothing, spending money, privacy, and her mother's attention. A theme of feeling neglected was emerging.

Later in therapy, the theme surfaced again. Cathie canceled her appointment because her boyfriend was coming to town, but the therapist could not reschedule with her during that week. When she arrived the following week, she was angry. She struggled to stay in contact with her feelings while stating how unfair it was that she could not obtain another appointment time, and how misunderstood she felt. The therapist listened and acknowledged her feelings.

After several minutes, he made an observation in an effort to communicate that he understood the significance of this issue. He suggested that she lived in fear of being treated unfairly, and not having her needs met. The failure to reschedule her therapy appointment symbolized yet another disappointment, which left her feeling dismissed and discounted. Cathie looked surprised by the therapist's forthrightness, but then responded even more directly. She acknowledged feeling discounted, and stated again that she wanted the therapist all for herself.

Cathie also said that her boyfriend constantly characterized all therapists as greedy, selfish people who just took advantage of others' weaknesses. It was difficult for her to know how she felt about therapy when she was with her boyfriend. Did she trust him or her own perceptions and experience? The therapist asked, "How is it to be saying these things to me?" Cathie acknowledged her fear of the strong dependent feelings that surfaced regularly in therapy. The previous week, for example, she had felt a strong need to pull back and thus canceled her regular appointment. Then, after canceling, she worried about disappointing the therapist and called back to reschedule.

Cathie was struggling to reconcile frozen images of her adopted brother, Michael, and her nonabusive biological sibling, Scott. The dichotomized images of a "bad" and a "good" brother were frequently reactivated in her close relationships with men. When she felt close to her boyfriend, she projected onto him more of the loving and protective qualities she associated with Scott; then, predictably, she perceived therapy as unsafe. Cathie, however, was also developing a reliable and trusting relationship with her therapist, which emphasized and reinforced the value of her own perceptions. The therapist acknowledged Cathie's courage in the face of these challenges. He relayed a growing confidence in her judgment and decision-making ability, and supported her willingness to consider another's point of view as she established her opinions on various issues.

The therapist asked, "Were there other times when you've had similar feelings?" With that, Cathie began to speak more about her brother, Scott. She cried for a long time while repeating how much she missed him. She then realized that none of her boyfriends since high school had felt safe to her, even when times were good. She chose men who had in common the quality of being both kind and abusive. She described Scott as the only man ever to support, compliment, and play with her without judgment or abuse. She wondered out loud if she would have been victimized as a child if Scott had been there to protect her.

The therapist suggested that Cathie create an image of Scott now as someone who would protect her. She relaxed considerably with the soothing mental image and was grateful for the opportunity to contact her overlooked feelings toward her brother. Later that evening, Cathie phoned her brother and spoke with him for the first time in eight years. She told him about her victimization as a child, and finally received support and acknowledgment from a member of her own family. She acknowledged her inability to have contact with him previously, and recognized that she blamed him for abandoning her when he left home. Cathie's anger and sense of betrayal had prevented her from maintaining a relationship with him all this time.

More regular contact with Scott and numerous experiences with her therapist enabled Cathie to internalize a more accurate view of both men in terms of their human limits as well as their strengths. Gradually she began to update the idealized frozen image of her brother Scott to include a wider range of positive and negative qualities. Simultaneously she also was more willing to assert her needs with her boyfriend and became more accepting of him in general.

FAMILY-OF-ORIGIN SESSIONS

Indications and contraindications for conducting family-of-origin meetings with adult survivors of incest have been addressed elsewhere (Trepper and Barrett, 1989). Such meetings with sibling offenders in attendance are distinctive and often complex. They should be held only if and when it is in the best interest of the survivor. Further, the therapist should be certain that an offender is capable of accepting full responsibility for the abuse and has apologized.

The danger of retraumatization is always present for victims when meeting with offenders. Extra caution may be appropriate in light of familial and societal tendencies to minimize or deny the harmful effects of sibling abuse. Some professionals, otherwise trained to treat adult survivors, have characterized sibling incest or assault as "less harmful than other kinds of abuse," "normal sexual exploration that maybe went a little too far," or "inevitable, given the dynamics in the family." Such attitudes convey an unspoken collusion with the sibling offender, and may contribute to the victim's potential retraumatization.

Structuring an apology session may be one purpose for a family-of-origin meeting. Salter (1995) has written extensively on the challenges of holding apology sessions with offenders and adult survivors. To be effective, the apology must be experienced by the victim as direct, heartfelt, and without excuses. Some offenders appear incapable of this kind of apology; in such cases, family apology meetings probably are not in the survivor's best interest. In addition to an apology, reparations—as determined by the survivor—sometimes can be an important step in recovery and empowerment.

Our clinical experience suggests that family-of-origin treatment without the offender present may benefit some adult survivors of sibling abuse. First, sibling incest and assault often go undetected by family members for years. Unlike some cases of parent-child incest or assault, it does not require collusion by the nonoffending parent. As stated earlier, parents may be unable to stop an offender determined to exploit his or her sibling. Further, many adult survivors were abused at a time when child abuse was not well recognized or acknowledged. As a result, few child victims received protection, intervention, or treatment at the time of the abuse. Adulthood therefore may be the time when former child victims first experience symptoms and when they need and seek psychological treatment (American Psychological Association, 1996).

Adult sibling abuse survivors, however, still face dismissal and disbelief from families and some professionals. Society's ambiguous response to sibling incest and assault contributes to survivors' remaining silent for years after the occurrence. Some survivors never reveal the abuse to original family members; this often interferes seriously with their ability to cope with trauma-related symptoms, and also may deprive them of potential sources of support or acknowledgment in their original family. Nonoffending siblings, in particular, can sometimes be important sources of comfort to survivors who feel disconnected from family members.

Sibling abuse may be part of a long transgenerational pattern. A family-of-origin meeting can provide the forum for discussing other secrets in the family's history, thus supplying context and under-standing for the survivor. In each case, survivors must determine the type of relationship with family members they want and can reason-ably expect before deciding whether to go forward with the meet-ing. An adult survivor must retain primary responsibility for the decision to hold a family-of-origin session, in conjunction with the therapist's assessment of the risks and the client's readiness. The clinician organizing the meeting should strive to create conditions such that the experience is empowering for the survivor.

Family-of-origin meetings are anxiety-provoking for survivors (for a multitude of reasons), and most choose not to hold them. Clinicians, however, by suggesting the meetings as an option, can increase the likelihood that such sessions are conducted when indicated and are productive. In doing so, they must clearly understand and explain the benefits. Framo (1993) mentions several ways in which clinicians can provide a constructive framework for the meetings. Perhaps the most crucial step is adequately preparing clients beforehand through individ-ual meetings focused on family-of-origin concerns. The strategy for the session is coconstructed with the therapist, but ultimate responsibil-ity for the agenda must rest with the client. The survivor should enter the meeting with a plan created after hours of preparation and based on confidence in the therapeutic alliance.

The goal is to minimize surprise as much as possible. The clini-cian should approach the meetings as a consultation with other fami-ly members about the client, and as an opportunity for the client to move toward some goals related to the family-of-origin, rather than viewing it as family therapy per se. An important aspect of prepara-tion is thoroughly evaluating the survivor's relationship with family-of-origin members and establishing sources of strength, support, and acknowledgment. Subsystem meetings with family members can often be useful as preparation for a family meeting, or as a valuable part of the recovery process in themselves. Acknowledgment of the survivor's perspective on the abuse within the family can be ex-tremely healing. The therapist also serves an important role in con-firming the client's reality about his or her family-of-origin.

Betty

Betty, thirty-eight years old and divorced, entered individual treatment for depression. In response to direct questioning, she disclosed that both she and her younger sister had been sexually abused as children by an older brother. Her brother and her father had died together twelve years earlier in an automobile accident. Although she had previously sought treatment, Betty kept the incest secret from both her family and her former therapist. She and her mother were fused intensely and often conflicted about family matters, but Betty was most troubled by her relationship with her sister, Michelle. They saw each other at family gatherings and holidays, but their contact was superficial and often was marked by competition and conflict. For example, conversations about work often contained veiled references to who was earning more money or traveling to more exotic places. Discussion of newsworthy events quickly became a struggle over who was more knowledgeable and held the "right" opinion on an issue. They did not speak to each other for long periods. Betty longed for a closer relationship. The therapist mentioned the possibility of a meeting with her remaining family-of-origin members at some point in the future, if Betty should be interested, and proceeded to address her current complaints.

Early Phases of Treatment

Initially treatment focused on the effects of the incest on Betty's functioning as an adult. She suffered from frequent bouts of depression, which had resisted several trials of medication. She also experienced trouble in her relationships with men, generally choosing partners who victimized and exploited her. By identifying abuse-related triggers (e.g., losing a sense of her needs and desires, rapidly sexualizing her attraction to a man) and their meaning in current relationships, Betty began to make sense of her depression. She seemed to benefit from speaking about the incest for the first time and processing some of her perceptions and feelings about the trauma.

As her depression subsided, Betty spent more time in treatment focusing on her current relationships with men. She also began to make more functional choices about how and when to become intimate with partners. She mourned the end of her marriage and struggled to make sense of mistreatment by her former spouse.

Betty initially felt responsible for the emotional abuse she had experienced in the marriage. A central therapeutic issue was the acceptance of responsibility only for her role in interactions with her former spouse, and not for his abusive behavior. This involved examining some of her long-standing beliefs about responsibility for the sibling incest. Her brother had told her that he could not stop himself from touching her because he "loved her too much." Because her body sometimes responded to the touching as pleasurable, Betty felt implicated as a coconspirator in the abuse and never told her parents. As an adult, she developed the belief that men could not control their advances toward her, and understood them as indicators of a man's strong, loving feelings. She became sexually involved with men almost as soon as she met them.

Processing Trauma-Related Effects
in the Therapy Relationship

Because of the immediate sexual involvement, Betty found it difficult to trust her perceptions of herself and the men she dated. It was probably inevitable that similar trust issues eventually extended to the therapeutic relationship.

During one meeting, Betty courageously struggled to understand feelings connected to being disappointed once again by a man she had thought she could trust. She was tired of feeling exploited, and also was beginning to recognize her role in the revictimizations. In the final moments of the session, she expressed her gratitude for the therapist's support and confidence in her ability to deal with her feelings. As she got up to leave, she moved toward him.

> **Betty:** Can I have a hug?
> **Therapist** (pausing for a moment)**:** You've really worked hard today and this has been a very productive meeting.
> **Betty:** Yes, thank you.
> **Therapist:** And a hug does feel like it might be a good way to acknowledge the hard work you've accomplished here. But I wonder if it might be too helpful.

Betty: I don't understand. Are you saying that you don't want to hug me?

Therapist: No, just that sometimes when you're in pain or working really hard in here, and you want me to hug you, that might be fine. But as your therapist, I need you to be able to describe your feelings as clearly as possible so that I can really understand what you are saying. And a hug would probably feel good, but it might also make your feelings disappear before we really have a chance to know them.

Betty (laughing nervously)**:** This is a first! You are the first guy who has ever wanted to talk to me like this, instead of touch me.

Therapist (smiling)**:** I think that not doing some of the things that friends do to comfort each other will be hard sometimes, but it is a pain we try to struggle through together in order to help you. And I know that this might feel like I'm withholding something. You aren't wrong to want a hug, and I feel bad about that part, but this is the best way I know to stay with the feelings. I think that you might benefit even more from therapy if we can continue to work toward understanding and describing your feelings, as we have today.

Finally, the therapist said that he understood the difficulty in saying this without time to discuss it further, and suggested that they continue talking about it at their next session. Later that day, he thought long and hard about the intervention. Intuitively, he felt right about it, but he worried that Betty might experience his decision not to hug her as a rejection.

Betty initiated a discussion about the hug midway through the next week's meeting. She said she had thought a lot during the week about the previous session, and at first was surprised and hurt by the therapist's decision not to hug her. But in the past twenty-four hours, she had come to understand it in light of her recent work in therapy. She stated tearfully that he was the first man she felt she could trust because he was paying attention to her needs and not his own. She confided that part of her still wanted to know if there was something wrong with her asking for the hug; the therapist assured her there was not. Mostly she wanted the therapist to know how grateful she was for his help.

Present-focused experiences in therapy, like this one, were instrumental in supporting change in Betty's intimate behavior with men. Her earlier template for intimate relations, shaped by the sibling incest, no longer served her. She was beginning to associate positive feelings with setting clearer boundaries around her contact, intimate and otherwise, with men.

Family-of-Origin Meetings

Later Betty raised the possibility of a meeting with family members. She wanted to begin with several conjoint sessions with her mother. After these had gone reasonably well, she expressed interest in preparing for a series of family-of-origin meetings with her mother and her sister, Michelle. After approximately ten preparatory meetings, the first of three family-of-origin sessions was held. The family sessions, in combination with individual therapy, helped Betty to place her abuse in its proper context. She began to view her abuse less as an indelible wound, and more as an interpersonal event with intrapsychic consequences.

By sharing the details of her abuse with her surviving family members, Betty was able to release the secret, along with associated feelings of guilt, shame, anger, and depression. There was particular potency in Betty's connection with her sister as someone who also had been molested by their brother. By revealing various perceptions of events related to their abuse, they provided missing information and confirmed each other's reality about key experiences. In one meeting, the siblings held a good-bye ritual to help them repair and heal unfinished mourning connected with the deaths of their brother and father.

In the following family meetings, Michelle observed how she resented Betty's overclose relationship to their mother. She felt that since the men in the family had died, Betty had assumed the role of surrogate parent. Rigid transgenerational roles developed in childhood often contribute to sibling friction; the mother, as a single parent, had relied on Betty for support, much as she had assumed a parentified role in her own original family. Listening to their mother share her family history, Betty and Michelle could understand the larger influences on their childhood relationship, and felt free to explore their own sibling connection unencumbered by historical patterns.

The sisters discovered that both were angry at their mother for not doing more to protect them from the abuse, and for contributing to a family climate that often placed Betty and Michelle at odds with each other. Periodic meetings were held so that the sisters could learn to separate their feelings toward each other from their loyalty to their parents, to resolve some of their angry feelings toward their mother, and to decrease the rigidity of the sibling roles held in their family since childhood. Private discussions of their respective abuse experiences outside therapy also helped to delineate and cement their connection.

KEY POINTS

- Our treatment of adult abuse survivors is based on a phenomenological approach that emphasizes and understands the survivor's subjective experience in the context of interactions between the survivor and the therapist.
- Paradoxically, change and growth are supported by focusing on what is actually and presently happening in therapy between the client and the therapist.
- Siblings may believe more readily that they were active participants in their abuse, and could have stopped it, because no generational boundary was violated. This may be a particularly salient concern for victims when an adopted or stepsibling offender committed the abuse.
- Nonabusive family-of-origin members who are available and willing to serve a supportive role can help to stabilize, facilitate, and expedite a survivor's healing process.
- Family intergenerational patterns of abuse are sometimes overlooked through a failure to screen for sibling abuse, even with clients for whom other abusive relationships have been disclosed.

Afterword

We conceived this book as an effort to increase awareness and understanding of sibling abuse and its long-lasting effects on victims and survivors, and to provide some guidelines for individual and family intervention with children and adults. Society's awareness of sibling incest and assault, and its response, have lagged behind other child abuse issues and concerns. This has practical consequences for prevention and treatment. In comparison with parent-child abuse, intersibling abuse is generally underreported by parents, teachers, mental health professionals, and the community. Child protective services and the legal system are reluctant to accept and respond to sibling abuse reports that are filed. It is generally believed that sibling incest and assault are less serious child welfare concerns than parent-child abuse and neglect. Protective or judicial protocols for responding to cases of sibling abuse are sparse throughout the country, and few treatment programs or private practitioners in the community have specialized knowledge and understanding of problems unique to sibling incest and assault.

In our book, we outlined an eclectic, multidimensional approach for conducting therapy with children, families, and adults abused by their brothers or sisters. We included clinical examples to illustrate fundamentals of treating sibling incest and assault victims and their families. Sometimes therapy does not proceed as planned, for many reasons, and often these cases teach us a great deal about how to provide improved treatment to others. Treatment for sibling incest and assault requires multidisciplinary cooperation and, usually, the coordination of services among several provider systems. Like child abuse treatment in general, it is complex and challenging work that requires ongoing specialized training and ability. The ultimate goal of a book like this, however, is to stimulate greater prevention efforts so that the various forms of family abuse, including intersibling incest and assault, no longer occur.

1

APPENDIXES

Appendix A

About the Research Project

This book began as a research project that aimed to describe the experience of intersibling incest or assault from the adult survivor's perspective. The original research included an in-depth interview study of seventy-three adult survivors of sibling incest and assault, which was the source of the family configurations described in the book. Interviews lasted approximately one and a half to two hours. The data include direct transcribed comments as well as information derived from the semistructured interviews with these seventy-three participants.

Our interviewees are not a random sample of sibling abuse victims or survivors; the participants are mostly white and middle class. This is a qualitative glimpse at the experiences of victims and survivors of sibling incest and assault, and of their families.

We were interested in the following questions: What family characteristics contribute to the development of abusive sibling relationships in childhood? How do various family configurations (e.g., stepfamily, single-parent, peripheral parent) affect the relationship between siblings in abusive dyads? How do sibling incest and assault in childhood affect adult survivors' relationships with their siblings?

We obtained our information from adults, who were a more convenient and more accessible group of participants than children. Interviewing children in their families might not have yielded complete information or provided us with a view of long-term effects of abuse. Nor would interviews with parents have been likely to provide complete information because research on other types of abuse, such as incest, tells us that children have difficulty in reporting their victimization while they live in the abusive family situation. With greater autonomy and distance from the family-of-origin, survivors might be better able to reflect on their experiences. Some of our study participants might not have been able to tell their abuse stories without the objectivity provided by years of distance from the events. Our research protocol, however, is also limited by its retrospective design. Survivors may not have recalled details of their childhood abuse experiences exactly as they occurred (Alexander, 1992; Beutler and Hill, 1992). Furthermore, our respondents were self-selected, and most had undergone some psychotherapy treatment. Therefore they may not be representative of the sibling abuse survivor population.

We accepted volunteers from several sources. First, we placed advertisements in local professional newsletters, such as those of the San Diego Psychological Association and the local chapter of the California Association of Marriage and Family Therapists, requesting that members of the professional community refer persons known to them to our study. Also, we sent personal announcements of our research project and a request for participants to approximately 200 colleagues in the San Diego mental health community. We also contacted colleagues belonging to local and state professional child abuse organizations (the San Diego Community Child Abuse Coordinating Council, the California Professional Society on the Abuse of Children), who agreed to assist us in our recruitment. In addition, we received permission to recruit individuals referred to the San Diego Department of Social Services (Child Protective Services) as voluntary participants in the study. Finally, the Marriage and Family Counseling Department at San Diego State University agreed to announce our study to their community and to help us obtain participants.

CHARACTERISTICS OF THE PARTICIPANTS

Figure A.1 depicts some general characteristics of the seventy-three participants in our study. Forty-nine (67 percent) female and twenty-four (33 percent) male adult survivors of sibling incest and assault agreed to participate. Participation was voluntary; each individual provided written informed consent. Participants' ages ranged from eighteen to fifty-four years, with a mean of thirty-eight for both men and women. Fifty-six participants (77 percent) identified themselves as Caucasian, ten participants (13 percent) as African American, and seven (10 percent) as Latino.

FREQUENCY OF SIBLING INCEST AND ASSAULT, BY CATEGORY OF ABUSE

Twenty-nine individuals (39 percent) were adult survivors of sibling incest; twenty-six (36 percent) identified themselves as survivors of sibling assault. In addition, eighteen men and women (25 percent) reported themselves as survivors of combined sibling incest and assault. We also determined initial frequencies of sibling incest and assault by gender of offender and victim; this information is presented in Figure A.2.

FIGURE A.1. Characteristics of Participants (*n* = 73)

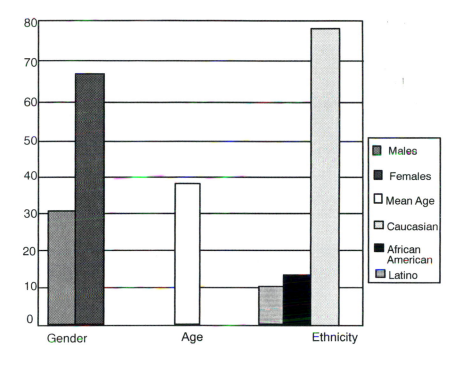

Incest

Women sexually abused by their brothers accounted for eighteen of the twenty-nine adult survivors of sibling incest (63 percent) in our study, the largest number of respondents in any one category. Adult survivors of brother-brother incest were the next largest group (20 percent) with six men in this category. Sister-brother incest survivors made up the third largest group with three adults (10 percent), and only two women in our study (7 percent) self-identified as survivors of sister-sister incest.

Assault

The greatest number of respondents in this category were survivors of brother-brother assault. Twelve men (45 percent) reported a history of physical assault by a brother. Eight women (30 percent) self-identified as

FIGURE A.2. Frequency of Sibling Incest and Assault, by Category of Abuse (*n* = 73)

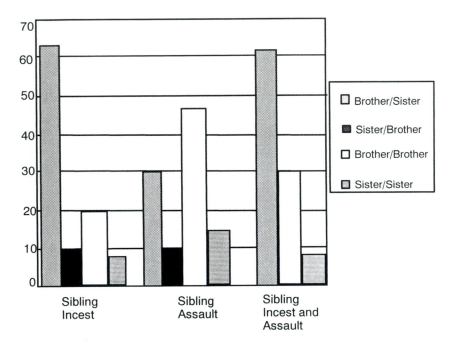

adult survivors of brother-sister assault. The next largest category consisted of four women (15 percent) who self-identified as survivors of sister-sister assault, and finally we interviewed two men (10 percent) who reported a history of sister-brother assault.

Incest and Assault

The second largest number of respondents in any category were eleven women (61 percent) self-identified as survivors of combined sibling incest and assault by a brother. Next most numerous in this category were five men (30 percent) who reported a history of brother-brother incest and assault, and two women (9 percent) self-identified as adult survivors of sister-sister incest and assault. There were no adult survivors of sister-brother incest and assault interviewed for our study. Consistent with the literature on family violence and gender (Graham-Bermann et al., 1994;

Russell, 1986; Saun-ders and Azar, 1989), survivors abused by females made up the smallest numbers in our study.

The number of participants in our study is relatively small, self-selected, and not necessarily representative of sibling abuse survivors in general. Nonetheless, the frequencies above are consistent with other reports for brother-sister incest (Laviola, 1992) and assault (Graham-Bermann et al., 1994), and for brother-brother assault (Goodwin and Roscoe, 1990).

Appendix B

Sibling Abuse Interview

SIBLING VICTIM

1. Do boys or girls have the most say in your family?
2. If you were to look at your family as being made up of two teams, who would be on each team?
3. When you have a fight with your brother or sister, who usually wins?
4. Pretend there is something that you and your sibling both really want, and only one of you can have it. Who gets it, and how?
5. How do you stand up for yourself when your sister or brother want you to do something that you do not want to do, or something that you know is wrong?
6. Does your sister or brother ask you to keep secrets about things that you know are wrong? (Elicit examples.)
7. What is something that your brother or sister has done to you that he or she would never do in front of your parents?
8. How often do you and your brother or sister argue with each other? How often does he or she yell at, insult, or criticize you?
9. Does your sibling ever embarrass or humiliate you in front of others?
10. Do you ever feel like a bad person because of something your brother or sister did or said to you?
11. How does your brother or sister react when you tell your parents something that she or he did not want you to reveal?
12. When your siblings get mad at you, what are you most afraid will happen? Are you ever afraid that your brother or sister might lose control when he or she is mad at you?

13. If your sibling is teasing you, or doing something to you that you don't like, will he/she stop when you ask him or her to?
14. Does your brother or sister ever say anything to you that makes you feel uncomfortable about your body?
15. Does your brother or sister ever touch you in a way that you don't like, or that makes you feel uncomfortable about your body?
16. When your brother or sister hits you or touches you in a way that's wrong, whose fault is it?
17. When your brother or sister hits you, are you able to go and tell your parents? Will they help you?
18. When a sibling shouts at you or teases you, do you believe that it is usually because you have done something to deserve it?

SIBLING OFFENDER

1. How do you know when people in your family are mad at you?
2. Brothers and sisters sometimes tease each other in mean ways. How do you and your siblings tease each other?
3. Who gets teased the most in your family? By whom?
4. What is the worst trouble you ever got into and what did your parents say and do?
5. How often do your parents punish you by hitting or spanking you? How do they do it?
6. Has anyone ever touched you in private ways without your permission?
7. Has your older brother or sister, or anyone else, ever touched you in a way that felt uncomfortable?
8. How are you able to get your sibling to do things that you want him or her to do?
9. What is one way that you let your brother or sister know that you don't like what he or she is doing?
10. When your brother or sister has something that you want, how do you get it?
11. How often do you hurt your sibling's feelings and make him or her cry or get angry? How do you do this?
12. How do you feel when your brother or sister feels sad?
13. Do you care a lot about what your sibling thinks of you?
14. When something positive happens to you, do you ever share it with your sister or brother?

15. How do you feel when your parents punish your sister or brother? Do you ever take the blame for something that your brother or sister did so that he or she doesn't get into trouble for it?

16. What is one of the worst days or experiences that you think your brother or sister has ever had? How do you imagine that she or he felt about it?

17. Do you ever think that you may have a problem with touching or hitting? And if you do, is it something that maybe you might like some help with?

18. I've heard that some of these things (from number 17) may be a problem for you, but I need to hear about it from you so I know the whole story. Tell me how it happens that you might end up:
    a. hitting/kicking your brother(s) or sister(s).
    b. hurting your brother or sister by _____ (fill in blank).
    c. touching your brother or sister in private places or in private ways, even if it might be by accident.

19. All brothers and sisters sometimes hurt the other one's feelings. What do you know about the ways that your brother or sister has said she or he was hurt by you? How do you feel about it?

20. Whose fault do you think it is?

21. How do you think your parents feel about it?

22. Has anyone inside or outside of your family ever bothered you a lot, made you feel scared, hit you, or hurt you in other ways? If so, who was it, and how did she or he hurt you? How did you feel about it?

23. What if something strange happened, and you were suddenly transformed into your brother or sister. Knowing how you treat him or her, how would you feel?

NONTARGETED SIBLINGS

1. If you and your brother or sister made the same mistake at home, would you each get punished in the same way?

2. Does it usually seem that the punishment "fits the crime" in your family?

3. When your brother or sister is punished, does it usually seem that he or she deserves it?

4. When you are punished, does it usually seem that you deserved it?

5. Sometimes kids are kind of relieved when a brother or sister gets punished after doing something wrong, because otherwise it

wouldn't feel fair. But sometimes it makes kids feel bad when their sisters or brothers are punished. Did you ever see your sister or brother being punished by Mom or Dad in a way that made you feel sad or afraid?

6. Did your brother or sister ever tell you about being punished or physically hurt by someone else in your family?

7. Have you ever seen a sister or brother being touched by another sister or brother (on her/his private parts) in a way that made you feel uncomfortable?

8. Have you ever seen your brother or sister being touched on his or her private parts by Mother or Father in a way that made you feel uncomfortable?

9. Have you ever wondered if this has happened, or has your brother or sister ever said things to you that made you think it maybe happened?

10. Has your brother or sister ever told you of this happening?

SIBLING SUBSYSTEM

1. What are some amusing, funny, interesting experiences that you have gone through together that are unique to your relationship as siblings?

2. What do you enjoy or like most about each other?

3. What are some of the good things and some of the bad things about growing up in your family?

4. When you do a good job at something—such as in school, work around the house, or things that your parents ask you to do—what does Dad usually do or say about that? What does Mom usually do or say?

5. When your Mom or Dad say that you will be rewarded for doing something, do you usually get the reward? Give some examples.

6. Pretend that this toy or game is one that both of you really want to play with right now. Decide who gets to play with it first.

7. Now, take your brother/sister's side in this conflict and pretend that you are speaking as him or her for a moment. How would you respond to what you have just heard?

8. How will you decide when it's time to allow your sister or brother to have a turn?

9. What does your mom do when you fight? What does your dad do?

10. Tell me about some times when you have been fighting, and describe how each of your parents have responded.

11. Who fights more, all of you or your parents? What do your parents do when they fight?

12. Sometimes kids get a little scared when their parents fight or argue. Are you ever afraid your parents will hurt each other, or you, when they fight? (Give examples of times when you felt afraid.)

13. During or after a fight between your parents, do your mom and dad ever still feel mad and take it out on you? If so, who do they get angry with the most?

14. What do the rest of you do when that happens?

15. Imagine that you and your brother or sister are fighting as characters in your favorite Saturday morning cartoon show (or movie). Which character would you each be? What would they be doing? How do you and your sibling resemble the characters in the cartoon, and what are the ways that you are different? How do the characters usually resolve their fights?

16. Could each of you describe your reaction to an important recent family event? You may choose the same or different events.

17. I'd like the rest of you to listen, and tell me afterward what new information you learned about your brother or sister.

18. How do you see yourselves as different and alike?

19. How do your parents tell you that you are different or alike? Do you agree with their perceptions of you?

20. Does anyone get blamed more than the others when something goes wrong at home? If so, how is that for the rest of you? How is it for the one who gets blamed more often?

21. Does one of you get to do things before the rest of your brothers or sisters? Is there someone among you who seems to be Mom or Dad's favorite?

22. Does your brother or sister treat you differently in front of his or her friends? Or when he or she is with friends and your parents aren't around?

23. How are you treated by your siblings when you are with your friends?

24. Do your siblings ever threaten to hurt you or tease you and try to humiliate you in front of your friends? Or when you are with your friends and your parents are not around?

25. In general, are your dad or mom around as much as you would like?

26. How much time do you and your brothers and sisters spend at home alone?

27. In every family, parents pay more attention to some problems than

to others. What are the family problems that your parents attend to most (shoes on the couch, messy rooms, etc.)?

28. What are some family problems that they don't pay that much attention to?

29. Do your parents discipline you and your siblings in the same ways? If not, how are they different with each of you?

30. When Mom and Dad say that you will be punished for something, do they always do what they say they will? Give some examples.

31. What are some rules or things your parents expect you to do or not do? Which of these rules or expectations seem fair and which seem unfair?

32. What sorts of things do each of you usually do with Dad during the week? On the weekend? How about with Mom? What do you each especially enjoy doing with Mom? With Dad?

33. What do you know about your brother or sister's abuse? How do you feel about it? Whose fault do you think it is? How do you think your parents feel about it?

34. Do your parents ever talk to any of you about each other, or about their fights?

35. Many families are sort of made up of teams; sometimes it's boys and Dad on one team with Mom and girls on the other; sometimes it's kids on one team with Mom and Dad on the other. Describe the different teams in your family (include extended-family members, if relevant).

36. We know every family sometimes has disagreements. When your family disagrees about something, whose side are you usually on? Who do your brothers and sisters usually side with?

37. In every family each person has a special role or place that he or she occupies (e.g., the smart one, funny one, the one who is usually in trouble, etc.). What roles do people have in your family?

38. Are there certain personal things, not related to safety (i.e., hurting self or others), that you share with each other and don't tell your parents? If so, what are some examples?

39. If you ever have children of your own, in what ways will you raise them like your parents have raised you? In what ways will you raise them differently?

40. If each of you could change anything about your family, what would you like to change? Why?

INDIVIDUAL PARENT INTERVIEWS

1. In every family, members have different roles, such as the smart one, the athletic one, the one who gets in trouble, etc. What roles did you and your siblings occupy in your family of origin?
2. What roles from your family of origin do you see yourselves and your children maintaining in your present family?
3. What are your relationships like with each of your siblings now?
4. At times in every family, a parent feels closer to one child than another. This may be related to the child's age, personality, physical appearance, or ability. Which of your children do you currently feel more connected to? Have you always felt closer to one child in particular?
5. Who do you children feel is the "favored" sibling in your family?
6. Which child believes that he or she is the "least favored"?
7. Have you ever had or do you have a current problem with alcohol or drug use? If yes, have you received or are you receiving treatment for this problem?
8. Were you abused as a child by a parent or sibling?
9. How do you and your spouse resolve conflict?
10. Does either of you ever physically strike the other when you're arguing?
11. Do you ever feel frightened of or intimidated by your partner?
12. Does your partner ever approach you in a sexual way in front of the children?
13. What specific sexual activities, and in what frequencies, are displayed in front of your children?
14. Are there sexually explicit materials in the house that might be accessible to your children?
15. Have you always been faithful to your current partner?
16. Do you have any doubts that your son's or daughter's abuse actually took place? If so, what are they?

PARENTAL SUBSYSTEM

1. Do each of you regularly confide in the other when struggling with something difficult, or when in need of love and support? If so, does your partner usually make himself/herself available to you when you need him or her? If not, do you think that she or he would be available if you needed support or some time together?

2. What are some of the ways that your partner lets you know that she or he is not available?
3. How much time do you spend together, apart from your children?
4. What activities do you participate in separately and as a couple?
5. How much time does each of you spend with your children?
6. How do you know when each of your children is angry, sad, afraid, happy, etc.?
7. How do you know what's going on in your children's lives? Who do you talk to or how else do you find out about things in your family?
8. Do your children ever have the advantage of watching the two of you argue, followed by compromise or agreement, and resolution of the conflict?
9. What does each of you do when you're angry with the other?
10. What do your children do when the two of you have an argument or fight?
11. How do they interact with each other both during and immediately following your disagreements or fights?
12. Are you each satisfied with how you resolve your anger with your partner? If not, what would you like to do differently? What would you like your partner to do differently?
13. How do you show affection for each other in front of your children?
14. What are some of the ways that you teach your children about sexuality? What are the differences in how you teach your boy and your girl children about sexuality?
15. Are there places in your house that are private and off-limits to the children?
16. Does your partner ever approach you in a sexual way in front of the children?
17. What specific sexual activities, and in what frequencies, are displayed in front of children?
18. Are there, or has there ever been, sexually explicit materials in the house that might be accessible to your children?
19. What parental sexual attitudes are directly expressed or implied in your family?
20. There are moments when siblings tease each other about their bodies, tickle each other, do things to embarrass one another, and maybe even touch each other sexually in an age-appropriate and playful way (e.g., playing doctor). Describe some of the times

you've witnessed or heard about such behavior involving your children, and your response to it.

21. What sexual activities are allowed between siblings in the family? At what point are sexual boundaries explicitly drawn?

22. Are you aware of your child's exposure to any recent external events that may have indirectly contributed to an environmental vulnerability for sibling abuse to occur? (e.g., invasive medical procedures, current events in the media, neighborhood, or school related to abuse, the abuse of another family member or friend, etc.)

23. Describe some of your children's "roughhousing" behavior.

24. How do you usually respond? Are you ever worried that one sibling will harm another?

25. How do you discipline your children? What are the differences between your styles of discipline?

26. Do either of you notice ways in which you might favor one child more than the others?

27. Which of your children generally "requires" more discipline? How is he or she disciplined differently than the others?

28. What are some ways in which you see your children as being similar to, or different from, each other?

29. How would you describe the relationships that each child has with his or her siblings? Explain.

30. What are some current sources of stress on you as parents? On the family as a whole?

31. What sources of outside support do you regularly rely on when family life becomes stressful?

32. Do you believe your child who says that he or she was physically or sexually abused by a brother or sister? If no, why not?

FAMILY INTERVIEW

1. Beginning with the adults in this family, I'd like each of you to go around and tell me two or three things you really like about each other.

2. What are two or three things you each really like about your family?

3. Every family has some problems from time to time. Your being here lets me know that now is one of those times for your family. I'd like to hear what each of you thinks the difficulties are that your family is struggling with now.

4. When one of you doesn't want your brothers, sisters, or parent to use something of yours, are your able to tell them?
5. Do they respect your wishes?
6. If something embarrassing happened to one of you that you didn't want your siblings or parents to share with people outside your family, would they disclose it anyway to family or friends?
7. If a family member started to say something that you wanted to keep private, and you asked him or her to stop, would he or she respect your wishes? And would your other family members also agree to not do this again?
8. Who would agree to maintain your privacy, and who would not?
9. If one of you is having private time in your room, the bathroom, or somewhere else in your house, does anyone ever intrude?
10. How do they intrude, and what happens when you ask them to stop?
11. What are some of the most important things for us to try to change in your family so that everyone feels better and is safe?

Appendix C

The Sibling Family-of-Origin Cartoon

This exercise can be used in family sessions to quickly gain a great deal of information and to generate conversation about a number of important properties of the family system. The cartoon is a crayon-and-paper task in which each family member is asked to divide his or her paper into four sections (see Figure C.1).

We tell family members that this is neither an art project nor a psycho-diagnostic exam. Families usually complete the drawing in about fifteen to twenty minutes. It is probably best to exclude children under age five, depending on their ability to complete and discuss the project. The cartoon is designed to explore relationships between family members, with an emphasis on sibling connections. Parents should complete the cartoon with regard to their sibling relationships in their original family. Children, of course, will draw relationships with current family members.

This cartoon provides parents with an opportunity to identify possible parallels between their own sibling relationships and their children's current sibling interactions. The cartoons usually reveal the presence of cross-generational coalitions and alignments, hierarchies or the lack thereof, parental favorites, scapegoats, and power differences in the family. Intergenerational family abuse patterns also frequently become more apparent.

FIGURE C.1. Sibling Family-of-Origin Cartoon

First Quadrant	**Second Quadrant**
Self and siblings in your family of origin	Self and best friend*
Third Quadrant	**Fourth Quadrant**
Self and parent you feel closest to	Other parent and sibling closest to him/her

*When using this exercise with adults, substitute "partner" for "best friend."

Appendix D

Semistructured Adult Sibling Abuse Survivor Questionnaire

We devised a twenty-nine-item semistructured questionnaire specifically for this study; it is designed to explore family relationships, relevant abuse, and the possible effects of abuse on the sibling relationship in the family of origin. The questionnaire also focuses on the possible effect of intrafamilial abuse on an individual's current relationship with a sibling or siblings. We used the questionnaire in the present study as a means of accessing information from participants and developing in-depth profiles of sibling relationships in abusive families. We did not use it to establish any form of empirical evidence. We content reviewed transcribed interviews for recurrent regularities in topics, themes, events, and dynamics.

INTERVIEW QUESTIONS

1. Describe your parents' relationship to one another as you were growing up.
2. Describe your parents' relationship to each of your siblings and yourself as you were growing up.
3. What was your birth position? What effect, if any, do you believe this and the positions of your sisters and brothers had on your relationships while you were growing up?
4. What is your earliest memory of each of your sisters and brothers?
5. If you have a younger sibling, can you remember how you felt when he or she was born?
6. What different parental messages did you and your brothers or sisters receive about what you could be or do when you grew up?
7. Please describe the closest or happiest you've ever felt with each of your siblings.

8. Describe the angriest or most distant you've ever felt with each of your brothers or sisters.

9. If you have brothers *and* sisters, how were your relationships with your brothers different than those with your sisters? Tell stories to illustrate.

10. What are some of the messages you received about your siblings regarding their conception, pregnancy, delivery, early months, etc.? Were there concerns related to temperament or personality? Use stories to illustrate whenever possible.

11. How did your parents influence your relationships with your siblings?

12. What were the messages your parents communicated to you and your siblings about your bodies, roughhousing, touching, or cuddling with parents and siblings?

13. What different parental messages about sexuality did you and your siblings receive while growing up? Were sexual roles clearly defined in your family?

14. When you began to go through puberty, what changes did you notice within your sibling relationships? How did your parents' behavior toward you change at that time—and what effect did this have on your relationship with your siblings?

15. Did you perceive your parents to use overly harsh discipline with you or any of your siblings as you were growing up? Choose one: (a) all the time; (b) frequently; (c) some of the time; (d) rarely. (Define harsh discipline: includes severe restrictions on behavior, humiliation and shaming, threatening, shouting, corporal punishment, and/or other forms of cruelty.)

16. Did you perceive any physical abuse occurring between a parent or other adult and child in your family as you were growing up? (Define physical abuse: causing nonaccidental physical harm or injury to a child. Includes hitting, shoving, striking with an object, kicking, etc.)

17. Did you perceive any sexual abuse occurring between a parent or other adult and child in your family as you were growing up? (Define sexual abuse: any sexual contact between an adult and a child including sexualized touch, masturbation, forcing child to touch an adult, viewing pornography, sexualized conversation, or intercourse.)
    If yes, then:

18. How did any physical or sexual abuse inflicted by a parent on you or your siblings affect your relationship with your brothers and sisters? How does it affect your relationship now?

19. Were any of your sisters or brothers protected from parental abuse? If so, how? By whom, and why? How did this affect the sibling relationships in your family?

20. Describe your relationship with your each of your siblings while you were growing up.

21. Did you feel picked on a lot by one sibling in particular while you were growing up?
    a. Did you perceive a higher level of conflict with a particular childhood sibling in the home than with others?
    b. Would you characterize a brother's or sister's interaction with you as physically abusive? (Define sibling assault: sibling causing physical harm or injury to a brother or sister. Includes pushing, hitting, kicking, biting, terrorizing, humiliating, exposing to violence or danger.)

22. Were you or any of your siblings sexually abused by any of your brothers or sisters while growing up? (Define sibling incest: sexual behavior between siblings that is not age-appropriate, transitory sexual exploration between developmental equals. May or may not include use of force or coercion, bribes, threats, mutual or dual masturbation, asking sibling to touch another sexually, forcing a sibling to witness masturbation, viewing pornography, fondling, sexualized conversation, oral copulation, or intercourse.)
    If yes, then:

23. How would the incest typically happen? Where, when?

24. How did the physical or sexual abuse affect your relationship with the sibling offender?

25. How is your relationship now with the brother or sister who abused you? Describe the nature of your current and previous contact.

26. Was the abuse acknowledged by someone in the family? Who? Did either parent try to protect you?

27. If you now have children of your own, how do you see the sibling abuse affecting your relationship with them?

28. If you could say anything you want to your brother or sister regarding the abuse that occurred in your family, what would it be?

29. Is there anything you would like to add to this interview that I haven't asked?

References

Abel, G.G. and Rouleau, J.L. (1990). The nature and extent of sexual assault. In W.L. Marshall, D.R. Laws, and H.E. Barbaree (Eds.), *Handbook of sexual assault: Issues, theories, and treatment of the offender* (pp. 9-21). New York: Plenum.

Abrahams, J. and Hoey, H. (1994). Sibling incest in a clergy family: A case study. *Child Abuse and Neglect*, 18, 1029-1035.

Achenbach, T.M. and Edelbrock, C. (1983). Manual for the child behavior checklist and revised child behavior profile. Burlington, VT: Queen City Printers.

Adams, B. (1968). *Kinship in an urban setting*. Chicago: Markham.

Adler, A. (1959). *Understanding human nature*. New York: Premier.

Adler, N. and Schutz, J. (1995). Sibling incest offenders. *Child Abuse and Neglect*, 19 (7), 811-819.

Ahrons, C.R. (1979). The binuclear family: Two households, one family. *Alternative Lifestyles*, 2 (4), 499-515.

Alexander, P.C. (1992). Application of attachment theory to the study of sexual abuse. *Journal of Consulting and Clinical Psychology*, 60 (2), 185-195.

Alpert, J. (1991, August). Sibling, cousin, and peer child sexual abuse: Clinical implications. Paper presented at the 99th Annual Convention of the American Psychological Association, San Francisco, CA.

Alston, R. and Turner, W. (1994). A family strength model of adjustment to disability for African Americans. *Journal of Counseling and Clinical Development*, 72, 378-383.

American Psychological Association. (1996). *Violence and the family*. Report of the APA Presidential Task Force on Violence and the Family, Washington, DC: Author.

Ammerman, R.T. (1989). Child abuse and neglect. In M. Hersen (Ed.), *Innovations in child behavior therapy* (pp. 353-394). New York: Springer.

Ammerman, R.T. (1991). The role of the child in physical abuse: A reappraisal. *Violence and Victims*, 6, 87-101.

Angel, R. and Angel, J.L. (1995). Mental and physical comorbidity among the elderly: The role of culture and social class. In D. Padgett (Ed.), *Handbook on ethnicity, aging, and mental health* (pp. 47-70). Westport, CT: Greenwood Press.

Bagley, C. and Young, L. (1987). Juvenile prostitution and child sexual abuse: A controlled study. *Canadian Journal of Community Mental Health*, 6 (1), 5-26.

Bank, S. and Kahn, M. (1982). *The sibling bond*. New York: Basic Books, Inc.

Barbaree, H.E., Marshall, W.L., and Hudson, J.M. (1993). *The juvenile sex offender*. New York: Guilford Press.

Baruth, L. and Manning, M. (1992). Understanding and counseling Hispanic American children. *Elementary School Guidance and Counseling*, 27, 113-122.

Baskett, L.M. (1984). Ordinal position differences in children's family interactions. *Developmental Psychology*, 20, 1026-1031.

Baskett, L.M. and Johnson, S.M. (1982). The young child's interactions with parents versus siblings: A behavioral analysis. *Child Development*, 53, 643-650.

Becker, J.V. (1988). The effects of child sexual abuse on adolescent sexual offenders. In G.E. Wyatt and G.J. Powell (Eds.), *Lasting effects of child sexual abuse* (pp. 193-207). Newbury Park, CA: Sage.

Becker, J.V. and Coleman, E.M. (1988). Incest. In V.B. Van Hasselt, R.L. Morrison, A.S. Bellack, and M. Hersen (Eds.), *Handbook of family violence* (pp. 187-205). New York: Plenum.

Becker, J.V. and Kaplan, M.S. (1988). The assessment of adolescent sexual offenders. In R.J. Printz (Ed.), *Advances in behavioral assessment of children and families: A research annual* (pp. 97-118). Greenwich, CT: JAI Press.

Belsky, J. (1980). Mother-infant interaction at home and in the laboratory: A comparative study. *Journal of Genetic Psychology*, 137 (1), 37-47.

Belsky, J. (1993). Etiology of child maltreatment: A developmental-ecological analysis. *Psychological Bulletin*, 114, 413-434.

Benson, M.J., Schindler-Zimmerman, T., and Martin, D. (1991). Accessing children's perceptions of their family: Circular questioning revisited. *Journal of Marital and Family Therapy*, 17 (4), 363-372.

Beutler, L.E. and Hill, C.E. (1992). Process and outcomes research in the treatment of adult victims of childhood sexual abuse: Methodological issues. *Journal of Consulting and Clinical Psychology*, 60 (2), 204-212.

Boney-McCoy, S. and Finkelhor, D. (1995). Psychosocial sequelae of violent victimization in a national youth sample. *Journal of Consulting and Clinical Psychology*, 63 (5), 726-736.

Bowen, M. (1978). *Family therapy in clinical practice*. New York: Jason Aronson.

Bowlby, J. (1973). *Attachment and loss: Vol. 2—Separation*. New York: Basic Books.

Bray, J.H., Williamson, D.S., and Malone, P.E. (1984). Personal authority in the family system: Development of a questionnaire to measure personal authority in intergenerational family processes. *Journal of Marital and Family Therapy*, 10, 167-178.

Briere, J. (1992). *Child abuse trauma*. Newbury Park, CA: Sage.

Briere, J. and Runtz, M. (1988). Post sexual abuse trauma. In G.E. Wyatt and G.J. Powell (Eds.), *Lasting effects of child sexual abuse* (pp. 85-99). Newbury Park, CA: Sage.

Briere, J. and Runtz, M. (1990). Differential adult symptomatology associated with three types of child abuse histories. *Child Abuse and Neglect*, 14, 357-364.

Brody, G.H., Stoneman, Z., and Burke, M. (1987). Family system and individual child correlates of sibling behavior. *Journal of the American Orthopsychiatric Association*, 57, 561-569.

Brody, G.H., Stoneman, Z., and Mackinnon, C. (1986). Contributions of maternal child-rearing practices and play contexts to sibling interactions. *Journal of Applied Developmental Psychology*, 7, 225-236.

Brody, G.H., Stoneman, Z., and McCoy, J.R. (1994). Contributions of family relationships and child temperaments to longitudinal variations in sibling relationship quality and sibling relationship styles. *Journal of Family Psychology*, 8 (3), 274-286.

Brody, G.H., Stoneman, Z., McCoy, J.R., and Forehand, R. (1992). Contemporaneous and longitudinal associations of sibling conflict with family relationship assessment and family discussions about sibling problems. *Child Development,* 63, 391-400.

Brown, G.W. and Harris, T. (1978). *Social origins of depression.* London: Tavistock.

Brown, J. and Dunn, J. (1992). Talk with your mother or your sibling? Developmental changes in early family conversations about feelings. *Child Development,* 63, 336-349.

Bryant, B. (1978). Cooperative goal structure and collaborative learning. *Teaching of Psychology*, 5 (4), 182-185.

Bryant, B.K. (1982). Sibling relationships in middle childhood. In M.E. Lamb and B. Sutton-Smith (Eds.), *Sibling relationships: Their nature and signif-icance across the lifespan* (pp. 87-121). Hillsdale, NJ: Lawrence Erlbaum.

Bryant, B.K. (1992). Conflict resolution strategies in relation to children's peer relations. *Journal of Applied Developmental Psychology*, 13 (1), 35-50.

Buhrmester, D. (1992). The developmental course of sibling and peer relationships. In F. Boer and J. Dunn (Eds.), *Children's sibling relationships: Developmental and clinical issues.* Hillsdale, NJ: Lawrence Erlbaum.

Burrell, B., Thompson, B., and Sexton, D. (1994). Predicting child abuse potential across family types. *Child Abuse and Neglect*, 18 (12), 1039-1049.

Butler, S. (1980, Summer). Incest: Whose reality, whose theory? *Aegis*, 48-55.

Canavan, M., Meyer, W., and Higgs, D. (1992). The female experience of sibling incest. *Journal of Marriage and Family Therapy,* 18 (2), 129-142.

Cantwell, H.B. (1988). Child sexual abuse: Very young perpetrators. *Child Abuse and Neglect*, 12, 579-582.

Chaffin, M. and Bonner, B. (1996). Managing teen offenders: Unsupportive families and family reunification. Workshop presented at American Professional Society on the Abuse of Children Fourth National Colloquium, Chicago, IL.

Cicchetti, D. and Lynch, M. (1993). Toward an ecological/transactional model of community violence and child maltreatment: Consequences for child development. In D. Reiss, J.E. Richters, and M. Radke-Yarrow (Eds.), *Children and violence* (pp. 96-118). New York: Guilford Press.

Cicirelli, V.G. (1980a). A comparison of college women's feelings toward their siblings and their parents. *Journal of Marriage and the Family*, 42, 95-102.

Cicirelli, V.G. (1980b). Sibling influence in adulthood: A lifespan perspective. In L.W. Poon (Ed.), *Aging in the 1980's*. Washington, DC: American Psychological Association.

Cicirelli, V.G. (1982). Sibling influence throughout the life span. In M. Lamb and B. Sutton-Smith (Eds.), *Sibling relationships: Their nature and significance across the life span.* Hillsdale, NJ: Erlbaum.

Cicirelli, V.G. (1985). Sibling relationships throughout the life cycle. In L. L'Abate (Ed.), *The handbook of family psychology and therapy.* Homewood, IL: Dorsey Press.

Cicirelli, V.G. (1989). Feelings of attachment to siblings and well-being in later life. *Psychology of Aging*, 4, 211-216.

Claussen, A. and Crittendon, P. (1991). Physical and psychological maltreatment: Relations among types of maltreatment. *Child Abuse and Neglect*, 15, 5-18.

Colonna, A.B. and Newman, L.M. (1983). The psychoanalytic literature on siblings. *Psychoanalytic Study of the Child*, 38, 285-309.

Conn-Caffaro, A. and Caffaro, J.V. (1993, July/August). Sibling affairs: The impact of abuse on sibling relationships. *The California Therapist*, 5 (4), 51-60.

Constantino, G., Malgady, R., and Rogler, L. (1994). Storytelling through pictures: Culturally sensitive psychotherapy for Hispanic children and adolescents. *Journal of Clinical Child Psychology*, 23, 13-20.

Courtois, C.A. (1988). *Healing the incest wound.* New York: W.W. Norton.

Cummings, E.M. (1987). Coping with background anger. *Child Development*, 58, 976-984.

Cummings, E. and Schneider, D. (1961). Sibling solidarity: A property of American kinship. *American Anthropologist*, 63, 408-507.

de Brock, A.J.L. and Vermulst, A.A. (1991, April). *Marital discord, parenting, and child dysfunctioning.* Paper presented at biennial meeting of the Society for Research in Child Development, Seattle, WA.

De Young, M. (1982). *The sexual victimization of children.* London: McFarland and Co.

DeJong, A. (1989). Sexual interactions among siblings: Experimentation or exploitation. *Child Abuse and Neglect*, 13, 271-279.

DePanfilis, D. and Wilson, C. (1996). Finding strengths in chaotic families. Workshop presented at American Professional Society on the Abuse of Children Fourth National Colloquium, Chicago, IL.

Doherty, W.J. (1988). Sibling issues in cotherapy and coauthoring. In Kahn, M.D. and Lewis, K.G. (Eds.), *Siblings in therapy: Lifespan and clinical issues.* New York: W.W. Norton.

Dornbusch, S., Carlsmith, J.M., Bushwall, S.J., Ritter, P.L., Leiderman, H., Hastorf, A.H., and Gross, R.T. (1985). Single parents, exended households, and the control of adolescents. *Child Development*, 56, 326-341.

Duncan, T., Duncan, S., and Hops, H. (1996). The role of parents and older siblings in predicting adolescent substance use: Modeling development via structural equation latent growth methodology. *Journal of Family Psychology*, 10 (2), 158-172.

Dunn, J. (1988). Sibling differences on childhood development. *Journal of Child Psychology and Psychiatry*, 29, 119-129.

Dunn, J. (1991). The developmental importance of differences in sibling's experiences within the family. In K. Pillimer and K. McCartney (Eds.), *Parent-child relations throughout life*. Hillsdale, NJ: Erlbaum.

Dunn, J. (1993). *Young children's close relationships: Beyond attachment*. Newbury Park, CA: Sage Publications.

Dunn, J. and Munn, P. (1985). Becoming a family member: Family conflict and the development of social understanding in the second year. *Child Development*, 56, 764-774.

Dunn, J. and Plomin, R. (1990). *Separate lives: Why siblings are so different*. New York: Basic Books.

Dunn, J., Stocker, C., and Plomin, R. (1990). Assessing the relationship between young siblings: A research note. *Journal of Child Psychology and Psychiatry and Allied Disciplines*, 31 (6), 983-991.

Elder, G.H., Caspi, A., and Burton, L.M. (1988). Adolescent transition in developmental perspective: Sociological and historical insights. In M.R. Gunnar and A.W. Collins (Eds.), *Development during the transition to adolescence*. Minnesota Symposia on Child Psychology, Vol. 21, (pp. 151-179). Hillsdale, NJ: Lawrence Erlbaum.

Falicov, C.J. and Karrer, B.M. (1983). Therapeutic strategies for Mexican-American families. *International Journal of Family Therapy*, 6 (1), 18-30.

Felson, R.B., and Russo, N. (1988). Aggression and violence between siblings. *Social Psychology Quarterly*, 46, 271-285.

Feschbach, N.D. (1975). Empathy in children: Some theoretical and empirical considerations. *Counseling Psychologist*, 5, 25-30.

Finkelhor, D. (1978). Psychological, cultural and family factors in incest and family sexual abuse. *Journal of Marriage and Family Counseling*, 4, 41-49.

Finkelhor, D. (1980). Sex among siblings: A survey on prevalence, variety, and effects. *Archives of Sexual Behavior*, 7, 171-194.

Finkelhor, D. (1984). *Child sexual abuse: New theory and research*. New York: Free Press.

Finkelhor, D. (1986). *A sourcebook on child sexual abuse*. Newbury Park, CA: Sage.

Finkelhor, D. (1987). The sexual abuse of children: Current research reviewed. *Psychiatric Annals*, 17 (4), 233-241.

Finkelhor, D. (1995). The victimization of children: A developmental perspective. *American Journal of Orthopsychiatry*, 63 (2), 177-193.

Finkelhor, D. and Browne, A. (1985). The traumatic impact of child sexual abuse: A conceptualization. *Journal of Orthopsychiatry*, 55, 530-541.

Finkelhor, D. and Dzuiba-Leatherman, J. (1994). Victimization of children. *American Psychologist*, 49 (3), 173-183.

Finkelhor, D., Hotaling, G., Lewis, I.A., and Smith, C. (1989). Sexual abuse and its relationship to later sexual satisfaction, marital status, religion, and attitudes. *Journal of Interpersonal Violence*, 4, 279-399.

Finkelhor, D., Hotaling, G., Lewis, I.A., and Smith, C. (1990). Sexual abuse in a national survey of adult men and women: Prevalence characteristics and risk factors. *Child Abuse and Neglect*, 14, 19-28.

Finkelhor, D. and Russell, D. (1984). Women as perpetrators in child sexual abuse: New theory and research. In D. Finkelhor (Ed.), *Child sexual abuse: New theory and research* (pp. 171-185). New York: Free Press.

Foa, E.B., Rothbaum, B.O., Riggs, D.S., and Murdock, T.B. (1991). Treatment of post-traumatic stress disorder in rape victims: A comparison between cognitive-behavioral procedures and counseling. *Journal of Consulting and Clinical Psychology*, 59, 715-723.

Fortenberry, D.J. and Hill, R. (1986). Sister-sister incest as a manifestation of multigenerational sexual abuse. *Journal of Adolescent Health Care*, 7, 202-204.

Forward, S. and Buck, C. (1978). *Betrayal of innocence: Incest and its devastation*. Los Angeles: J.P. Tarcher.

Foster, G.M. (1945). *Sierra popolucan folklore and beliefs*. University of California Publications in American Archaeology and Ethnology, 42, 177-250.

Framo, J.L. (1993). *Family of origin therapy*. New York: Brunner/Mazel.

Freud, A. and Dann, S. (1951). An experiment in group upbringing. *The Psychoanalytic Study of the Child*, 6, 127-168.

Friedrich, W.N. (1988). Behavior problems in sexually abused children: An adaptational perspective. In G. Wyatt and G. Powell (Eds.), *Lasting effects of child sexual abuse*. Newbury Park, CA: Sage.

Friedrich, W.N. (1990). *Psychotherapy of sexually abused children and their families*. New York: W.W. Norton.

Friedrich, W.N., Beilke, R., and Urquiza, A.J. (1988). Behavior problems in young sexually abused boys: A comparison study. *Journal of Interpersonal Violence*, 3, 21-28.

Furman, W. and Buhrmester, D. (1990). Perceptions of sibling relationships during middle childhood and adolescence. *Child Development*, 61 (5), 1387-1398.

Furstenberg, F., Morgan-Philip, S., and Allison, P. (1987). Paternal participation and children's well-being after marital dissolution. *American Sociological Review*, 57, 695-701.

Garbarino, J. (1986). Can we measure success in preventing child abuse? Issues in policy, programming and research. *Child Abuse and Neglect*, 10 (2), 143-156.

Garbarino, J. and Vondra, J. (1987). Psychological maltreatment: Issues and perspectives. In M.R. Brassard, R. Germain, and S.N. Hart (Eds.), *Psychological maltreatment of children and youth* (pp. 25-44). New York: Pergamon Press.

Gelles, R. J. and Cornell, C.P. (1985). *Intimate violence in families*. Beverly Hills, CA: Sage.

Gelles, R. J. and Straus, M.A. (1988). *Intimate violence*. New York: Simon and Schuster.

Gelles, R.J. and Straus, M.A. (1990). The medical and psychological costs of family violence. In M.A. Straus and R.J. Gelles (Eds.), *Physical violence in*

American families: Risk factors and adaptations to violence in 8,145 families (pp. 425-430). New Brunswick, NJ: Transaction.

Gil, E. (1996). *Systemic treatment of families who abuse.* San Francisco, CA: Jossey-Bass, Inc.

Goodwin, M.P. and Roscoe, B. (1990). Sibling violence and agonistic interactions among middle adolescents. *Adolescence*, 25, 451-467.

Graham-Bermann, S.A. (1994). The assessment of childhood sibling relationships: Varying perspectives on cooperation and conflict. *The Journal of Genetic Psychology*, 155, 457-469.

Graham-Bermann, S.A. and Cutler, S.E. (1992, August). Sibling violence and abuse: Prevalence, emotional and social outcome. Paper presented at the 100th Annual Convention of the American Psychological Association, Washington, D.C.

Graham-Bermann, S. and Cutler, S. (1994). The brother-sister questionnaire: Psychometric assessment and discrimination of well-functioning from dysfunctional relationships. *Journal of Family Psychology*, 8, 224-238.

Graham-Bermann, S., Cutler, S., Litzenberger, B., Schwartz, W. (1994). Perceived conflict and violence in childhood sibling relationships and later emotional adjustment. *Journal of Family Psychology*, 8, 85-97.

Greenbaum, S. (1989). *School bullying and victimization.* NSSC resource paper. Malibu, CA: National School Safety Center.

Gully, K.J., Dengerink, H.A., Pepping, M. and Bergstrom, D. (1981). Research note: Sibling contribution to violent behavior. *Journal of Marriage and the Family*, 43, 333-337.

Hamlin, E. and Timberlake, E. (1979). Sibling group treatment. *Clinical Social Work Journal*, 9, 101-110.

Harlan, S., Rogers, L., and Slattery, B. (1981). *Male and female adolescent prostitutes.* Washington, DC: Huckelberry House Sexual Minority Youth Services Project, Youth Development Bureau, U.S. Department of Human Services.

Harry, B. (1992). Making sense of disability: Low-income, Puerto Rican parents' theories of the problem. *Exceptional Children*, 59, 27-40.

Hart, S.N. and Brassard, M.R. (1987). A major threat to children's mental health: Psychological maltreatment. *American Psychologist*, 42 (2), 160-165.

Helfer, R.E. (1987). The developmental basis of child abuse and neglect: An epidemological approach. In Helfer, R.E. and Kempe, R.S. (Eds.), *The battered child,* Fourth Edition (pp. 60-80). Chicago: University of Chicago Press.

Herman, J. (1981). *Father-daughter incest.* Cambridge, MA: Harvard University Press.

Herman, J. (1990). Sex offenders: A feminist perspective. In W.L. Marshall, D.R. Laws, and H.E. Barbaree (Eds.), *Handbook of sexual assault: Issues, theories, and treatment of the offender* (pp.177-193). New York: Plenum.

Herman, J. (1992). *Trauma and recovery.* New York: Basic Books.

Hetherington, E.M. (1994). Siblings, family relationships, and child development: Introduction. In Special Section: Siblings, family relationships, and child development. *Journal of Family Psychology*, 8 (3), 251-253.

Hetherington, E.M. and Clingempeel, W.G. (1992). Coping with marital transitions. *Monographs of the Society for Research in Child Development*, 57, (2-3, Serial No. 227).

Hinde, R.A. and Stevenson-Hinde, J. (1988). Epilogue. In R.A. Hinde and J. Stevenson-Hinde (Eds.), *Relationships within families: Mutual influences.* Oxford, UK: Clarendon.

Horwitz, A.V. and Reinhard, S.C. (1995). Ethnic differences in caregiving duties and burdens among parents and siblings of persons with severe mental illnesses. *Journal of Health and Social Behavior*, 36 (2), 138-150.

Hotaling, G. T., Straus, M.A., and Lincoln, A.J. (1990). Intrafamily violence and crime and violence outside the family. In M.A. Straus and R.J. Gelles (Eds.), *Physical violence in American families: Risk factors and adaptations to violence in 8,145 families.* New Brunswick, N.J.: Transaction.

Howes, C. and Espinosa, M.P. (1985). The consequences of child abuse for the formation of relationships with peers. *Child Abuse and Neglect*, 9, 397-404.

Hunter, J., Lexier, L. Goodwin, D., Browne, P., and Dennis, C. (1993). Psychosexual, attitudinal, and developmental characteristics of juvenile female sexual perpetrators in a residential treatment setting. *Journal of Child and Family Studies*, 2 (4), 317-326.

Jaffe, P., Wolfe, D.A., and Wilson, S.K. (1990). *Children of battered women.* Newbury Park, CA: Sage.

Kagan, S. (1977). Social motives and behaviors of Mexican American and Anglo American children. In J.L. Martinez (Ed.), *Chicano psychology.* New York: Academic Press.

Kaufman, J. and Cicchetti, D. (1989). The effects of maltreatment on school-aged children's socioemotional development: Assessments in a day-camp setting. *Developmental Psychology,* 25, 516-524.

Kaufman, J. and Zigler, E. (1987). Do abused children become abused parents? *Journal of Orthopsychiatry,* 57 (2), 186-192.

Kendall-Tackett, K. and Simon, A. (1987). Perpetrators and their acts: Data from 365 adults molested as children. *Child Abuse and Neglect*, 11, 237-245.

Kilpatrick, D.G., Saunders, B.E., Amick-McMullan, A., Best, C.L., Veronen, L.J., and Resnick, H.S. (1989). Victim and crime factors associated with the development of crime-related post-traumatic stress disorder. *Behavior Ther-apy*, 20, 199-214.

Knight, G. and Kagan, S. (1982). Siblings, birth order, and cooperative-competitive social behavior. *Journal of Cross-Cultural Psychology*, 13 (2), 239-249.

Kolko, D., Kazdin, A., and Day, B. (1996). Children's perspectives in the assessment of family violence: Psychometric characteristics and comparison to parent reports. *Child Maltreatment*, 1 (2), 156-167.

Koss, M. and Harvey, M. (1987). The rape victim: Clinical and community approaches to treatment. Lexington, MA: Stephen Greene Press.

Kreppner, K. and Lerner, R.M. (1989). *Family systems and life-span development.* Hillsdale, NJ: Lawrence Erlbaum.

Kromelow, S., Harding, C., and Touris, M. (1990). The role of the father in the development of stranger sociability during the second year. *American Journal of Orthopsychiatry*, 60 (4), 521-530.

Kubo, S. (1959). Research and studies on incest in Japan. *Hiroshima Journal of Medical Sciences*, 8, 99-159.

Lamb, M.E. (1978). Interactions between eighteen-month-olds and their pre-school aged siblings. *Child Development*, 49, 51-59.

Laredo, C.M. (1982). Sibling incest. In S.M. Sgroi (Ed.), *Handbook of clinical intervention in child sexual abuse*. Lexington, MA: Free Press.

Lavigueur, H. (1976). The use of siblings as an adjunct to the behavioral treatment of children in the home with parents as therapists. *Behavior Therapy*, 7, 602-613.

Laviola, M. (1992). Effects of older brother-younger sister incest: A study of the dynamics of 17 cases. *Child Abuse and Neglect*, 16, 409-421.

Lewis, K.G. (1988). Sibling therapy: A blend of family and group therapy. *The Journal for Specialists in Group Work*, 13 (4), 186-193.

Loeber, R., Weissman, W., and Reid, J.B. (1983). Family interactions of assaultive adolescents, stealers and nondelinquents. *Journal of Abnormal Child Psychology*, 11, 1-14.

Main, M. and George, C. (1985). Responses of abused and disadvantaged toddlers to distress in agemates studied in the day care setting. *Developmental Psychology*, 21, 407-412.

Mangold, W. and Koski, P. (1990). Gender comparisons in the relationship between parental and sibling violence and nonfamily violence. *Journal of Family Violence*, 5 (3), 225-235.

Margolin, G. (1995). Research documents trauma of abuse. In *APA Monitor*, 26 (4), 34.

McCarty, L. (1986). Mother-child incest: Characteristics of the offender. *Child Welfare*, 65, 447-458.

McClintock, E., Bayard, M.P., and McClintock, C.G. (1979). Socialization of prosocial orientations in the Mexican American family. Paper presented at the National Symposium on the Mexican American Child, University of California, Santa Barbara, CA.

McGoldrick, M. (1995). *You can go home again*. New York: W.W. Norton.

Meiselman, K. (1978). *Incest: A psychological study of causes and effects with treatment recommendations*. San Francisco: Jossey-Bass.

Minuchin, S. (1985). Families and individual development: Provocations from the field of family therapy. *Child Development*, 56, 289-302.

Navarre, E.L. (1987). Psychological maltreatment: The core component of child abuse. In M.R. Brassard, R. Germain, and S. N. Hart (Eds.), *Psychological maltreatment of children and youth* (pp. 45-56). New York: Pergamon.

Newberger, C.M. and DeVos, E. (1988). Abuse and victimization: A life-span developmental perspective. *American Journal of Orthopsychiatry*, 58, 505-511.

O'Brien, M. (1989). *Characteristics of male adolescent sibling incest offenders: Preliminary findings*. Orwell, VT: The Safer Society Program.

O'Brien, M. (1991). Taking sibling incest seriously. In Patton, M. (Ed.), *Understanding family sexual abuse*, Newbury Park, CA: Sage.

Pagelow, M.D. (1989). The incidence and prevalence of criminal abuse of other family members. In L. Ohlin and M. Tonry (Eds.), *Family violence* (pp. 263-314). Chicago: University of Chicago Press.

Panton, J. (1979). MMPI profile configurations associated with incestuous and non-incestuous child molesters. *Psychological Reports*, 45 (1), 335-338.

Paredes, A. (1970). *Folktales of Mexico*. Chicago: University of Chicago Press.

Patterson, G.R. (1986). The contribution of siblings to training for fighting: A microsocial analysis. In D. Olweus, J. Block, and M. Radke-Yarrow (Eds.), *Development of antisocial and prosocial behavior. Research, theories, and issues*. Orlando, FL: Academic Press.

Patton, M. (1991). *Understanding family sexual abuse*. Newbury Park, CA: Sage.

Pence, D.M. (1993). Family preservation and reunification in intrafamilial sexual abuse cases: A law enforcement perspective. *Journal of Child Sexual Abuse*, 2 (2), 103-108.

Piaget, J. (1965). *The moral judgement of the child*. New York: Academic Press.

Pulakos, J. (1987). Brothers and sisters: Nature and importance of the adult bond. *Journal of Psychology*, 121 (5), 521-522.

Putnam, F.W. (1990). Disturbances of "self" in victims of childhood sexual abuse. In R. Kluft (Ed.), *Incest-related syndromes of adult psychopathology* (pp. 113-131). Washington, DC: American Psychiatric Press.

Raffaelli, M. (1991, April). Interpersonal conflict with siblings and friends: Implications for early adolescent development. Paper presented at biennial meeting of the Society for Research in Child Development, Seattle, WA.

Rausch, K. and Knutson, J. (1991). The self-report of personal punitive childhood experiences and those of siblings. *Child Abuse and Neglect*, 15, 29-36.

Reid, W. and Donovan, T. (1990).Treating sibling violence. *Family Therapy*, 27 (1), 49-59.

Roscoe, B., Goodwin, M., and Kennedy, D. (1987). Sibling violence and agonistic interactions experienced by early adolescents. *Journal of Family Violence*, 2, 121-138.

Rosenberg, B.G. (1982). Life span personality stability in sibling status. In M.E. Lamb and B. Sutton-Smith (Eds.), *Sibling relationships: Their nature and significance across the lifespan* (pp. 167-224). Hillsdale, NJ: Lawrence Erlbaum.

Rosenberg, M.S. (1984). The impact of witnessing interparental violence on children's behavior, perceived competence, and social problem-solving activities. Unpublished doctoral dissertation, University of Virginia.

Rosenthal, P.A. and Doherty, M.B. (1984). Serious sibling abuse by preschool children. *Journal of the American Academy of Child Psychiatry*, 23 (2), 186-190.

Ross, H., Filyer, R., Lollis, S., Perlman, M., and Martin, J. (1994). Administering justice in the family. *Journal of Family Psychology*, 8 (3), 254-273.

Ross, H.G. and Milgram, J.I. (1982). Important variables in adult sibling relationships: A qualitative study. In M.E. Lamb and B. Sutton-Smith (Eds.), *Sibling relationships: Their nature and significance across the lifespan.* Hillsdale, NJ: Lawrence Erlbaum.

Russell, D. (1986). *The secret trauma: Incest in the lives of girls and women.* New York: Basic Books.

Salter, A. (1988). *Treating child sex offenders and victims: A practical guide.* Newbury Park, CA: Sage.

Salter, A. (1995). *Transforming trauma.* Thousand Oaks, CA: Sage.

Sanday, P.R. (1981). *Female power and male dominance: On the origins of sexual inequality.* New York: Cambridge University Press.

Saunders, D.G. and Azar, S. (1989). Treatment programs for family violence. In L. Ohlin and M. Tonry (Eds.), *Family violence: Crime and justice—A review of research* (pp. 481-546). Chicago: University of Chicago Press.

Schacter, F. (1985). Sibling deidentification in the clinic: Devil vs. angel. *Family Process,* 24 (3), 415-427.

Schlegel, A. (1977). Toward a theory of sexual stratification. In A. Schlegel (Ed.), *Sexual stratification* (pp. 1-40). New York: Columbia University Press.

Smith, H. and Israel, E. (1987). Sibling incest: A study of the dynamics of 25 cases. *Child Abuse and Neglect,* 11, 101-108.

Sontag, J. and Schacht, R. (1994). An ethnic comparison of parent participation and information needs in early intervention. *Exceptional Children,* 60, 422-433.

Steinmetz, S.K. (1977). The use of force for resolving family conflict: The training ground for abuse. *The Family Coordinator,* 26 (1), 19-26.

Steinmetz, S.K. (1978). Sibling violence. In J.M. Eskelaan and S.N. Katz (Eds.), *Family violence: An international and interdisciplinary study.* Toronto: Butterworths.

Steinmetz, S.K. (1981). A cross-cultural comparison of sibling violence. *International Journal of Family Psychiatry,* 2, 337-351.

Stewart, R.B. (1983). Sibling attachment relationships: Child-infant interactions in the strange situation. *Developmental Psychology,* 19, 192-199.

Stocker, C.M. and McHale, S.M. (1992). The nature and family correlates of preadolescents' perceptions of their sibling relationships. *Journal of Social and Personal Relationships,* 9, 179-195.

Stolba, A. and Amato, P.R. (1993). Extended single-parent households and children's behavior. *Sociological Quarterly,* 34, 543-549.

Stolorow, R. , Brandchaft, B., and Atwood, G. (1987). *Psychoanalytic treatment: An intersubjective approach.* Hillsdale, NJ: Analytic Press.

Stoneman, Z., Brody, G.H., and Burke, M. (1989). Marital quality, depression, and inconsistent parenting: Relationship with observed mother-child conflict. *American Journal of Orthopsychiatry,* 59, 105-117.

Straus, M. (1979). Measuring intrafamily conflict and violence: The Conflict Tactics Scale. *Journal of Marriage and the Family,* 41, 75-88.

Straus, M.R. and Gelles, R.J. (1990). *Physical violence in American families: Risk factors and adaptations to violence in 8,145 families.* New Brunswick, NJ: Transaction.

Straus, M.R., Gelles, R.J., and Steinmetz, S.K. (1980). *Behind closed doors.* New York: Doubleday.

Sullivan, H.S. (1953). *The interpersonal theory of psychiatry.* New York: W.W. Norton.

Sutton-Smith, B. and Rosenberg, B.G. (1970). *The sibling.* New York: Holt, Rinehart and Winston.

Taggart, J. (1992). Gender segregation and cultural constructions of sexuality in two Hispanic societies. *American Ethnologist,* 19 (1), 75-92.

Teti, D.M. and Ablard, K.E. (1989). Security of attachment and infant-sibling relationships: A laboratory study. *Child Development,* 60, 1519-1528.

Trepper, T. and Barrett, M. (1989). *Systemic treatment of incest.* New York: Brunner/ Mazel.

Urquiza, A. (1988). The effects of childhood sexual abuse in an adult male population. Unpublished doctoral dissertation, University of Washington, Seattle.

Urquiza, A. and Capra, M. (1990). The impact of sexual abuse: Initial and long-term effects. In M. Hunter, *The sexually abused male* (pp. 105-135), Lexington, MA: Lexington Books.

Weinberg, S.K. (1955). *Incest behavior.* New York: Citadel.

Wiehe, V. (1990). *Sibling abuse: Hidden physical, emotional, and sexual trauma.* New York: Lexington Books.

Wiehe, V. (1996). *The brother/sister hurt.* Brandon, VT: Safer Society Press.

Wolfe, D.A. (1987). *Child abuse: Implications for child development and psychopathology.* Newbury Park, CA: Sage.

Worling, J.R. (1995). Adolescent sibling incest offenders: Differences in family and individual functioning when compared to adolescent nonsibling sex offenders. *Child Abuse and Neglect,* 19 (5), 633-643.

Wright, P. (1982). Men's friendships, women's friendships and the alleged inferiority of the latter. *Sex Roles,* 8, 1-20.

Index

Page numbers followed by the letter "t" indicate tables; those followed by the letter "f " indicate figures.

Order Your Own Copy of
This Important Book for Your Personal Library!

SIBLING ABUSE TRAUMA
Assessment and Intervention Strategies for Children, Families, and Adults

_____ in hardbound at $49.95 (ISBN: 0-7890-6007-8)

_____ in softbound at $24.95 (ISBN: 0-7890-0491-7)

COST OF BOOKS_____

OUTSIDE USA/CANADA/
MEXICO: ADD 20%_____

POSTAGE & HANDLING_____
*(US: $3.00 for first book & $1.25
for each additional book)
Outside US: $4.75 for first book
& $1.75 for each additional book)*

SUBTOTAL_____

IN CANADA: ADD 7% GST_____

STATE TAX_____
*(NY, OH & MN residents, please
add appropriate local sales tax)*

FINAL TOTAL_____
*(If paying in Canadian funds,
convert using the current
exchange rate. UNESCO
coupons welcome.)*

☐ **BILL ME LATER:** ($5 service charge will be added)
(Bill-me option is good on US/Canada/Mexico orders only;
not good to jobbers, wholesalers, or subscription agencies.)

☐ Check here if billing address is different from
shipping address and attach purchase order and
billing address information.

Signature_____

☐ **PAYMENT ENCLOSED: $**_____

☐ **PLEASE CHARGE TO MY CREDIT CARD.**

☐ Visa   ☐ MasterCard   ☐ AmEx   ☐ Discover
☐ Diners Club
Account #_____

Exp. Date_____

Signature_____

Prices in US dollars and subject to change without notice.

NAME_____

INSTITUTION_____

ADDRESS_____

CITY_____

STATE/ZIP_____

COUNTRY_____ COUNTY (NY residents only)_____

TEL_____ FAX_____

E-MAIL_____
May we use your e-mail address for confirmations and other types of information? ☐ Yes   ☐ No

Order From Your Local Bookstore or Directly From
The Haworth Press, Inc.
10 Alice Street, Binghamton, New York 13904-1580 • USA
TELEPHONE: 1-800-HAWORTH (1-800-429-6784) / Outside US/Canada: (607) 722-5857
FAX: 1-800-895-0582 / Outside US/Canada: (607) 772-6362
E-mail: getinfo@haworthpressinc.com
PLEASE PHOTOCOPY THIS FORM FOR YOUR PERSONAL USE.

BOF96